1992-1993 SUPPLEMENT
NINTH EDITION

ACCOUNTING
DESK BOOK

THE ACCOUNTANT'S EVERYDAY
INSTANT ANSWER BOOK

Tom M. Plank

PRENTICE HALL
Englewood Cliffs, New Jersey 07632

Prentice-Hall International (UK) Limited, London
Prentice-Hall of Australia Pty. Limited, Sydney
Prentice-Hall Canada, Inc., Toronto
Prentice-Hall Hispanoamericana, S.A., Mexico
Prentice-Hall of India Private Limited, New Delhi
Prentice-Hall of Japan, Inc., Tokyo
Simon & Schuster Asia Pte. Ltd., Singapore
Editora Prentice-Hall do Brasil, Ltda., Rio de Janeiro

© 1993 by
PRENTICE-HALL, Inc.
Englewood Cliffs, NJ

10 9 8 7 6 5 4 3 2 1

Library of Congress Cataloging-in-Publication Data

(Revised for 1992–1993 Suppl.)
Plank, Tom M., 1919–
    Accounting desk book.

    Kept up to date by supplements.
    Includes indexes.
    1. Accounting.   2. Tax accounting—United States.
3. Tax accounting—Law and legislation—United States.
II. Title.
HF5635.B668   1989   657'.02'02   88-39352
ISBN 0-13-003559-9
ISBN 0-13-005448-8 (1990 suppl.)
ISBN 0-13-006917-5 (1991 suppl.)

ISBN 0-13-096561-8

PRENTICE HALL
Professional Publishing
Englewood Cliffs, NJ 07632
Simon & Schuster. A Paramount Communications Company

Printed in the United States of America

How to Use This Supplement

The purpose of this update Supplement is to furnish users of the *Accounting Desk Book, 9th Edition,* and other accountants and financial practitioners, with the latest developments in financial accounting and significant federal accounting laws in the 1991, 1990, 1989, 1988, 1987, and 1986 tax legislation, as they apply to the three major forms of business organizations—corporations, S corporations, and partnerships. The tax responsibilities relevant to accountants' needs are explained in detail, as the space in the ninth edition of the book (772 pages) was limited to a broad coverage of the twelve different sections covering 144 major sections and subtopics of financial and tax accounting principles.

Most significant are the changes in the rules governing the financial presentation of cash flows in financial reports and the numerous changes in the tax accounting rules. Specifically, Sections 1, 11, and 12 in the book are substantially expanded in detail by the information in this Supplement.

This publication is divided into four parts. Part I covers the requirements in the *accounting rules* for cash flows and accounting for taxes, complete with illustrations of their presentation in financial statements.

Part I can be considered an addition to Section 1 in the book *(The Accountant and Accounting)* and to Section 12 *(Tax Accounting).*

Part II discusses the requirements of the 1991, 1990, 1989, and 1988 tax legislation, with emphasis on **immediate** answers to practical tax accounting, finance, and other accountant's questions in these areas that are relevant.

Part III discusses the 1987 and 1986 tax bills, with emphasis on the Tax Reform Act of 1986, considered to be the broadest overhaul of federal tax legislation since the war-time Revenue Act of 1942.

Parts II and III are additions to Section 11 of the book *Summarizing Tax Legislation 1986–1990.*

Part IV updates the significant tax accounting requirements for S corporations, Partnerships, Depreciation, Interest Expense, Corporation Net Operating Losses, Deducting Business Expenses, and RICs, REITs, REMICs.

The discussions throughout the four parts of the Supplement are self-contained; an explanation of a topic does not require any reference, nor is it linked to a preceding topic in another location in the *Supplement.*

The contents topical listing includes the major topics discussed in the *Supplement,* and the user will find the index particularly helpful. It is constructed in substantial detail in order to provide a ready-reference guide to the location of topics and subtopics. Every major and minor topic in the manual is listed in the index and referenced by page number.

It is recommended that the initial use of the manual is a thorough review of the index; this will enable the user to see the subject matter of each topic in the detailed listing of the 540 topics discussed in the *Supplement.*

About the Author

Tom M. Plank is President of Pasadena Business Institute, Inc., a consulting firm. He holds his degrees from the Graduate School of Management, University of California (Los Angeles).

Mr. Plank is a specialist in SEC Accounting Rules and Regulations, new security issues registrations, and annual report filings with the SEC. He gives in-house seminars on accounting rules and SEC disclosure requirements to the accounting personnel of companies in commerce and industry and in public accounting firms.

In addition, Mr. Plank has served on the accounting and finance faculties of various major universities in Chicago and Los Angeles. His business experience includes that of an officer for a large commercial bank, a securities analyst for an investment banking firm, and a consultant for various corporations.

Mr. Plank has published over 25 articles in various journals and is the author of 10 business books: *SEC Accounting Rules and Regulations, The Age of Automation, The Science of Leadership,* and 7 accounting books. He is an accounting editor for a major publishing house.

Contents

Real Property   Reserve Method for Deducting Bad Debts
Educational Assistance Programs and Group Legal Plans
Dependent Care Assistance Programs   Employee Achievement
Awards   Depreciation   Modification of ACRS   Section 179
Deduction, Election to Expense Certain Depreciable Business
Assets   Tax Credits   Investment Tax Credit   Corporations
Environmental Tax   Relief from Underpayment of Estimated Tax
Penalty   Employee Benefit Plans   New Annual Limit on Elective
Deferrals   Treatment of Excess Deferrals   Keogh Plans
Tax-Sheltered Annuities   Profit-Sharing Plans   Limits on
Contributions and Benefits   Leased Employees   Reversion of
Plan Assets to Employer   Plan Amendments—Not Required Until
1989   Employer Must Report Employee's Coverage by Plan
Coverage by Defined Contribution and Defined Benefit Plans
Changes in Penalties   Accounting Periods and Methods
S Corporation Tax Year   Personal Service Corporation Tax
Year   Cash Method of Accounting   Allocation of Sales Price of
Business Assets   Transactions Between Related Parties
Employment Taxes—Independent Contractor   Real Estate
Reporting   Partnerships and S Corporations: Meals, Travel, and
Entertainment Expenses   Capitalizing Sales Tax

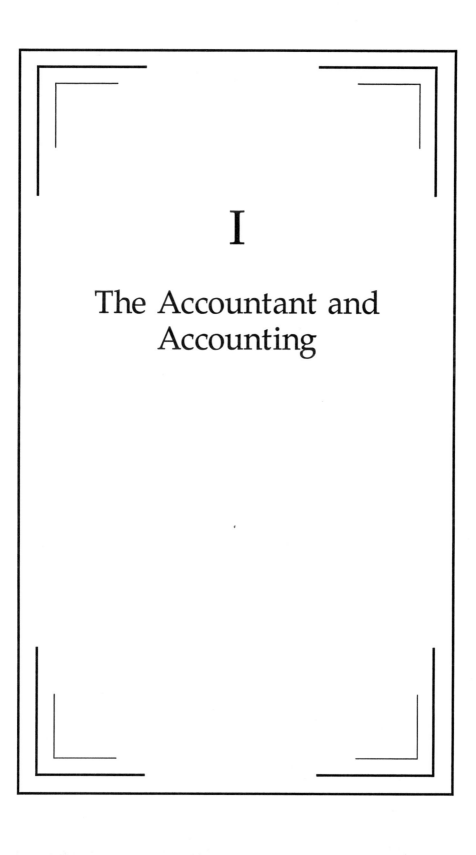

I

The Accountant and Accounting

CONCEPTUAL FRAMEWORK

Six Statements of Financial Accounting Concepts have been adopted by the Financial Accounting Standards Board. These concepts form the basis for financial accounting standards from the standpoint of the nature, function, and limits of financial accounting.

FASB Concepts Statements

1) *Objectives of Financial Reporting by Business Enterprises* covers information useful to anyone (whether externally or internally) needing to review financial statements, including creditors and investors.

Thus, the aims of this statement are twofold: to provide a general purpose external financial reporting method by business enterprises, and at the same time, satisfy the needs of internal users who are not in a position to provide the information necessary to carry out their responsibilities, but must rely upon the information that management has chosen to furnish them.

2) The *Qualitative Characteristics of Accounting Information Statements* provides step-by-step guidelines for acceptable accounting methods, including the amount and types of information to be disclosed, and the appropriate form for that information. The FASB emphasizes that relevance and reliability are the key words in providing useful accounting information. Only slightly less vital qualities are consistency and the ease with which the relevant information can be verified or used in comparison studies.

3) *Elements of Financial Statements of Business Enterprises* is superseded by Concept No. 6.

4) *Objectives of Financial Reporting by Nonbusiness Organizations.* The Statement prescribes the external financial reporting by nonbusiness organizations, such as governmental entities and government-sponsored entities, including hospitals, universities, and utilities.

5) *Recognition and Measurement in Financial Statements of Business Enterprises.* This Statement specifies what information should be included in financial statements and when that information should be collected and reported. It deals with four basic assumptions relevant to financial accounting:

1) A going concern.
2) A monetary unit.
3) An economic entity.
4) Periodicity.

6) *Elements of Financial Statements.* Ten elements germane to financial statements are defined and described in this Statement. Included are economic terms used in financial reporting relevant to investment, credit, and other resource allocation decisions. These ten interrelated key words vital to financial statements are:

1) Assets.
2) Liabilities.
3) Equity.
4) Investments by Owners.
5) Distributions to Owners.
6) Comprehensive Income.
7) Revenues.
8) Expenses.
9) Gains.
10) Losses.

NOTE: The concepts are not a rigid outline for specific accounting procedures or disclosure practices required by GAAP, but attempt to provide a broad perspective useful in setting up acceptable accounting standards and procedures, as well as in evaluating and/or improving existing ones.

ECONOMIC PERFORMANCE RULE

All-Events Test. In determining whether an amount for any item has been incurred during a taxable year, the *all-events test* will not be deemed to have been met before economic performance of the item occurs. The all-events test is adjudged to have been met with respect to any item if all events have occurred which determine the fact of liability, and it is possible to determine the amount of liability with a reasonable degree of accuracy.

The time frame in which economic performance takes place can be determined under the following principles:

1) When the liability of the taxpayer originates with services provided for the taxpayer by another person, economic performance occurs when the services have in fact been provided.
2) When the liability of the taxpayer is the result of another person providing *property* to the taxpayer, economic performance occurs at the time the person provides the property.
3) When the liability of the taxpayer results from the **use** of property by the taxpayer, economic performance occurs when the taxpayer uses that property. An item is treated as incurred during any taxable year if:
   a) The all-events test when applied to that item is met during the taxable year.
   b) The economic performance occurs:
      1. Within a reasonable period after the close of the taxable year; or
      2. 8½ months after the close of the taxable year, whichever is shorter;

c) It is a recurring item and the taxpayer consistently treats said items as incurred in the taxable year in which the requirements of the all-events test relating to them are met.

Also, the all-events test can be considered met if either the item is not a material item, or the accrual of the item in the taxable year in which the requirements of the all-events test are met results in costs more closely matching income than in accruing the item in the taxable year in which economic performance occurs.

Under the accrual method of tax accounting, an expenditure is taken into account for deduction or capitalization purposes in the year in which all events have occurred that determine the **fact** of the liability, and its amount can be estimated with reasonable accuracy.

The *Economic Performance Rule* establishes an additional standard for determining when an expenditure may be taken into account—the *economic performance test.* Expenditures of a recurring nature may be taken into account in advance of economic performance if the taxpayer adopts a special method applicable to qualifying items, provided that economic performance for the expenditure occurs within a stated period after year-end.

The economic performance rule could have a deleterious effect upon the taxpayer. For example, deductions for accrued property taxes prior to payment are prohibited unless a special method appropriate for recurring expenditures has been adopted in reference to the time in question and the relevant taxes are paid usually within $8^{1}/_{2}$ months after the end of the year in which they become due, or would have become due. The rule also provides for the timing of the income recognition of taxpayers who are subject to the long-term contract rules. Under the percentage-of-completion method, the portion of the contract price on a long-term contract is to be recognized income as a percentage of estimated total income:

1) That actual costs bear to total costs after giving effect to recent estimates of costs to complete.

2) As indicated by other appropriate measures of progress to completion.

Under the percentage-of-completion method, current assets may include costs and recognized income not yet filled for certain contracts. Liabilities (usually current liabilities) may include billings in excess of costs and recognized income with regard to other contracts.

The regulations provide that economic performance on costs associated with long-term contracts has occurred 1) if at the earlier time, payment is made, or 2) the time at which the taxpayer **actually receives** the related property or services. Thus, income recognition can be accelerated if the taxpayer must pay for property or services before they are delivered.

To illustrate, assume the total cost of building 25 houses at the same fixed price in a development includes $500,000 for required costs at the end of the project in five years. Under prior law, if four of the houses were finished and sold during the first year, the costs of building the four houses, as well as $100,000 (20% × $500,000) could be applicable to the future costs. Now, the application of the economic performance rule would result in a deferral of any deduction for the future costs until the end of the construction when the entire development is completed.

ACCOUNTING PRINCIPLES BOARD (APB) OPINIONS

Omnibus Opinion

(*NOTE:* portions of this Opinion are superseded by APB 14, which immediately follows.)

APB 12 requires allowances for depreciation and depletion to be deducted from the assets to which they specifically relate. In line with this rule, the following disclosures should be made:

1) Depreciation expense for the period.

2) Balances of the major classes of depreciable assets should be according to the function of the assets being depreciated.

3) Depreciation should be accumulated either by classes or in total.

4) The accounting procedures used in computing depreciation for all the major classes.

Deferred Compensation Contracts.   When a deferred compensation contract is involved, the following steps should be taken:

1) The estimated amounts to be paid under each contract should be accrued in a systematic manner extending over the entire period of actual employment from the time the contract becomes effective.

2) Some deferred compensation contracts provide for periodic payments to employees or surviving spouses for life with provisions for a minimum lump sum settlement in the event of the early death of one or all of the beneficiaries. However, in estimating future payments, calculations should be based on life expectancy of each individual concerned or on the estimated cost of an annuity contract rather than on the minimum amount paid in the event of early death(s).

3) Amounts relating to deferred compensation contracts with active employees which have not been accrued as stated in item 1) should be accrued over the employees' remaining term of employment.

In noting *capital changes,* when both financial position and the results of operations are presented, changes in stockholders' equity accounts and changes in the number of shares outstanding should be disclosed either in separate statements or in the basic financial statements

Accounting for Convertible Debt and Debt Issued with Common Stock Warrants

APB 14 covers GAAP for the issuance of convertible debt and debt issued with stock purchase warrants. When warrants to purchase stock are issued with bonds but are detachable, that portion of the proceeds that may be allocated to the warrants should be accounted for as paid-in capital. Any bond discount or premium resulting should be accounted for by the same procedure. The allocation should be based on the relative values of the two securities at the time of issue. If the warrants are not detachable, the bonds are convertible debt.

In addition:

1) No portion of the proceeds from the convertible debt issue should be accounted for as associated with the conversion feature.

2) The inseparability of the debt and the conversion feature are the principal reason for accounting for convertible debt solely as debt.

Other reasons are:

1) Both choices cannot be consummated.

2) The monetary value of the conversion option presents problems because the market values are not established.

3) Material adjustments which result from retroactive adoption of this option should be treated as a prior period adjustment.

Intangible Assets

APB 17 reviews GAAP in accounting for intangibles. A company should record as assets the costs of those intangibles acquired from outside sources:

1) Cost of developing, maintaining, or restoring intangible assets which (a) are not specifically identifiable, (b) have indeterminate lives, or (c) are inherent in a continuing business and related to an enterprise as a whole and should be deducted from income at the time the expense is incurred.

2) Individually acquired intangible assets should be recorded at cost at the time of acquisition. Cost is measured by:
   a. The amount of cash disbursed;
   b. The fair value of other assets distributed;
   c The present value of amounts to be paid for liabilities incurred; or
   d. The fair value of consideration received for any stock issued.

Intangible assets in this category, including those acquired as a part of a major acquisition, should also be recorded at cost at the time of acquisition. Cost is calculated in a different manner for specifically identifiable intangible assets and those which cannot be specifically identified. Since the cost of identifiable intangible assets is an assigned part of the total cost of the group of assets or enterprise acquired, usual procedure is to base the cost on the stated fair values of the specific, individual assets. On the other hand, the cost of unidentifiable intangible assets is measured by the difference between the cost of the group of assets or enterprise acquired and the sum of the assigned costs of individual tangible and identifiable assets acquired less liabilities assumed. Costs should be assigned to all specifically identifiable intangible assets; cost of identifiable assets should not be included in goodwill.

Because the value of intangible assets eventually disappears, the recorded costs of those assets should be amortized by systematic charges to income over a period during which they are deemed to have a beneficial effect. Elements which must be kept in mind when estimating the useful lives of intangible assets include:

1) Legal, regulatory, or contractual provisions may set maximum limits upon them.

2) Provisions for renewal or extension may alter a stated limit.

3) Results of obsolescence, demand, competition, and other economic factors may shorten the anticipated useful period.

4) A useful life may be tied to the service-life expectancies of key individuals or groups of employees.

5) Anticipated actions and/or reactions of competitors and others may reduce existing competitive advantages.

6) An apparently unlimited useful life may be so indefinite that benefits cannot be reasonably projected with any degree of accuracy.

The cost of each type of intangible asset should be amortized on the estimated life of that specific asset and should not be written off at the time it is acquired. After critical analysis, most intangible assets can be assigned a reasonably accurate useful life. Even when this approach proves to be overly subjective, a reasonable estimate of the useful life may at times be based on upper and lower limits. However, the period of amortization should not exceed an upper limit of 40 years. Analysis may show that the indeterminate lives of some of the intangible assets will probably exceed 40 years. In such cases, at the time of acquisition, it should be established that the cost of these assets will be amortized over 40 years, not a shorter period of time.

Unless a company can show that another amortization method is more appropriate, the straight-line method should be applied. The method and period of amortization should be disclosed in the financial statements. A timing difference is not created by the amortization of acquired goodwill and of other acquired intangible assets not deductible in computing income taxes payable. An allocation of income taxes is inappropriate.

Disclosure of Accounting Policies

APB 22 covers *Disclosure of Accounting Policies.* A description of all significant accounting policies of the reporting entity should be included as an integral part of all financial statements. Whether these statements are issued in presenting the entity's financial position, changes in the financial position, or in showing results of operations in accordance with GAAP, a description of all significant accounting policies, methods and practices of the reporting entity should be included as an integral part of all financial statements. When it is appropriate to issue one or more basic financial statements without the others, these statements should also comprise the pertinent accounting policies. Not-for-profit entities should also present details of their accounting policies as an integral part of their financial statements.

Content and Format of Disclosures

1) Disclosure of accounting policies should identify and describe the accounting principles employed by the reporting business and the methods of applying those principles which are important in the determination of financial position, changes in financial position, or results of operations. The disclosure should include decisions concerning applicability of principles relating to recognition of revenue and allocation of asset costs to current and future periods. The disclosure statement should comprise all the reasoning behind the choice of, or an explanation of, the accounting principles and methods employed that involve any of the following:
   a) Selection of one practice over another from existing acceptable alternatives.
   b) Principles and methods peculiar to the industry of the reporting firm, even when such principles and methods are characteristically followed in that industry.
   c) Unusual or innovative applications of generally accepted accounting principles or of practices and methods peculiar to that industry.
2) Examples of disclosures commonly required in regard to accounting policies include those relating to basis of consolidation, depreciation methods, amortization of intangibles, inventory pricing, accounting for research and development costs and the basis for amortization thereof, translation of foreign currencies, recognition of profit on long-term construction-type contracts, recognition of revenue from franchising and leasing operations, and any other items deemed pertinent to give a complete picture of a firm's financial status.
3) The format follows a plan of having a separate *Summary of Significant Accounting Policies* preceding the notes to the financial statements or, in some cases, as the initial note of the statement.

Early Extinguishment of Debt

APB 26 covers the extinguishment of **all** debt other than debt that has been extinguished through a troubled restructuring and convertible debt that is converted to equity securities of the debtor.

The reacquisition of any form of debt security or debt instrument before the scheduled maturity date, other than through conversion by the holder of the said debt obligation, is classified as early extinguishment. This is true whether the debt is considered as terminated or is held as so-called treasury bonds. All open-market or mandatory reacquisitions of debt securities in order to meet sinking fund requirements are considered to be extinguishments. Three definitions which may be helpful in understanding APB 26 are:

1) *Difference* as used in this opinion is the excess of the reacquisition price over the net carrying amount or the excess of the net carrying amount over the acquisition price.

2) *Net carrying amount of debt* is the amount due at maturity, adjusted for unamortized premium, discount and cost of issuance.

3) *Reacquisition price of debt* is the amount paid on early extinguishment including a call premium and miscellaneous costs of reacquisition. If early extinguishment is achieved by a direct exchange of new securities, the reacquisition price is the total present value of the new securities.

All extinguishments of debt before their scheduled maturity dates are basically the same. Therefore, accounting for these transactions is the same despite differing methods used to bring about extinguishments. Any difference between the reacquisition price and the net carrying amount of the extinguished debt should be recognized in income for the period during which extinguishment occurs. That difference is to be recorded as losses or gains and recorded as a separate item.

The extinguishment of convertible debt before maturity does not change its nature in relation to its classification as debt or equity at that time. Hence, any difference between the cash acquisition price of the debt and its net carrying amount is to be recognized in income during the period of extinguishment as a loss or gain, as the case may be.

FINANCIAL ACCOUNTING STANDARDS BOARD (FASB) STATEMENTS

Reporting Gains and Losses from Extinguishment of Debt

1) FASB Statement No. 4 specifies that gains and losses from extinguishment of debt should be aggregated and, if material, classified as an extraordinary item in the income statement.

2) Statement 4 requires the following disclosures in financial statements in which debt extinguishments are reported as extraordinary items:

   a) A description of the extinguishment transaction, including the sources of any funds used to extinguish debt.

   b) The income tax effect in the period of extinguishment.

   c) The per share amount of the aggregate gain or loss, net of related income tax effect.

3) Paragraph 8 of FASB Statement No. 4 says, in part:

> "Gains and losses from extinguishment of debt that are included in the determination of net income shall be aggregated and, if material, classified as an extraordinary item, net of related income tax effect. That conclusion shall apply whether an extinguishment is early or at scheduled maturity date or later."

This portion of the Statement amends APB Opinion No. 30 in that material gains and losses from extinguishment of debt are to be classified as an extraordinary item in the income statement.

4) *Types of Extinguishment of Debt:*

   a) Retirement of debt serially—includes serial bonds as well as debt payable in periodic installments (e.g., term loans and notes payable to insurance company).

   b) Refinancing—replacing existing debt with new debt.

   c) Early extinguishment of debt at a discount.

   d) Early extinguishment of debt at a premium.

   e) Sinking-fund purchase.

5) *Disclosure Requirements:* The Statement concludes that gains or losses from extinguishment of debt that are reported as extraordinary items should be described sufficiently to enable users of financial statements to evaluate their significance. The following disclosures are required:

   a) A description of the extinguishment transactions, including the sources of any funds used to extinguish debt.

   b) The income tax effect in the period of extinguishment.

   c) The per share amount of the aggregate gain or loss, net of related income tax effect.

Accounting for Contingencies

FASB Statement No. 5 establishes new accounting criteria for an estimated loss from a contingency and carries forward existing criteria for an estimated gain from a contingency. To comply with the Statement, many companies which have made accruals for contingent losses will be required to reverse the accruals and credit the balance to income in the year of change. Other companies will be required to begin accruing for loss contingencies and charge income in the year of change.

1) The key provisions of the Statement are:

a) An estimated loss from a contingency should be charged to income only if **both** of the following conditions are met.

1. It is **probable** that a future event or events will occur confirming the likelihood that an asset had been impaired or a liability had been incurred as of the balance sheet date;

2. The amount of the loss can be **reasonably estimated**.

b) Contingencies which might result in gains usually are not recorded prior to realization.

c) Reserves for catastrophe losses, general contingencies (i.e., general or unspecified business risks), and self-insurance reserves or accruals for workmen's compensation and other employment-related costs which are excluded from the scope of the Statement.

2) Disclosure:

a) For accrued loss contingencies, disclosure of the nature of the accrual and, in some circumstances, the amount accrued may be necessary for the financial statements not to be misleading.

b) For contingencies which represent at least a "reasonable possibility" of loss, but which are not accrued because both conditions for accrual (probable and reasonable estimate) are not met, the Statement requires disclosure of:

1. The nature of the contingency;

2. An estimate of the possible loss or range of loss or a statement that an estimate cannot be made.

3) *Contingency:* An existing condition, situation, or set of circumstances involving uncertainty as to possible gain or loss to an enterprise that will ultimately be resolved when one or more future events occur or fail to occur. Resolution of the uncertainty may confirm the acquisition of an asset, or the reduction of a liability, or the loss or impairment of an asset, or the incurrence of a liability.

4) In determining whether an accrual is required for a loss contingency, it is first necessary to assess the outcome of the contingency in terms of the likelihood of occurrence of the future event or events that will confirm the loss.

a) The Statement uses three terms in discussing the likelihood of occurrence:

1. *Probable*—The future event or events are likely to occur.

2. *Reasonably possible*—The chance of the future event or events occurring is more than remote but less than likely.

3. *Remote*—The chance of the future event or events occurring is slight.

b) If it is probable that a loss will result from a contingency and the amount of the loss can be *reasonably estimated,* the estimated loss should be accrued by a charge to income. *Both* conditions must be met if a loss contingency is to be accrued.

c) Companies which currently have contingency reserves that do not meet both conditions for accrual (e.g., general contingencies, self-insurance, catastrophe losses) will be required to reverse the reserves; other companies will be required to begin accruing for loss contingencies that meet both conditions (e.g., warranty obligations).

5) Examples of Loss Contingencies—loss related to:

a) Collectibility of receivables.

b) Obligations related to product warranties and product defects.

c) Risk of loss or damage of enterprise property by fire, explosion, or other hazards.

d) General or unspecified business risks.

e) Risk of loss from catastrophies assumed by property and casualty insurance companies including reinsurance companies.

f) Threat of expropriation of assets.

g) Pending or threatened litigation.

h) Actual or possible claims and assessments.

i) Guarantees of indebtedness of others.

j) Obligations of commercial banks under "standby letters of credit."

k) Agreements to repurchase receivables (or the related property) that have been sold.

6) Examples of Items Not Affected by the Statement:

a) Pension costs.

b) Deferred compensation contracts.

c) Capital stock issued to employees.

d) Group insurance.

e) Vacation pay.

f) Workmen's compensation.

g) Disability benefits.

7) The Statement continues existing accounting and disclosure requirements for the following items:

a) Net losses on long-term, construction-type contracts.

b) Write-down of carrying amount of operating assets because questionable recovery of cost.

c) Unused letters of credit.

d) Long-term leases.

e) Assets pledged as security for loans.

f) Pension plans.

g) Existence of cumulative preferred stock dividends in arrears.

h) Commitments for plant acquisition.

i) Commitments to reduce debts, maintain working capital, or restrict dividends.

8) Product Warranty Liabilities: The Statement categorizes warranty obligations as contingencies because of the uncertainty surrounding future claims. An accrual for warranty obligations is required if it is probable that customers will make valid warranty claims and the aggregate amount of the claims can be reasonably estimated. The Statement suggests that a reasonable estimate may be based on individual or overall claims and will usually depend on the company's warranty experience.

Accounting for Certain Marketable Securities

1) FASB Statement No. 12 affects the year-end reporting of companies which own marketable equity securities by requiring such securities to be carried at the lower of aggregate cost or market value. Only not-for-profit organizations, mutual life insurance companies, and employee benefit plans are exempted from the new requirements.

2) Separate rules are provided for companies in industries that follow specialized accounting practices with respect to marketable securities (broker-dealers, investment companies, and insurance companies).

3) Marketable equity securities should be carried at the lower of aggregate cost or market value, as determined at each balance sheet date. Companies in industries in which the market value is an accepted practice may elect that practice.

4) Generally, for purposes of comparing aggregate cost and market value, securities are to be grouped into two portfolios according to their current or noncurrent classification in classified balance sheets.

a) Transfers between the current and noncurrent classifications should be made at the lower of cost or market value at the date of transfer.

b) If market value is less than cost, the difference is accounted for as a realized loss.

c) In unclassified balance sheets, all marketable equity securities would be considered noncurrent.

5) Realized gains and losses are to be included in net income in the period in which they occur unless industry practice allows different treatment.

a) Any change in the excess of aggregate cost over market value for securities classified as current assets should be included in the determination of net income; however, any change in such excess for **noncurrent** securities should be included as a separate item in the equity section of the balance sheet.

b) Subsequent recoveries in market price (up to the amount of original cost) would be credited to income in the case of current securities and for noncurrent securities would be used to reduce the accumulated net unrealized loss shown in the equity section of the balance sheet.

6) For companies **not following** specialized industry accounting practices:

a) Aggregate cost and aggregate market value, as of the date of each balance sheet presented, segregated between current and noncurrent securities when a classified balance sheet is presented.

b) Net realized and net unrealized gains and losses during each year for which an income statement is presented with separate disclosure of the amounts included in the equity section of the balance sheet and in determining net income. Also, the basis on which cost was determined in computing realized gains and losses.

7) For companies **following** specialized industry accounting practices:

a) The amount by which equity has been increased or decreased as a result of unrealized gains and losses for each period for which an income statement is presented.

8) For **all** companies:

a) Gross unrealized gains and losses as of the date of the latest balance sheet presented, segregated between current and noncurrent securities when a classified balance sheet is presented.

b) Significant net realized and net unrealized gains and losses arising after the date of the financial statements, but prior to their issuance.

9) Exempted Entities:

a) Not-for-profit organizations.

b) Mutual life insurance companies.

c) Employee benefit plans.

10) This Statement does apply to mutual savings banks and other for-profit mutual enterprises.

11) Generally, the reporting requirements apply only to *marketable equity securities. Equity securities* are defined as those instruments that represent:

a) Ownership shares (e.g., common, preferred, and other capital stock).

b) The right to acquire ownership shares at a fixed or determinable price (e.g., warrants, rights, and call options).

c) The right to dispose of ownership shares at fixed or determinable prices (e.g., put options).

d) Marketable means that a sales price or bid and ask prices are currently available on a national securities exchange or in the over-the-counter market. In the over-the-counter market, quotations may be reported by the National Association of Securities Dealers Automatic Quotations System or by the National Quotations Bureau, Inc. In the latter case, quotations must be made available from at least three dealers for the equity security to be considered marketable.

e) Equity securities traded in foreign markets are considered marketable when such markets are of a breadth and scope comparable to a national securities exchange or the over-the-counter market in the United States.

12) This Statement does not apply to the following securities:

a) Treasury stock.

b) Preferred stock that must be redeemed by the issuer or that is redeemable at the option of the investor.

c) Convertible bonds.

d) Restricted stock.

e) Investments accounted for by the equity method.

13) The Statement defines "restricted stock" as those securities for which sale is restricted by a governmental or contractual requirement unless such requirement terminates within one year or the holder has the power to cause the requirement to be met within one year. Further, any portion of restricted stock which can reasonably be expected to qualify for sale within one year (e.g., under the SEC's Rule 144) is not considered restricted.

14) Companies that do not follow specialized industry accounting practices should account for marketable equity securities as follows:

a) The carrying amount should be the lower of the aggregate cost or market value, determined at the balance-sheet date. According to the FASB, aggregate market value simply represents the number of shares owned times the quoted market price per share.

b) Any excess of aggregate cost over market value at the balance-sheet date is accounted for as a valuation allowance.

c) Realized gains and losses and changes in the valuation allowance related to current asset securities should be included in determining net income in the period in which they occur.

d) Accumulated changes in the valuation allowance relating to noncurrent asset securities (including those presented in an unclassified balance sheet) should be included as a separate item in the equity section of the balance sheet.

e) The cost of any security to which d) applies should be written down to market value by a charge to income if a market value decline is judged to be other than temporary. The amount to which the security is written down becomes its new cost basis for subsequent application of this Statement. Recoveries in market value in excess of new cost may not be recognized.

15) When it is determined that permanent impairment in value has occurred, the cost of the individual security should be written down and the difference treated as a realized loss.

16) Although this Statement gives little guidance for determining the existence of permanent impairment, consideration should be given to such factors as the length of time the security has been owned, the length of time and the extent to which the security has been owned, the length of time and the extent to which the market value has been less than cost, the financial condition and prospects of the issuer, the financial condition and prospects of the holder, and the size of the decline in relation to net income and stockholders' equity of the holder.

17) The Statement says unrealized gains and losses on marketable securities are timing differences as defined in APB Opinion No. 11, *Accounting for Income Taxes*. Therefore, the provisions of that Opinion should be applied to determine whether the applicable income tax effect should be recorded for a net unrealized gain or loss (whether included in income or reflected directly in the equity section of the balance sheet). The Statement reiterates the conclusion in Opinion No. 11 that tax effects of unrealized capital losses should be recognized only when realization of the benefit by an offset of the loss against capital gains is assured beyond a reasonable doubt.

Foreign Currency Translation

FASB 52 covers accounting for the translation of foreign currency statements and the gain and loss on foreign currency transactions. Foreign currency transactions and financial statements of foreign entities include branches, subsidiaries, partnerships and joint ventures, which are consolidated, combined, or reported under the equity method in financial statements prepared in accordance with U.S. generally accepted financial principles.

The rapid expansion of international business activities of U.S. companies and dramatic changes in the world monetary system created the need to reconsider the accounting and reporting for foreign currency translation. In considering this topic, the FASB issued FASB Statement No. 52, *Foreign Currency Translations*.

1) Foreign currency transactions include buying or selling on credit goods or services whose prices are denominated in a foreign currency; i.e., currency other than the currency of the reporting entity's country.

2) Being a party to an unperformed foreign exchange contract.

3) Borrowing or lending funds denominated in a foreign currency.

4) For other reasons, acquiring assets or incurring liabilities denominated in foreign currency.

Statement 52 also applies to a foreign enterprise which reports in its currency in conformity with U.S. generally accepted accounting principles. For example, a French subsidiary of a U.S. parent should translate the foreign currency financial statements of its Italian subsidiary in accordance with Statement 52. The objective of translation is to measure and express in dollars, and in conformity with U.S. generally accepted accounting principles, the assets, liabilities, revenues, or expenses that are measured or denominated in foreign currency. In achieving this objective, translation should remeasure these amounts in dollars without changing accounting principles. For example, if an asset was originally measured in a foreign currency under the historical cost concept, translation should remeasure the carrying amount of the asset in dollars at historical cost, not replacement cost or market value.

The most common foreign currency transactions result from the import or export of goods or services, foreign borrowing or lending, and forward exchange contacts. Import or export transactions can be viewed as being composed of two elements—a sale or purchase and the settlement of the related receivable or payable. Changes in the exchange rate, which occur between the time of sale or purchase and the settlement of the receivable or payable, should not affect the measurement of revenues from exports or the cost of imported goods or services.

Foreign currency statements should be translated based on the exchange rate at the end of the reporting year. Translation gains and losses are presented in the stockholders' equity section. Also important is the accounting treatment of gains and losses resulting from transactions denominated in a foreign currency. These are shown in the current year's income statement.

Definitions.   An understanding of this rather complex accounting rule can be aided by becoming familiar with the terms used in the Statement. The following list of definitions will enable the accountant to apply the accounting procedures and methods which are covered in the brief of the rule following the definitions.

Attribute—For accounting purposes, the quantifiable elements of items.

Conversion—Exchanging one currency for another.

Currency Exchange Rate—The rate at which one unit of a currency can be exchanged or converted into another currency. For purposes of translation of financial statements, the current exchange rate is the rate at the end of the period covered by the financial statements, or the dates of recognition in the statements for revenues, expenses, gains and losses.

Currency Swap—An exchange between enterprises of the currencies of two different countries with a binding commitment to reverse the exchange of the two currencies at the same rate of exchange on a specified future date.

Current Rate Method—All assets and liabilities are translated at the exchange rate in effect on the balance sheet date. Capital accounts are translated at *historical exchange rates.*

Discount or Premium on a Forward Contract—The foreign currency amount of a contract multiplied by the difference between the contracted forward rate and the spot rate at the date of inception of the contract.

Economics Environment—The nature of the business climate in which an entity *primarily* generates and expends cash.

Entity—In this instance, a party to a transaction which produces a monetary asset or liability denominated in a currency other than its functional currency.

Exchange Rate—The ratio between a unit of one currency and the amount of another currency for which that unit can be exchanged at a particular time. The appropriate exchange rate for the translation of income statement accounts is the rate for the date on which those elements are recognized during the period.

Foreign Currency—A currency other than the functional currency of the entity being referred to. For example, the dollar could be a foreign currency for a foreign entity. Composites of currencies, such as the Special Drawing Rights (SDRs), used to set prices or denominate amounts of loans, etc., have the characteristics of foreign currency for purposes of applying Statement 52.

Foreign Currency Transaction—A transaction the terms of which are denominated in a currency other than an entity's functional currency. Foreign currency transactions arise when an enterprise buys or sells goods or services on credit at prices which are denominated in foreign currency; when an entity borrows or lends funds and the amounts payable or receivable are denominated in foreign currency; acquires or disposes of assets, or incurs or settles liabilities denominated in a foreign currency.

Foreign Currency Translation—Amounts that are expressed in the reporting currency of an enterprise that are denominated in a foreign currency. An example is the translation of the financial statements of a U.S. company from the foreign currency to U.S. dollars.

In the translation of balance sheets, the assets and liabilities are translated at the *current exchange rate,* e.g., rate at the balance sheet date. Income statement items are translated at the *weighted-average exchange rate* for the year.

There are two steps in translating the foreign country's financial statements into U.S. reporting requirements:

1) Conform the foreign country's financial statements to GAAP.
2) Convert the foreign currency into U.S. dollars, the reporting currency.

Foreign Entity—An operation (subsidiary, division, branch, joint venture, etc.) whose financial statements are prepared in a currency other than the currency of the reporting enterprise. The financial statements are combined and accounted for on the equity basis in the financial statements of the reporting enterprise.

Foreign Exchange Contract—An agreement to exchange at a specified future date, currencies of different countries at a specified rate, which is the *forward rate.*

Functional Currency—The currency of the primary economic environment in which an entity operates; that is, the currency of the environment in which an entity primarily generates and expends cash.

Hedging—An effort by management to minimize the effect of exchange rate fluctuations on reported income, either directly by entering into an exchange contract to buy or sell one currency for another, or indirectly by managing exposed net assets or liabilities' positions by borrowing or billing in dollars rather than the local currency. An agreement to exchange different currencies at a specified future date and at a specified rate referred to as the *forward rate.*

Highly Inflationary Economy—Economies of countries in which the *cumulative* local inflation rate over a three-year period exceeds approximately 100 per cent, or more.

Historical Exchange Rate—A rate, other than the current or a forward rate, at which a foreign transaction took place.

Inflation—Not defined by specific reference to a commonly quoted economic index. Management can select an appropriate method for measuring inflation. An annual inflation rate of about 20 percent for three consecutive years would result in a cumulative rate of about 100 percent.

Intercompany Balance—The foreign currency transactions of the parent, the subsidiary, or both. An intercompany account denominated in the local foreign currency is a foreign currency transaction of the **parent**. An intercompany account denominated in dollars is a foreign currency transaction of a foreign entity whose functional currency is a currency **other than** the U.S. dollar.

Local Currency—The currency of a particular country.

Measurement—Measurement is the process of measuring transactions denominated in a unit of currency (e.g., purchases payable in British pounds).

Remeasurement—Measurement of the functional currency financial statement amounts in other than the currency in which the transactions are denominated.

Reporting Currency—The currency used by an enterprise in the preparation of its financial statements.

Reporting Enterprise—An entity or group whose financial statements are being referenced. In Statement 52, those financial statements reflect a) the financial statements of one or more foreign operations by combination, consolidation, or equity accounting; b) foreign currency transactions; c) both a) and b).

Self-Contained Operations—Operations which are integrated with the local economic environment, and other operations which are primarily a direct or integral component or extension of a parent company's operations.

Speculative Contracts—A contract that is intended to produce an investment gain (not to hedge a foreign currency exposure).

Spot Rate—An exchange for *immediate delivery* of the currencies exchanged.

Transaction Date—The date at which a transaction, such as a purchase of merchandise or services, is recorded in accounting records in conformity with GAAP. A long-term commitment may have more than one transaction date; for example, the due date of each progress payment under a construction contract is an *anticipated transaction date* credited to shareholder's equity.

Translation Adjustment—Translation adjustments translate financial statements from the entity's functional currency into the reporting currency. The amount necessary to balance the financial statements after completing the translation process. The amount is charged or credited to shareholder's equity.

Unit of Measure—The currency in which assets, liabilities, revenues, expenses, gains and losses are measured.

Weighted Average Rates—Determined on a monthly basis by an arithmetic average of daily closing rates, and on a quarterly and an annual basis by an arithmetic average of average monthly rates.

Because of the proliferation of multinational companies, expanding international trade, business involvement with foreign subsidiaries, and joint ventures, FASB 52, *Foreign Currency Translation,* was established, in effect, by popular demand. The stated aims of Statement 52 are to a) provide information that is generally compatible with the expected effects of a rate change on an enterprise's cash flows and equity and b) reflect in consolidated statements the financial results and relationships of the individual consolidated entities as measured in their functional currencies, whether the U.S. dollar or a specified foreign currency, in conformity with U.S. generally accepted accounting principles.

The method adopted to achieve these aims is termed the *functional currency approach* which is the currency of the primary economic environment in which the entity carries on its business; in substance, where it generates and expends cash. The Statement permits a multiple measurement basis in consolidated financial statements (depending upon the country in which the subsidiary operates) because business enterprises made up of a multinational enterprise operate and generate cash flows in diverse economic environments, each with its own functional currency. When an enterprise operates in several of these environments, the results of business transactions are measured in the functional currency of the particular environment. "Measured in the functional currency" has the specific meaning that gains and losses comprising income are determined only in relation to accounts denominated in the functional currency.

Mechanically, the functional currency approach calls for eventual translation of all functional currency assets and liabilities into dollars at the current exchange rate. Use under Statement 52 of the current rate for all accounts resolves both the economically compatible results and operating margins distortions. In the past, these distortions came about with the translation of nonmonetary accounts at historical rates. The volatility of earnings distortions is alleviated by recording the translation adjustments directly into shareholders' equity.

The functional currency approach presumes the following:

1) Many business enterprises operate and generate cash flows in a number of different countries (different economic environments).

2) Each of these operations can usually be identified as operating in a single economic environment: the local environment or the parent company's environment. The currency of the principal economic environment becomes the functional currency for those operations.

3) The enterprise may be committed to a long-term position in a specific economic environment and have no plans to liquidate that position in the foreseeable future.

Because measurements are made in multiple functional currencies, decisions relating to the choice of the functional currency of a specific foreign operation will in all likelihood have a significant effect upon reported income. Even though the management of the business enterprise is entitled to a degree of latitude in its weighing of specific facts, the thinking behind adoption of this Statement is that the functional currency is to be determined based on the true nature of the enterprise and not upon some arbitrary selection which management feels might be of particular advantage to the reporting entity.

Determining the Functional Currency. Multinational companies are involved with foreign business interests either through transactions or investments in foreign entities operating in a number of different economic environments. Each of these endeavors may be associated with one primary economic environment whose currency then becomes the functional currency for that operation. On the other hand, in a foreign country where the economic and/or political environment is so unstable that a highly inflationary economy is likely, it may be deemed wise to carry on the enterprise with the dollar as the functional currency. If the operations in situations of this nature are remeasured on a dollar basis, further erosion of nonmonetary accounts may be avoided.

When there is a reasonably stable economic situation, the national environment of each operation should be considered as the primary economic environment of the particular operation since national sovereignty is a primary consideration in relation to currency control.

Industry practice, on the other hand, may in some instances be instrumental in the determination of a primary economic environment and functional currency. If it is an industry-wide practice that pricing or other transaction attributes are calculated in a specific currency, such as prices set in dollars on a worldwide basis, that fact may be more of a determinant than local currency considerations.

The actual decisions in determining a functional currency depend to a large extent upon the operating policy adopted by the reporting company. Two broad classes of foreign operations are to be considered:

1) Those in which a foreign currency is the functional currency. This designation will have been made after receiving the facts and determining that this particular aspect of foreign business operations is largely autonomous and confined to a specific foreign economic environment. That is, ordinary operations are not dependent upon the economic environment of the parent company's functional currency, nor does the foreign operation primarily generate or expend the parent's functional currency.

2) When the workaday business of the foreign operation is deemed to be in actuality just an extension of the parent company's operation and dependent upon the economic environment of the parent company, the dollar may be designated as the functional currency. In substance, most transactions can reasonably be in dollars, thus obviating the need for foreign currency translation.

One of the objectives of Statement 52 is to provide information that is generally compatible with the expected economic effects of a rate change on an enterprise's cash flow and equity in a readily understood manner. If a foreign operation's policy is to convert available funds into dollars for current or near-term distribution to the parent, selection of a dollar functional currency may be expedient.

Therefore, reporting for investments expected to be of short-term duration, such as construction or development joint ventures, the dollar should probably be designated the functional currency. If the nature of an investment changes over a period of time, future redetermination of the appropriate functional currency may become necessary. Such redetermination is permissible only when, in actual fact, significant changes in economic facts and/or circumstances have occurred. The operative functional currency cannot be redetermined merely because management has "changed its collective mind." It becomes evident that functional currency determination should be carefully considered with the decision weighted in favor of the long-term picture rather than short-term expectations.

In the event that redetermination is necessary, three procedures should be kept in mind:

1) When the functional currency has been changed, Statement 52 provides that the prior year's financial statement need not be restated for a change in functional currency.

2) When the functional currency change is from the local currency to the dollar, historical costs and exchange rates are to be determined from translated dollar amounts immediately prior to the change.

3) When the functional currency change is from the dollar to the local currency, nonmonetary assets are to be translated at current exchange rates, charging the initial translation adjustment to equity similar to that produced when Statement 52 was adopted.

Translation. Translation is the process of converting financial statements expressed in one unit of currency to a different unit of currency (the reporting currency). In short, translation as used in Statement 52 is the restatement into the reporting currency (the U.S. dollar) of any/all foreign currency financial statements utilized in preparing the consolidated financial statements of the U.S. parent company.

Thus, the focus for the preparation and subsequent translation of the financial statements of individual components of an organization is, as previously stated, to:

1) Provide information that is generally compatible with the expected economic effects of a rate change on the enterprise's cash flows and equity, and

2) Reflect in consolidated statements the financial results and relationships of the individual consolidated entities as measured in their functional currencies in conformity with U.S. generally accepted accounting principles.

Measurement is the process of stating the monetary value of transactions denominated in a particular unit of currency (e.g., purchases payable in British pounds). These transactions may also be figured in a unit of currency other than that in which they are denominated. This process then becomes remeasurement and is accomplished by assuming that an exchange of currencies will occur at the exchange rate in effect at the time of the remeasurement. As is evident, should the exchange rate fluctuate between the date of the original transaction and the date of the exchange, a foreign exchange gain or loss will result. The gains or losses so recorded vary little from other trading activities and are, therefore, included in income.

It is important to note that while translations were formerly based on the premise that financial statements of a U.S. enterprise should be measured in a single unit of currency—the U.S. dollar—translation was under the Old Rule, a one-step process that included both remeasurement and reporting in dollars. In the newer context of the functional approach, multiple units of measure are permitted so that remeasurement is required only when 1) the accounts of an entity are maintained in a currency other than its own functional currency, or 2) an enterprise is invoiced in a transaction which produces a monetary asset or liability not denominated in its functional currency.

The subsequent translation to dollars under FASB 52 is the second step of a two-step process necessary to prepare U.S. dollar financial statements.

Foreign currency transactions. Foreign currency transactions are those denominated in a currency other than the entity's functional currency. These transactions include:

1) Buying or selling goods priced in a currency other than the entity's functional currency.
2) Borrowing or lending funds (including intercompany balances) denominated in a different currency.
3) Engaging in an unperformed forward exchange contract.

As becomes evident, companies with foreign subsidiaries can readily become engaged in foreign currency transactions which must be considered when financial statements are prepared. But, in addition, companies which have no foreign branches may also in the everyday course of business become involved in foreign currency transactions.

Regardless of whether the company is entirely domestic-based or not, at the transaction date, each resulting asset, liability, revenue, expense, gain, or loss not already denominated in the entity's functional currency must be so measured and recorded. At the close of each subsequent accounting period, all unsettled monetary balances are to be remeasured using the exchange rates in effect on the balance-sheet date. Gains and losses from remeasuring or settling foreign currency transactions are accounted for as current income. However, with certain restrictions, hedging losses and gains may be excluded from net current income.

Hedging. Hedging is planning to enter into a forward exchange contract to buy or sell one currency for another, or to manage an exposed net asset or liability position, such as borrowing or billing in dollars instead of in a local currency.

Hedging gains and losses can be excluded from net income when the transaction is *designated* as a hedge by management and is effective as such. Foreign currency transactions can be used in addition to, or in place of, forward exchange contracts to hedge a firm's foreign currency commitments. Under FASB 8, the deferral of unrealized translation gains and losses was permitted only when the commitment was hedged by forward exchange contracts and they, in turn, had to match the commitment dates. On the other hand, FASB 52 permits maintenance of a hedge for any desired period of time. Furthermore, management now also has the option of removing a hedge and later reestablishing it. Qualifying as hedges are foreign currency cash balances and certificates of deposit, foreign currency loans, foreign currency swaps, and intercompany account balances.

Gains and losses from hedges of firm commitments in foreign currency, such as a contract to buy equipment, are deferred and included in the measurement of the related foreign currency transaction, e.g., the cost of the equipment at the date of the actual purchase. However, hedging losses may not be deferred if it appears likely that deferral will have the effect of recognizing losses in later periods. When a firm commitment is hedged, the translation gains or losses which are deferrable are limited to the amount that provides a hedge on an after-tax basis.

FASB Statement 91, *Accounting for Nonrefundable Fees and Costs Associated with Originating or Acquiring Loans and Initial or Direct Costs of Leases*

FASB Statement 91 prescribes accounting for nonrefundable fees and costs associated with lending, committing to lend, or purchasing a loan or group of loans. The Statement also details the accounting methods to be used for initial direct costs connected with leasing.

Loan fees may be deferred and recognized over the life of the loan as an adjustment of yield. Also, some organization costs are to be deferred and amortized over the life of the loan and appear as a reduction in yield. Deferred fees and costs are customarily figured using the interest method.

Costs which may be deferred are spelled out in the Statement and must be related to an actual loan or commitment. The new rules do away with the practice of deferring all or some portion of costs related to a particular lending activity or unit, such as the mortgage loan department, regardless of the volume of business generated. Payroll and other costs related to unsuccessful, rejected applications, or idle time, are considered as current expense. Fees and costs must normally be accounted for on a loan-by-loan basis, but under specified conditions, fees and costs can be grouped.

Although not mentioned in Statement 91's title, the Statement also covers the accounting procedures for discounts and premiums related to purchased debt securities, such as corporate bonds.

FASB Statement 92, *Regulated Enterprises— Accounting for Phase-In Plans*

FASB Statement 92 outlines procedures for regulated enterprises to recover allowable cost of construction of a new plant under a phase-in plan adopted by a regulator. Further, it specifically relates to allowable costs deferred for future recovery under phase-in plans for plants completed before January 1, 1988, or plants on which substantial physical construction was performed prior to that date.

Capitalization of the costs is required if each of the following criteria is met:

1) The regulator has agreed to the plan.
2) The plan specifies recovery time.
3) Allowable costs deferred will be recovered within 10 years of beginning the deferral

4) The percentage increases in scheduled rates for each succeeding year is less than, or equal to, the percentage increases in rates of the prior year.

If each of these criteria is not met, capitalization of the allowable costs deferred under the plan would not be permitted.

FASB Statement 92 applies to phase-in plans that do not meet the criteria for capitalization of deferred allowable costs set forth in the Statement. The costs can be deferred if the regulated enterprise has filed, or plans to file, a rate application to amend the phase-in plan to meet the criteria for capitalization, and it is reasonably possible the regulator will change the phase-in plan. The Statement should be applied to those plans when the regulator amends or refuses to amend the plan.

FASB Statement 93, *Recognition of Depreciation by Not-for-Profit Organizations*

FASB Statement 93 provides that all not-for-profit organizations must recognize depreciation on all long-lived, tangible assets in general-purpose external financial statements. Thus, the Statement eliminates previously allowed exemptions from depreciation accounting for landmarks, monuments, cathedrals, certain historical treasures, and structures such as churches or temples used primarily as houses of worship.

However, rare works of art and historical treasures that have exceptionally long lives will continue to be exempt from depreciation accounting; but to be in line for this exemption, these assets must have recognized cultural, aesthetic, or historical value, and normally will already have had a long existence, and be expected to retain this value far into the future.

Statement 93 also requires not-for-profit organizations to disclose depreciation expense periodically. The financial statement is to include:

1) Depreciation expense for the current reporting period.
2) Balance of major classes reported by nature or function.
3) Accumulated depreciation by major class or in total.
4) Description of accounting methods employed in figuring depreciation.

FASB Statement 95, *Cash Flow Accounting*

Definitions of the terminology used in the cash flow accounting rule (which establishes standards for reporting cash flows in financial statements) are given below. Following the definitions is a summary of the significant points of the new rule which supersedes APB 19. Cash receipts and payments are classified, cash flows are illustrated, and illustrations are given for both the direct and indirect methods of the computations required for statement presentation.

Definitions. These definitions of terms relating specifically to the new rule are helpful for understanding the new requirements.

Cash—Includes currency on hand, demand deposits in banks, and accounts with financial institutions having demand deposits, e.g., a depositary that accepts deposits and permits withdrawals without prior notice or penalty.

Cash Equivalent—Short-term, highly liquid investments that are readily convertible into known amounts of cash and close to maturity (see *Original Maturity,* below), so that a change in the interest rate structure could result in only minimal risk of changes in their value.

Cash Flow—Cash receipts and payments which result from on-going financing or operating activities.

Direct Method—The principal components are the operating cash receipts and payments.

Financing Activities—In general, transactions which acquire capital or require repayment of capital.

Indirect Method—Computation starts with net income adjusted for revenue and expense items that are *not* the result of operating cash transactions. Net income is then reconciled with net cash flow from operating activities. (This method does not disclose operating cash receipts and payments.)

Investing Activities—Making loans; collecting loans; acquiring and disposing of debt; acquiring and disposing of equity; acquiring and disposing of productive assets, such as plant and equipment.

Net Cash Flow—Gross cash receipts and gross cash payments which result in the net cash flow from *operations.*

Noncash and Investing Activities—Investing and financing activities which affect assets or liabilities, but do not result in cash receipts or cash payments.

Operating Activities—All transactions that are not investing or financing activities. Cash flows from activities which enter into the determination of net income.

Original Maturity—Investments purchased three months, or more, before the maturity date. An investment purchased more than three months before maturity is not a cash equivalent, even if its remaining maturity on the date of the financial statement comes under the three months' rule.

Summary.

• Statement 95 provides information in financial statements detailing the cash receipts and cash payments of an enterprise during a specified accounting period.

- The statement of *cash flows* reports the cash results of an enterprise's operations, investing, and financing transactions.
- Related disclosures detail the effect of investing and financing transactions upon the enterprise's financial position, but do not directly affect its cash flow.
- Net income and net cash flow from operating activities are reconciled to show the net effect of operating transactions and other financial activities.
- The cash flows statement explains the change during a specified accounting period in cash and cash equivalents.
- The Statement requires enterprises with foreign currency transactions (e.g., cash receipts and payments) to report the dollar equivalent of foreign currency cash flows. This is done by applying the exchange rates in effect at the time of the cash flows. (A weighted average exchange rate for the period is permissible as specified in FASB No. 52, Para. 12.)

Classification of Cash Receipts and Cash Payments Resulting from Operating Activities

CASH INFLOWS	CASH OUTFLOWS
Receipts from sale of goods and services.	Payments to suppliers.
Collections on accounts.	Payments on accounts.
Collections on short- and long-term notes, and other credit arrangements.	Principal payments on short- and long-term payables.
Interest and dividend receipts.	Interest payments.
Other cash receipts that do not originate from investment or financing activities.	Other cash payments that do not originate from investment or financing activities.
Generally, the cash effects of transactions that enter into the determination of net income.	Payments to employees, tax payments, etc.

Resulting from Investing Activities

CASH INFLOWS	CASH OUTFLOWS
Principal collections on loans.	Loans made. Payment for debt instruments of subsidiaries.
Sale of equity securities of other enterprises.	Purchases of equity securities of other enterprises.
Sale of plant, equipment, property, and other productive assets	Purchases of plant, equipment, and other productive assets

Resulting from Financing Activities

CASH INFLOWS

Proceeds from new securities issues.

Bonds, mortgages, notes, and other indebtedness.

CASH OUTFLOWS

Repurchase of enterprise's equity securities.

Debt repayments; dividend payments.

Direct method—discussion and illustration. Reporting the three major classes of gross cash receipts and gross cash payments and their arithmetic sum is required in order to disclose the *net cash flow* from operating activities. The reconciliation of net income to net cash flow from operating activities must be exhibited in a separate schedule. (See Figures 1 and 2.)

Indirect method—discussion and illustration. The indirect method (also termed the reconciliation method) requires *net cash flow* to be

FIGURE 1 Statement of Cash Flows
Increase (Decrease) in Cash and Cash Equivalents (Direct Method)
Year Ended December 31, 19xx

Cash flows from operating activities:		
Cash received from customers	$ 435,000	
Interest received	5,000	
Cash provided by operations		440,000
Cash paid to employees and suppliers	(382,000)	
Interest paid	(13,000)	
Taxes paid	(20,000)	
Cash disbursed by operations		(415,000)
Net cash flow from operations		$ 25,000
Cash flows from investing activities:		
Marketable securities purchases	$(32,500)	
Proceeds-marketable securities sales	20,000	
Loans made	(8,500)	
Loan collections	6,000	
Plant purchase	(80,000)	
Proceeds-sale of plant assets	37,500	
Net cash used in investing activities		$(57,500)
Cash flows from financing activities:		
Loan proceeds	$ 22,500	
Debt repayments	(27,500)	
Proceeds-Bond issue	50,000	
Proceeds-Common Stock issue	25,000	
Dividends paid	(20,000)	
Net cash provided by financing activities		$ 50,000
Net increase (decrease) in cash		$ 17,500

FIGURE 2 Statement of Cash Flows
Increase (Decrease) in Cash and Cash Equivalents (Direct Method)
Year Ended December 31, 19xx

Cash flow from operations:		
Cash from receivables	$ 10,000,000	
Dividend receipts	700,000	
Cash provided		10,700,000
Cash paid to suppliers	2,000,000	
Wage & salary payments	4,000,000	
Interest payments	750,000	
Taxes	1,000,000	
Cash disbursed		7,750,000
Net cash flow from operations		$ 2,950,000
Cash flow from investing activities:		
Property and plant purchases	(4,000,000)	
Proceeds from sale of equipment	2,500,000	
Acquisition of Corporation X	(900,000)	
Securities purchases	(4,700,000)	
Securities sales	5,000,000	
Borrowings	(7,500,000)	
Collections on notes receivable	5,800,000	
Net cash outflow from investments		$(3,800,000)
Cash flow from financing activities:		
Increase in customer deposits	1,100,000	
Short-term borrowings (increase)	75,000	
Short-term debt payments	(300,000)	
Long-term debt proceeds	(1,250,000)	
Lease payments	(125,000)	
Common stock issue	500,000	
Dividends to shareholders	(450,000)	
Net cash provided by financing		$ 2,050,000
Foreign exchange rate change		100,000
Net increase (decrease) in cash		$ 1,300,000
Schedule—Noncash Investing and Financing Activities:		
Incurred lease obligation .... $	750,000	
Acquisition of Corporation X:		
Working capital acquired (except cash)	(100,000)	
Property and plant acquired	3,000,000	
Assumed long-term debt	(2,000,000)	
Cash paid for acquisition .... $	900,000)	
Common stock issued in payment of long-term debt ...... $	250,000	

reported indirectly. Net income is adjusted and is then reconciled to net cash flow from operating activities. The adjustment requires:

- The removal from net income of the effects of all deferrals of past operating cash receipts and payments.
- The removal from net income of the effects of all accruals of expected future operating cash receipts and payments.
- The removal from net income of the effects of all items of investing and financing cash flows.

The reconciliation can be reported either within the statement of cash flows or in a separate schedule, with the statement of cash flows reporting only the net cash flow from operating activities. However, if the reconciliation is disclosed in the cash flow statement, the adjustments to net income must be identified as reconciling items. This is illustrated in Figure 1.

Figure 2 is a Statement of Cash Flow from operations applying the *direct* method and is more comprehensive than the preceding illustration. This approach includes the disclosure of noncash transactions in a separate schedule formatted after the statement.

Figure 3 on the next page is a Statement of Cash Flow from operations applying the indirect method. This approach includes the disclosure of noncash transactions in a separate schedule formatted below the statement.

FASB Statement 97, *Accounting and Reporting by Insurance Enterprises*

FASB Statement 97 amends Statement 60 by concluding that the accounting methods required by Statement 60 are not appropriate for insurance contracts in which the insurer can vary amounts charged or credited to the policyholder's account or the policyholder can vary the amount of premium paid.

The Statement outlines the accounting methods for three different classifications of long-duration life and annuity products. These classifications are:

1) Universal life-type policies.
2) Limited payment policies.
3) Policies not covering significant mortality or morbidity risks.

Universal life-type policies.   Universal life-type policies must utilize a retrospective deposit method. The liability for this type of policy will be equal to the gross account balances before deduction of surrender charges. Revenues reported will be made up of charges assessed against the policy for mortality, expenses, and surrenders. These charges are presumed to be earned in the period during which they were assessed; however, charges, such as front-end fees, for example, assessed a limited number of times are deferred as unearned revenue

FIGURE 3   Statement of Cash Flows
(Indirect Method) Year Ended December 31, 19xx

Net cash flow from operations		$ 2,950,000
Cash flow from investing activities:		
Property and plant purchases	(4,000,000)	
Proceeds from sale of equipment	2,500,000	
Acquisition of Corporation X	(900,000)	
Securities purchases	(4,700,000)	
Securities sales	5,000,000	
Borrowings	(7,500,000)	
Collections on notes receivable	5,800,000	
Net cash outflow from investments		$(3,800,000)
Cash flow from financing activities:		
Increase in customer deposits	1,100,000	
Short-term borrowings (increase)	75,000	
Short-term debt payments	(300,000)	
Long-term debt proceeds	1,250,000	
Lease payments	(125,000)	
Common stock issue	500,000	
Dividends to shareholders	(450,000)	
Net cash provided by financing		$ 2,050,000
Foreign exchange rate change		100,000
Net increase (decrease) in cash		$ 1,300,000
Schedule—Earnings to Net Cash Flow Reconciliation from Operations:		
Net income	$ 3,000,000	
Noncash expenses, revenues, losses, and gains included in income:		
Depreciation and amortization	1,500,000	
Deferred taxes	150,000	
Net increase in receivables	(350,000)	
Net increase in payables	(200,000)	
Net increase in inventory	(300,000)	
Accrued interest earned	(350,000)	
Accrued interest payable	100,000	
Gain on sale of equipment	(600,000)	
Net cash flow from operations		$ 2,950,000

For universal life-type policies, acquisition costs will be deferred and amortized in relation to present value of estimated future gross profits. Interest accrues to the unamortized balance of the deferred acquisition costs. The estimated gross profits are computed from estimated future mortality charges minus the estimated benefit claims exceeding:

1) The related account balances.

2) Expense charges minus the policy's estimated administration costs.

3) Estimated surrender charges.

4) Estimated future earnings based on investment yields of the policyholder's account balances, minus the estimated interest to be credited to account balances.

When the estimates of future gross profits are reevaluated, the amortization of deferred acquisition costs accrued to date must be adjusted and recognized in current operations. Any deferred revenues, including deferred front-end fees, are recognized as income on the same basis as the amortization of deferred acquisition costs.

Limited-payment policies. Limited-payment policies consist of life insurance and annuity policies with fixed and guaranteed terms having premiums that are payable over a period shorter than the period during which benefits are paid. The premiums for this type of policy are reported as revenues (reserves are computed in accordance with rulings set forth in Statement 60). However, the accumulated profit, formerly shown as a percentage of premiums, is deferred. The amount of coverage must be related to life insurance in force or expected future annuity benefit payments.

Policies not covering significant mortality or morbidity risk. Policies not covering significant mortality or morbidity risks, such as *guaranteed investment contracts* (GICs) and some types of annuities, are shown as interest-bearing or other financial instruments, rather than as insurance contracts. Therefore, the accounting for these policies would show the account balance as a liability, and premiums as deposits rather than as revenues. Deferred acquisition costs would primarily be amortized in relation to future interest margins.

Policies including accident and health insurance not falling under one of these three classifications remain within the requirements of Statement 60.

Statement 97 also requires that property/casualty and stock life insurance companies must provide one-step income statements for realized investment gains or losses instead of the currently required two-step statement. The latter shows operating income after taxes but before net realized investment gains or losses. The one-step income statement presents realized investment gains or losses on a pretax basis with revenues, investment income, and expenses to show income before taxes.

FASB Statement 98, *Accounting for Leases*

Sale-Leaseback Transactions Involving Real Estate, Sales-Type Leases of Real Estate, Definition of the Lease Term, Initial Direct Costs of Direct Financing Leases (FASB 98).

Statement 98 specifies the accounting by a seller-lessee for a sale-leaseback transaction involving real estate or real estate with equipment. The Statement also modifies the lease-term provisions of FASB Statement 13 with respect to all leases, as well as the accounting by a lessor for sales-type leases of real estate that provide for the transfer of title, and the accounting for initial direct costs of direct financing leases.

The Statement clarifies that a seller-lessee can use sales-leaseback accounting for a transaction involving real estate or real estate with equipment only if the transaction qualifies for sales treatment under FASB Statement 66, "Accounting for Sales of Real Estate." The Statement indicates that any continuing involvement with the property by the seller-lessee, other than a normal leaseback, would preclude accounting for the transaction as a sale. A "normal leaseback" would involve the active use of the property during the lease term in the seller-lessee's trade or business.

Amended are the lease-term provisions of Statement 13 for all leases to include all renewal periods during which a loan related to the leased property from the seller-lessee to the buyer-lessor is expected to be outstanding. The definition of the lease term also is expanded to include all renewal periods for which a significant penalty, defined in the Statement, would be incurred by the lessee if the lease were cancelled. These amendments will result in lease terms that generally are longer than previously contemplated.

Statement 98 also amends the definition of a "sales-type" lease that involves real estate, including real estate with equipment. Under the amended definition, a sales-type lease involving real estate must transfer title to the property at or shortly after the end of the lease term. Otherwise, the lease would be classified and accounted for as an operating lease.

The Statement clarifies the amendment in FASB Statement 91 to specify that initial direct costs associated with direct financing leases are to be capitalized separately from the gross investment in the lease and amortized to income over the lease term so as to produce a constant periodic rate of return.

FASB Statement 101, *Accounting for Regulated Enterprises (Discontinuation of FASB Statement 71)*

FASB Statement 101 specifies that an entity that no longer meets the criteria for application of FASB Statement 71, *Accounting for the Effects of Certain Types of Regulation,* to all or part of its regulated operations, should discontinue application of Statement 71 and adjust the affected items and amounts reported in its balance sheet to reflect what they would have been if Statement 71 had never been applied.

However, the carrying amounts of plant, equipment, and inventory measured and reported in line with provisions of Statement 71 should not be adjusted unless they would be impaired. In that eventuality, the carrying amounts of the assets should be reduced to reflect the impairment. The net effect of these adjustments would be included in income during the transition period and classified as an extraordinary item. The Statement takes into consideration that reasonable estimates may be used when determining the effect resulting from discontinuing the provisions of Statement 71, as long as the results would be in line with those that would result from a detailed application of the Statement.

FASB Statement 106, *Employers Accounting for Postretirement Benefits Other than Pensions*

FASB Statement 106 requires a company's accounting for retiree benefits, particularly in relation to health-care costs. The statement is to take effect in 1993 for most companies, but will be delayed until 1995 for private companies with fewer than 500 participants in a plan and for non-U.S. plans.

Companies are apprehensive about the effects on earnings and the time and cost involved in implementing the requirements for complying with Statement 109, *Accounting for Income Taxes*. Statement 106 may cause a decline in earnings as businesses begin to accrue the cost of the benefits on their balance sheets instead of using a cash-basis method which is a pay-as-you-go approach.

Statement 106 is expected to cause problems for companies with large nonaccrued liabilities. When U.S. companies adopt the new rules, a decline in their reported pretax earnings and an increase in their balance sheet liabilities will result.

Where companies must now separate the cost of retiree benefits from those of active workers, they could formerly combine them. To estimate future obligations in addition to current costs, company estimates will be required which could easily be far off the mark. The forward-looking estimates will necessitate a number of subjective considerations, including the projected cost of medical benefits. During the last decade, the number of retirees and the average life expectancy have increased appreciably while the cost of health care has grown much faster than other sectors of the economy.

To add further to the problem, a reduction of federal and state Medicare and Medicaid benefits has resulted in private companies having to absorb the increase in medical costs and has forced health-care reimbursement plans to cover a larger share of these costs. As a result, earnings' pressures may cause companies to consider reducing or cancelling health-care benefits perhaps to the detriment of the company.

Those who in the past have offered generous postretirement benefits and who have high ratios of retirees to active employees are probably already beginning to feel profit pressures even under cash-basis accounting; new, rapidly growing companies having low turnover, young workers and few retirees may well begin to feel the pressures under this rule.

To alleviate some of the problems, the new Statement will not go into effect until the fiscal year beginning after 1992, thus giving companies the opportunity to study and analyze options available for recording the transition obligation and amortizing gains and losses. After analyzing the options, companies will be able to choose those that minimize the effects on their operating results.

Decisions about transition obligations relating to those benefits deemed earned at the time FASB 106 is adopted, but not yet expensed under cash-basis accounting, may be weighed and considered. For example, subject to certain limitations, when a company converts to the accrual method, the transition obligation can be recognized immediately through a one-time charge to income.

Another choice could be to extend the transition obligations over succeeding years, using a straight-line method applied to the average remaining service period of active participants or twenty years, whichever time is longer.

Added to the effect on pretax profits, the decision on the transition obligation may have implications for after-tax profits as well if a company is using the previously mentioned FASB method of accounting for income taxes. This method limits the amount of deferred tax benefits which can be recognizable.

Along with forcing companies to take a long look at accounting alternatives, FASB 106 will undoubtedly cause them to take more than a cursory glance at costs in relation to health-care plans.

When taking into account years of benefit coverage, an important element in computing possible payouts, an estimate must include the number of retirees and dependents eligible for benefits multiplied by the number of years each will probably be covered. These projections require using data on current employees and retirees, including age, gender, and number of dependents, as well as actuarial assumptions for retirement age, employee turnover, and life expectancy. As is readily apparent, these variables are subject to wide margins of error, but they are not the only element for errors in projection.

Another difficult determinant of plan payouts is the number of times each of the medical services covered under existing plans may be used by the retirees and their dependents and the net cost to the company. This can be projected by estimating plan variables, such as the deductible factor, level of participant contributions, number and length of hospital stays and frequency of doctor visits by a similar sector of the population.

Among important factors is the price paid by participants, net of relevant reimbursements such as Medicare. These costs must be estimated using actuarial projections of medical cost increases.

If a company changes its benefits and updates its assumptions, there will be an immediate effect on the annual service costs of employees' OPEB by producing actuarial gains and losses. Similar to pensions, a practice can be adopted that will either recognize or defer the changes. If deferral is used, amortization of the deferral is required only when the cumulative amount exceeds a prescribed minimum. The main effect of deferrals is to help eliminate volatility due to the need to use assumptions.

The major **tax impact** will arise from federal income taxes, although other taxes may also be affected for certain funding approaches. Federal tax deductions for OPEB are generally allowed only at the time the benefits are paid; under limited conditions, deductions can be allowed when the obligation is prefunded.

Companies will find it prudent to consider very carefully the timing of their tax deductions when choosing the best way to record the transition obligation. If an immediate charge is selected, the result will probably be that it is difficult to deduct the full expense for tax obligations.

Another tax to consider is the unrelated business tax, which could be imposed on earnings of assets used to fund OPEB liabilities.

FASB Statement 107, *Disclosure About Fair Value of Financial Statements*

Financial Statement 107, *Disclosure About Fair Value of Financial Statements* defines fair value to mean the amount at which a financial instrument could be exchanged in a current transaction between willing parties, other than a forced or liquidation sale.

The rule is a broad approach to help issuers of financial statements understand what is required of them in meeting the newer, improved disclosure requirements, as well as to help minimize the costs of providing that information. Of course, the reasoning behind the stipulations in this Statement is to ensure a clearer, better defined picture of the fair value of financial instruments than has been provided in the past. This truer picture of an entity's financial activities should be of value to creditors, current and potential investors, and others in making informed decisions concerning granting credit to, investing in, or investigating more thoroughly, a particular entity.

Other impetus for enactment of this rule comes from a desire to provide another useful indicator of the solvency of a financial institution. A recent report issued by the U.S. Treasury Department has suggested that further market value information about various financial institutions could be of aid in regulatory supervision.

Since in many instances generally accepted accounting principles already necessitate disclosure, the term *fair value* use in FASB 107 in no way supersedes or modifies the set of figures obtained using *current value, mark-to-market,* or simply *market value.* It is simply an attempt to get more accurate information about financial instruments—both their assets and liabilities whether on or off the balance sheet—available for easy access.

For the purposes of this Statement, a financial instrument is cash, an ownership interest in an entity, or a contract that imposes on one entity a contractual obligation to deliver cash or another financial instrument to a second entity, or to exchange other financial instruments on potentially unfavorable terms with the second entity. The agreement gives the second entity a contractual right to receive cash or another financial instrument from the first entity, or to exchange other financial instruments on potentially favorable terms with the first entity.

If available, open-market prices are the best and easiest to obtain a measure of fair value of financial instruments. If quoted market prices or other established values are not available, estimates of fair value can be based on the quoted market price of a financial instrument with similar characteristics. Estimates can also be based on valuation techniques, such as the present value of estimated future cash flows using a discount rate commensurate with the risks involved, or using option pricing models. If it is not practicable to estimate the fair value of a particular financial instrument, reasons why it is not practicable must be thoroughly explained.

In all instances, descriptive material must be included detailing the method(s) and the basis for assumptions utilized in arriving at a stated fair value or in failure to do so. In any event, failure to do so is not to be considered final. A continuing effort to arrive at a practicable (without incurring excessive cost) fair value should be carried out.

Because the Board realizes that the cost of attempting to compute fair value in some instances would become excessive, certain types of financial instruments have been excepted from the requirements of Statement 107. These are:

- Obligations of employers and plans for pension benefits, other postretirement benefits including health care and life insurance benefits, employee stock option, and stock purchase plans.
- Extinguished debt and assets held in trust in connection with a defeasance of that debt.
- Insurance contracts, other than financial guarantees and investment contracts.
- Lease contracts as defined in FASB Statement 13.
- Warrant obligations and rights.
- Unconditional purchase obligations.
- Investments accounted for under the equity method.
- Minority interests in consolidated subsidiaries.
- Equity investments in consolidated subsidiaries.
- Equity instruments issued by the entity and classified in stockholders' equity in the statement of financial position.

Tax Accounting

The new rule for tax accounting (FASB 109) supersedes all existing accounting rules for income tax accounting, particularly APB Opinion No. 11 and FASB 96 *Accounting for Income Taxes.* The new rule also supersedes or amends other rules associated with income tax accounting.

Definitions.   There are a number of terms relevant only to FASB 109. The following definitions will aid the practitioner in implementing the new rule.

Assumption—Reported assets that will be recovered and liabilities that will be settled.

Current Tax Expense or Benefit—Income taxes paid or payable (or refundable) for a year.

Deferred Tax Asset—The amount of deferred taxes caused by temporary differences that will result in net tax deductions in future years.

Deferred Tax Expense or Benefit—The net change during the year in an enterprise's deferred tax liability.

Deferred Tax Liability—The amount of deferred taxes resulting from temporary differences that will result in future years.

Gains and Losses Included in Comprehensive Income but Excluded from Net Income—This category includes certain changes in market value of investments in marketable equity securities classified as noncurrent assets, certain changes in adjustments from recognizing certain additional pension liabilities, and foreign currency translation adjustments. Future changes in GAAP might modify what is included in this category.

Income Tax Expense (Benefit)—The sum of current tax expense (benefit) and deferred tax expense (benefit).

Loss Carrybacks or Carryforwards—An excess of tax deductions over gross income during a specific year that may be carried back or forward to reduce taxable income in other years.

Operating Loss Carryforward for Financial Reporting—The amount of an operating loss carryforward for tax purposes (a) **reduced** by the amount of offsets for temporary differences that will result in net taxable amounts during the carryforward period, and (b) **increased** by the amount of temporary differences that will result in net tax deductions.

Public Enterprise—An enterprise (a) whose debt or equity securities are traded in a public market, or (b) whose financial statements are filed with a regulatory agency in preparation for the sale of securities.

Statutory Limitations—Limits for the amount by which certain deductions or tax credits may reduce taxable income (or income taxes payable).

Taxable Income—The amount of taxable revenues which exceed tax deductible expenses and exemptions for the year.

Tax Credit Carryback or Carryforward—Tax credits which exceed statutory limitations and may be carried back or forward to reduce taxes payable in other years.

Temporary Differences—A difference between the tax basis of an asset or liability and its reported amount in the financial statement.

Computation of deferred tax liabilities or assets.

• Compute all existing differences between the financial reporting basis of assets and liabilities. These are the temporary differences.

• Estimate the specific future years in which temporary differences will result in taxable or deductible amounts.

• Calculate the net taxable or deductible amount in each future year.

• Deduct operating loss carryforwards from net taxable amounts scheduled for future years and included in the loss carryforward period.

• Carryback or carryforward the net deductible amounts occurring in particular years to offset net taxable amounts scheduled for prior or subsequent years.

• Schedule the expected reversal of existing temporary differences.

• Calculate the tax effects of reversals based on existing tax laws and rates.

• Recognize a deferred tax asset for the tax benefit of net deductible amounts that could be realized by loss carryback from future years 1) to reduce a current deferred tax liability, and 2) to reduce taxes paid in the current or prior year.

• Calculate the tax for the remaining net taxable amounts scheduled to occur in future years. Apply current tax rates to the amount of net taxable amounts scheduled for each of those years.

• Deduct tax credit carryforwards from the amount of tax calculated for future years that are included in the carryforward periods.

• Recognize a deferred tax liability for the remaining amount of taxes payable for each future year.

The effects on deferred taxes of changes in tax rates and laws should be recorded when the changes occur as a component of tax expense for the period of the change. For accounting purposes, the change occurs the day the new law is enacted.

FASB Statement 109, *Accounting for Income Taxes*

Statement 109 *Accounting for Income Taxes* has been issued by the FASB to supersede Statement 96. The new Statement applies to those fiscal years beginning after December 15, 1992. Accounting for income taxes should address 1) the amount of taxes payable or refundable during the current year and 2) the deferred tax liabilities and assets for future tax consequences of entries that have been recognized in an enterprise's financial statements and/or tax returns.

Statement 109 signals a marked departure from the manner in which companies have previously accounted for income taxes. Prior standards, including APB Opinion 11 and FASB Statement 96, failed to provide adequate simplified direction; Opinion 11 also failed to provide useful guidelines. In addition to being much too complicated and erring by being too specific, Statement 96 further failed to make provision for recognition of tax benefits expected to be realized in future years.

The FASB has promulgated Statement 109 in an attempt to remedy the criticism of these earlier rulings. It is a further departure from APB 11 which related tax to pretax income. FASB 109, like FASB 96, utilizes the balance sheet as the focal point for tax determination. FASB 109 requires an asset and liability approach for financial accounting and reporting for income taxes. When employing a balance sheet approach, deferred taxes represent the expected effects of existing book/tax differences on those taxes which will be due in the future rather than the effects on taxes previously paid. Therefore, deferred taxes are to be adjusted for tax rate changes when the new rulings or laws become effective.

However, many companies will now be forced into making difficult, rather subjective decisions in relation to assessing the likelihood of tax asset realization. The situation arises from the fact that in line with the new statement, tax assets (that must be recorded) are to be reduced by a reserve fund if impairment is apt to occur and the tax asset is never actually realized.

Several other aspects of the new ruling will also be instrumental in a specific enterprise's decisions regarding adoption options and the related effect upon facets of the enterprise including working capital: owners' equity, earnings trends; and various financial ratios, such as the current ratio, debt-equity ratio, and other balance sheet and income statement ratios.

Loss carryforwards and accruals for postretirement benefits, other than pensions (OPEBs), will derive the most advantage from the less stringent criteria for tax benefits in FASB 109. Benefits of loss carryforwards, according to this Statement, will be subject to the same recognition criteria as other potential tax benefits where, according to the interpretation under FASB 96, it was not possible to recognize any benefits from book loss carryforwards.

Since accrual accounting for OPEBs will be mandatory for most companies by 1993, and for foreign plans and some specific private companies in 1995, it will now be easier to recognize the related tax benefits whether a particular concern decides to record the entire transition liability immediately or amortize it over 20 years; regardless, the greater the ability to recognize the related tax benefits under FASB 109, the more vital a factor this will become in a company's decision.

It is fairly obvious that Statement 109 could bring about some changes in an enterprise's income statement. One change could result from adjustments of deferred taxes for newly enacted tax rate changes since these will show up immediately in the company's continuing operations. Companies may find that after accrual accounting is adopted for OPEBs and the provisions of FASB 109, they have net deferred tax assets rather than net deferred tax liabilities. Additional income would result from an enacted increase in tax rates while an expense would result from an enacted decrease in tax rates. Change in the income statement could also be caused by reassessments of the valuation allowance for an enterprise's deferred tax assets.

Companies may find it advantageous to adopt implementation of the New Rule early if that approach fortuitously reduces deferred tax liabilities or increases deferred tax assets.

In the event a company has not previously implemented the OPEB standard (FASB 106), it may be beneficial to adopt it and the income tax ruling, FASB 109, within the same fiscal year so that the accounting department (in particular) and management (in general) will be faced with what could be fairly drastic accounting alterations within one year rather than in two different years. An additional advantage is that simultaneous adoption also increases the ability to record the tax benefit resulting from the OPEB charge.

If, for whatever reasons, enterprises prefer to maintain the historical record rather than restate the financial statements for previous years, they will select prospective adoption. However, if for budgeting, planning, reporting, or other accounting reasons, it is important to make previous years' statistical results readily comparable to the current and future years, restatement will be the method selected.

The number of prior years restated, if restatement is chosen, will depend to some extent on the availability of pertinent records and the value of the statistical data weighed against the time, effort, and cost involved.

Reporting the tax benefit of tax deductible dividends paid on shares already earned by employees under an employee stock ownership plan (ESOP), according to requirements of Statement 109, is the same as for tax deductible dividends paid to other shareholders and recorded in net income. The requirements for tax deductible dividends paid on shares held by an ESOP but not yet earned by employees follow the same course under FASB 109 as laid down by Statement 96 and Opinion 25. An ESOP and a stock option plan are similar: The tax benefits of both are reported as a credit to shareholders' equity inasmuch as they are compensation methods which at times resulted in tax deductions that were not recognized as compensation expense in the financial statements.

The reasoning behind the differentiation is that tax deductions received for the payment of dividends, except for those paid on unallocated shares held by an ESOP, represent an exemption from taxation of an equivalent amount of earnings. Therefore, the tax benefit is to be shown as a reduction of tax expense and is not allocated directly to shareholders' equity. A tax benefit cannot be recognized, however, for tax deductions or favorable tax rates related to future dividends on undistributed earnings for which deferred tax liability has not been recognized. For disclosure purposes, favorable tax treatment would be reflected in the unrecognized deferred tax liability.

When recording a valuation allowance for deferred tax assets, there will be many circumstances where tax benefits are likely to be realized in the future. There will also be circumstances where the judgment will be difficult, as the judgments are especially critical and should involve top-level management as well as the accounting department.

Opportunities can develop to record the benefit of tax assets, especially for future deductions in jurisdictions where there are significant carryback/carryforward periods. Some enterprises may feel that if a valuation reserve is recorded rather than recognition of the full benefit, shareholders, financial analysts, and employees may consider this as grounds for concern about the company's viability in the future. At the same time, if the asset is not eventually realized, litigation could be forthcoming. When a valuation allowance is necessary, a full explanation of the reasoning behind and interpretation of the change in the accounting and reporting procedures should be made.

Liability method illustrated.   The liability method of computation measures the future tax effects of existing timing differences awaiting reversal.

In the balance sheet, deferred taxes are assets or liabilities. They must present the estimated effects on taxes receivable or payable for the period in which the differences are expected to reverse.

The deferred tax expense for a tax period is derived from the changes for the period in the balance sheet's deferred tax receivables or payables.

Deferred taxes on existing timing differences are computed using tax rates expected to be in effect when the timing differences reverse. Existing deferred taxes are adjusted when tax rates change or future rate changes become known. If there are no legislative changes in the tax law or rates, current rates are used; that is, no estimate or prediction of rate changes is made.

The liability method is not too involved, as the cumulative timing differences are simply multiplied by the current tax rate. The result is a deferred tax liability or asset. The change in that amount for a year is the deferred tax expense for the year. The total tax currently payable plus deferred tax expense is the income tax expense for the year.

Assume a taxpayer has a deferred tax liability of $50,000 on a cumulative timing difference of $100,000 at the beginning of the year. Taxable income for the year is $200,000; the only timing difference is ACRS tax deductions over book depreciation. At year-end the net book value of depreciable assets is $500,000. The tax basis is $350,000. Pretax book income is $250,000.

Taxable Income	$200,000
Tax Rate	50%
Tax Currently Payable	$100,000
Book basis of depreciable assets	$500,000
Tax basis of depreciable assets	350,000
Cumulative timing differences	150,000
Tax Rate	50%
Deferred tax liability at end of year	$ 75,000
Deferred tax liability at beginning of year	50,000
Deferred Tax Expense	25,000
Tax Currently Payable	100,000
Tax Expense	$125,000

The second illustration below compares the computations for the deferred method with the liability method, including a change in the tax rate in 1988.

Deferred Method

	1987	1988
Pretax Book Income	$1,000,000	$1,000,000
Taxable Income	200,000	200,000
Tax Rate	40%	50%
Taxes Payable	$ 320,000	$ 400,000
Deferred Tax		
($200,000 × 40%)	80,000	
($200,000 × 50%)		100,000
Tax Expense	$ 400,000	$ 500,000
Cumulative Deferred Tax Credit	$ 80,000	180,000

Applying the liability method and using the same data, the tax provisions and balance sheet amounts for the two years are calculated as follows:

Liability Method

	1987	1988
Taxes Payable	$320,000	$400,000
Tax Effects of Timing Differences ($200,000 × 50%)	100,000	100,000
Tax Expense....................	$420,000	$500,000
Cumulative liability for future taxes	$100,000	$200,000

Disclosure requirements. Without regard for any particular sequence or organization, several salient features of the disclosure requirements are listed below.

1) The deferred tax consequences of temporary differences scheduled to reverse during the next year must be disclosed as current. The tax effects scheduled to reverse the following year are considered as noncurrent.

2) The amount of income tax expense for benefit from continuing operations is computed separately from any other category of earnings shown on the income statement. Income taxes are allocated among other categories, such as the cumulative effect of accounting changes, discontinued operations, and extraordinary items. The taxes are based on the incremental effect that each category has on income tax expense.

3) The tax benefits resulting from operating loss and tax credit carryforwards are categorized according to the type of income that results in the current period.

4) When the Statement is adopted, a cumulative catchup adjustment will occur which can be disclosed by either:

   a) Actively restating financial statements for prior years; or

   b) Including the adjustment in net income as of the beginning of the year of adoption.

5) Amounts of refundable income taxes, income taxes currently payable, and deferred taxes must still be disclosed.

6) Deferred taxes continue to be categorized as current and noncurrent amounts, and the computing of current and noncurrent amounts must be consistent with the liability method.

7) The current amount is the net deferred tax asset or deferred tax liability caused by timing differences reversing in the year following the balance sheet date. Remaining net deferred taxes would be the noncurrent amounts. This results in a change from the old rule which required the current or

noncurrent classification of most deferred taxes to follow the classification of the related asset or liability, if any.

8) A change caused by the liability method does not permit deferred tax liability and assets attributable to different tax jurisdictions to be offset.

9) For interim reporting, the entire effect of a change in tax rates is reported in the interim period in which the change is introduced. It should not be allocated over either prior or future interim periods.

10) The components of income tax expense or benefit resulting from continuous operations must be disclosed in the financial statement, or in footnotes. These include:

a) Current tax expense or benefit.

b) Deferred tax expense or benefit.

c) Investment tax credits and grants.

d) The benefit of operating loss carryforwards which result in a reduction of income tax expense.

e) Adjustments of a deferred tax liability or asset resulting from changes in the tax laws, or rates, or the status of the enterprise (for example, from nontaxable to taxable or vice versa).

f) SEC requirements are not affected by the new rule.

11) Disclosure is required for the amounts and expiration dates of operating loss and tax credit carryforwards for financial reporting purposes and for tax purposes.

12) a) Income tax expense or benefit allocated to other than continuing operations must be disclosed.

b) Included among these are extraordinary items and the foreign currency translation component of equity.

II

The 1991, 1990, 1989, and 1988 Tax Legislation

1991 TAX LEGISLATION

In 1991 Congress made a number of changes in the tax law. This section of the *Supplement* covers corporate taxes, which together with a review of the 1986 Tax Reform Act will provide a useful update for users.

DEFINITIONS

Because the tax law uses unfamiliar terms, definitions of terms that appear in the code and regulations can help a user understand the meaning of words and phrases used by IRS. The objective of this section is to provide rewrites in simplified explanations of the significant regulations to help the user better understand the law associated with various topics of corporate requirements.

Definitions.   Since the precise meaning of tax terminology can be helpful, definitions of tax terms follow.

Carrybacks—Deductions or credits that cannot be utilized on the tax return during a year that may be carried back to reduce taxable income or taxes payable in a prior year. An operating loss carryback is an excess of tax deductions over gross income in a year; a tax credit carryback is the amount by which tax credits available for utilization exceed statutory limitations. Different tax jurisdictions have different rules about whether excess deductions or credits may be carried back and the length of the carryback period.

Carryforwards—Deductions or credits that cannot be utilized on the tax return during a year that may be carried forward to reduce taxable income or taxes payable in a future year. An operating loss carryforward is an excess of tax deductions over gross income in a year; a tax credit carryforward is the amount by which tax credits available for utilization exceed statutory limitations. Different tax jurisdictions have different rules about whether excess deductions or credits may be carried forward and the length of the carryforward period. The terms *carryforward, operating loss carryforward,* and *tax credit carryforward* refer to the amounts of those items, if any, reported in the tax return for the current year.

Current tax expense or benefit—The amount of income taxes paid or payable or refundable for a year as determined by applying the provisions of the enacted tax law to the taxable income or excess of deductions over revenues for that year.

Deductible temporary difference—Temporary difference that results in deductible amounts in future years when the related asset or liability is recovered or settled.

Deferred tax asset—The deferred tax consequences attributable to deductible temporary differences and carryforwards. A deferred tax asset is measured using the applicable enacted tax rate and provisions of the enacted tax law. A deferred tax asset is reduced by a valuation allowance if, based on the weight of evidence available, it is more likely than not that some portion or all of a deferred tax asset will not be realized.

Deferred tax consequences—The future effects on income taxes as measured by the applicable enacted tax rate and provisions of the enacted tax law resulting from temporary differences and carryforwards at the end of the current year.

Deferred tax expense or benefit—The change during the year in an enterprise's deferred tax liabilities and assets; for deferred tax liabilities and assets acquired in a purchase business combination during the year, it is the change since the combination date. Income tax expense or benefit for the year is allocated among continuing operations, discontinued operations, extraordinary items, and items charged or credited directly to shareholders' equity.

Deferred tax liability—The deferred tax consequences attributable to taxable temporary differences. A deferred tax liability is measured using the applicable enacted tax rate and provisions of the enacted tax law.

Event—A happening of consequence to an enterprise. The term encompasses both transactions and other events affecting an enterprise.

Gains and losses included in comprehensive income but excluded from net income—Under present practice, gains and losses included in comprehensive income but excluded from net income include:

1) Certain changes in market values of investments in marketable equity securities classified as noncurrent assets.
2) Certain changes in market values of investments in industries having specialized accounting practices for marketable securities.
3) Adjustments from recognizing certain additional pension liabilities.
4) Foreign currency translation adjustments.

Future changes to generally accepted accounting principles can change what is included in this category.

Income taxes—Domestic and foreign federal (national), state and local (including franchise) taxes based on income.

Nonpublic enterprise—An enterprise other than one:

1) Whose debt or equity securities are traded in a public market, including those traded on a stock exchange or in the over-the-counter market (including securities quoted only locally or regionally); or
2) Whose financial statements are filed with a regulatory agency in preparation for the sale of any class of securities.

Taxable income—The excess of taxable revenues over tax deductible expenses and exemptions for the year as defined by the governmental taxing authority.

Taxable temporary difference—Temporary differences that result in taxable amounts in future years when the related asset or liability is recovered or settled. (Also refer to *Temporary difference.*)

Tax consequences—The effects on income taxes, current or deferred, of an event.

Tax planning strategy—An action, including elections for tax purposes, that meets certain criteria and that would be implemented to realize a tax benefit for an operating loss or tax credit carryforward before it expires. Tax planning strategies are considered when assessing the need for an amount of a valuation allowance for deferred tax assets.

Temporary difference—A difference between the tax basis of an asset or liability and its reported amount in the financial statements that will result in taxable or deductible amounts in future years when the reported amount of the asset or liability is recovered or settled. Some temporary differences cannot be identified with a particular asset or liability for financial reporting, but those temporary differences:

1) Result from events that have been recognized in the financial statements.
2) Will result in taxable or deductible amounts in future years based on provisions of the tax law.

Some events recognized in financial statements do not have tax consequences. Certain revenues are exempt from taxation and certain expenses are not deductible. Events that do not have tax consequences do not give rise to temporary differences.

Valuation allowance—The portion of a deferred tax asset for which it is more likely than not that a tax benefit will not be realized.

Usually persons such as lawyers contractors, subcontractors, public stenographers, auctioneers, and others who follow an independent trade, business, or profession in which they offer their services to the general public, are generally not employees. However, whether such people are *employees* or *independent contractors* depends on the facts in each case. The general rule is that an individual is an independent contractor if the employer has the right to control or direct only the result of the work and not the means and methods of accomplishing the result. The employer does not have to withhold or pay taxes on payments made to independent contractors.

Under common-law rules, every individual who performs services subject to the will and control of an employer, as to both what must be done and how it must be done, is an employee. It does not matter that the employer allows the employee discretion and freedom of action, so long as the employer has the *legal right* to control both the method and the result of the services.

Two usual characteristics of an employer-employee relationship are that the employer has the right to discharge the employee and the employer supplies the employee with tools and a place to work.

It makes no difference how the relationship is described in an employer-employee relationship. It does not matter if the employee is called an employee, partner, agent, or independent contractor. It also doesn't matter how the payments are measured, how they are made, or what they are called; nor does it matter whether the individual is employed full- or part-time.

No distinction is made between classes of employees. Superintendents, managers, and other supervisory personnel are all employees. An officer of a corporation is generally an employee, but a director is not. An officer who performs no services or only minor services, and neither receives nor is entitled to receive any pay, is not considered an employee. It may be necessary to withhold and pay taxes on wages paid to common-law employees.

If an individual is not an employee under the common-law rules, federal income taxes need not be withheld; however, for social security and Medicare taxes, the term *employee* includes any individual who works for pay in one of the following four categories:

1) A driver (an agent or paid on commission) who distributes meat products, vegetable products, fruit products, bakery products, or beverages other than milk; or if the driver picks up and delivers laundry or dry cleaning.

2) A full-time insurance sales agent whose principal business activity is selling life insurance or annuity contracts, or both, primarily for one life insurance company.

3) An individual who works at home on materials or goods supplied by a company and which must be returned to the company or to a person named by the company, and, if a company furnishes specifications for the work to be done.

4) A full-time traveling or city salesperson who works on behalf of a company and submits orders to the company from wholesalers, retailers, contractors, or operators of hotels, restaurants, or other similar establishments. The goods sold must be merchandise for resale or supplies for use in the buyers' business operation. The work performed must be the salesperson's principal business activity.

For social security and Medicare taxes, individuals within any of the above four categories are employees if:

- The service contract states or implies that almost all of the services are to be performed by the individual.

- The individual has little or no investment in the equipment and property used to perform the services, other than an investment in transportation facilities.
- The services are performed on a continuing basis.

Two categories of statutory nonemployees have been established: *direct sellers* and *licensed real estate agents*. They are treated as self-employed for federal income taxes and employment tax purposes if:

- Substantially all payments for their services as direct sellers or real estate agents are directly related to sales or other output, rather than to the number of hours worked.
- Their services are performed under a written contract providing that they will not be treated as employees for federal tax purposes.

Direct sellers are persons:

1) Engaged in selling or soliciting the sale of consumer products in the home or at a place of business other than in a permanent retail establishment.
2) Engaged in selling or soliciting the sale of consumer products to any buyer on a buy-sell basis, a deposit-commission basis, or any similar basis prescribed by regulations, for resale in the home or at a place of business other than in a permanent retail establishment.

Direct selling includes activities of individuals who attempt to increase direct sales activities of their direct sellers and who earn income based on the productivity of their direct sellers. Such activities include providing motivation and encouragement, imparting skills, knowledge or experience, and recruiting.

To help a company determine whether an individual is an employee under the common-law rules, 20 factors have been identified that indicate whether sufficient control is present to establish an employer-employee relationship. The degree of importance of each factor varies depending on the occupation and the context in which the services are performed. It does not matter that the employer allows the employee freedom of action, so long as the employer has the right to control both the method and the result of the services. If an employer treats an employee as an independent contractor and the relief provisions do not apply, the person responsible for the collection and payment of withholding taxes can be held personally liable for an amount equal to the employee's income, social security, and Medicare taxes that should have been withheld.

The 20 factors are:

1) *Instructions.* An employee must comply with instructions about when, where, and how to work. Even if no instructions are given, the control factor is present if the employer has the right to give instructions.

2) *Training.* An employee is trained to perform services in a particular manner. Independent contractors ordinarily use their own methods and receive no training from the purchasers of their services.

3) *Integration of services.* An employee's services are integrated into the business operations because the services are important to the success or continuation of the business. This shows that the employee is subject to direction and control.

4) *Services rendered personally.* An employee renders services personally. This shows that the employer is interested in the methods as well as the results.

5) *Hiring assistants.* An employee works for an employer who hires, supervises, and pays assistants. An independent contractor hires, supervises, and pays assistants under a contract that requires providing materials and labor and responsibility only for the result.

6) *Continuing relationship.* An employee has a continuing relationship with an employer. A continuing relationship may exist where work is performed at frequently recurring although irregular intervals.

7) *Set hours of work.* An employee has set hours of work established by an employer. Independent contractors are masters of their own time.

8) *Full-time work.* An employee normally works full time for an employer. An independent contractor can work when and for whom he or she chooses.

9) *Work done on premises.* An employee works on the premises of an employer, or works on a route or at a location designated by an employer.

10) *Order or sequence set.* An employee must perform services in the order or sequence set by an employer. This shows that the employee is subject to direction and control.

11) *Reports.* An employee submits reports to an employer. This shows that the employee must account to the employer for his or her actions.

12) *Payments.* An employee is paid by the hour, week, or month. An independent contractor is paid by the job or on a straight commission.

13) *Expenses.* An employee's business and travel expenses are paid for by an employer. This shows that the employee is subject to regulation and control.

14) *Tools and materials.* An employee is furnished significant tools, materials, and other equipment by an employer.

15) *Investment.* An independent contractor has a significant investment in the facilities he or she uses in performing services for someone else.

16) *Profit or loss.* An independent contractor can make a profit or suffer a loss.

17) *Works for more than one person or firm.* An independent contractor performs services to two or more unrelated persons or firms at the same time.

18) *Offers services to general public.* An independent contractor makes other services available to the general public.

19) *Right to fire.* An employee can be fired by an employer. Independent contractors cannot be fired as long as they produce a result that meets the specifications of the contract.

20) *Right to quit.* An employee can quit his or her job at any time without incurring liability. An independent contractor usually agrees to complete a specific job and is responsible for its satisfactory completion, or is legally obligated to make good for failure to complete it.

The following are excerpts of the general tax laws that apply to corporations. They are briefs intended to clarify significant portions of the law so that a requirement can more easily be understood. The information provided does not cover every regulation of the corporate tax code, but rather many of the significant parts of the law that relate regularly to the annual corporate tax return—Form 1120.

A *corporation* for federal income tax purposes includes associations, joint stock companies, insurance companies, trusts, and partnerships that actually operate as associations or corporations. Organizations of doctors, lawyers, and other professional people organized under state professional association acts or corporation statutes are generally recognized as corporations for federal income tax purposes. To be classified as a corporation, a professional service organization must be both organized and operated as a corporation. All states and the District of Columbia have professional association acts.

Unincorporated organizations having certain corporate characteristics are classified as associations that are taxed as corporations. To be treated as a corporation for tax purposes, the organization must have associates, be organized to carry on business, and divide the gains from the business. In addition, the organization must have a majority of the following characteristics:

1) Continuity of life.
2) Centralization of management.
3) Limited liability.
4) Free transferability of interests.

The presence or absence of these characteristics must be taken into account in determining whether an organization is an association. The facts in each case determine whether or not the characteristics are present. However, other factors may be significant in classifying an organization as an association. An organization is treated as an association if its corporate characteristics make it more nearly resemble a corporation than a partnership or trust.

An *estimated tax penalty* applies to the underpayment of an installment of estimated tax. The underpayment of any installment is the amount required to be paid minus the amount paid by the due date.

For tax years beginning in 1992, the amount required to be paid in installments is the lesser of:

1) 93% of the tax shown on the return for the tax year, or, if no return is filed, 93% of the tax for the year; and

2) 100% of the tax shown on the return for the preceding year, if that year was a 12-month tax year and a return for that year was filed showing a tax liability.

Cash payments over $10,000.   A new definition of cash now applies in determining if a Form 8300, *Report of Cash Payments over $10,000 Received in a Trade or Business,* must be filed. Cash is defined as:

1) The coins and currency of the United States and of any other country.

2) Certain cashier's checks, bank drafts, traveler's checks, and money orders received on or after February 3, 1992, if they have a face amount of $10,000, or less, and they are received in:

a) Any transaction in which it is known that the payer is trying to avoid the reporting of the transaction on Form 8300.

b) A designated reported transaction.

A designated reporting transaction is the retail sale of any of the following:

1) A consumer durable, such as an automobile or boat. A consumer durable is any property, other than land or buildings, that:

a) Is suitable for personal use.

b) Can reasonably be expected to last at least one year of ordinary use.

c) Has a sale price of more than $10,000.

d) Can be seen or touched.

2) A collectible, such as a work of art, rug, antique, metal, gem, stamp, or coin.

3) Travel or entertainment, if the total sales price of all items sold for a trip or entertainment event includes the sales price of items such as airfare, hotel rooms, and admission tickets.

The term *retail sale* means any sale made in the course of a trade or business that consists mainly of making sales to ultimate consumers. Thus, if a business consists mainly of making sales to ultimate consumers, all sales made in the course of that business are retail sales, including any sales of items that will be resold.

A cashier's check, bank draft, traveler's check, or money order received in a designated reporting transaction generally is not treated as cash **if** it is the proceeds from a bank loan, is received in payment on a promissory note or an installment sales contract, or is received under certain down payment plans.

The exclusion for employer-provided *educational assistance payments* has been extended to tax years beginning before July 1, 1992. For tax years beginning in 1992, the exclusion applies only to amounts paid before July 1, 1992.

The exclusion from employees' income for *employer-provided legal service plans* is extended through June 30, 1992. The exclusion will not apply to tax years beginning after June 30, 1992. However, for tax years beginning in 1992, the exclusion applies only to amounts paid before July 1, 1992, for periods before that date.

The *standard mileage rate* is 28 cents per mile for all business miles. The special rate for rural mail carriers is 42 cents per mile for 1992. The standard mileage rate for charitable contributions remains at 12 cents per mile, and the rate for medical and moving expenses remains at 9 cents per mile.

Total deduction and depreciation on a vehicle used in the taxpayer's business and first placed in service in 1991 is $2,660. The depreciation cannot exceed $4,300 for the second year of recovery, $2550 for the third year of recovery, and $1,575 for each later tax year.

Whether an individual is an employee or self-employed, *expenses for the business use of a home* generally cannot be deducted. A limited deduction for its business use can be taken if the following tests are met:

1) Exclusive use.
2) Regular use.
3) Principal place of business.
4) Place to meet customers, clients, or patients.
5) Separate structures.
6) Trade or business use.

To take a deduction for the use of part of a home in business, that part must be used exclusively and regularly:

1) As the principal place of business for any trade or business in which the taxpayer engages.
2) As a place to meet or deal with customers, clients, or patients in the normal course of trade or business.
3) In connection with a trade or business, if a separate structure is used that is not attached to the house or residence.

Even if all of the use tests are met, no deduction can be taken based on the business use of the home if the taxpayer is an employee and either of the following two situations applies to the taxpayer:

1) The business use of a home is not for the convenience of the employer. Whether the home's business use is for the employer's convenience depends on all the facts and circumstances. However, business use is not considered for an employer's convenience merely if it is appropriate and helpful; or

2) All or part of the home is rented to the taxpayer's employer and the rented portion is used to perform services as an employee.

A corporation is allowed a deduction for a *percentage of certain dividends received* during the tax year.

Dividends from domestic corporations.   A corporation can deduct, with certain limitations, 70% of the dividends received if the corporation receiving the dividend owns less than 20% of the distributing corporation.

Twenty percent or more owners can take a deduction for 80% of the dividends received or accrued if they own 20% or more of the paying domestic corporation. Such a corporation is referred to as a 20%-owned corporation.

Ownership.   Ownership, for these rules, is determined by the amount of voting power and value of stock, other than certain preferred stock, owned by the corporation.

Small business investment companies.   Small business investment companies can deduct 100% of the dividends received from a taxable domestic corporation.

Affiliated corporations.   If certain conditions are met, members of an affiliated group of corporations may deduct 100% of the dividends received from a member of the same affiliated group. The term *affiliated group* means one or more chains of includible corporations connected through stock ownership with a common parent corporation.

Dividends from regulated investment companies.   Regulated investment company dividends received are subject to certain limits. Capital gain dividends do not qualify for the deduction.

Dividends on preferred stock of public utilities.   A corporation can deduct 41.176% of the dividends it receives on certain preferred stock issued before October, 1942 of a less than 20%-owned taxable public utility. For a 20% or more owned taxable utility, 47.059% can be deducted.

Dividends from Federal Home Loan Bank.   Certain dividends from Federal Home Loan Banks qualify for the dividend received deduction.

Dividends from foreign corporations.   A corporation can deduct a percentage of the dividends it receives from 10%-owned foreign corporations.

Dividends on debt-financed portfolio stock.   For dividends received on debt-financed portfolio stock of domestic corporations, the 70% (80% for any dividend received from a 20%-owned corporation) dividends received deduction is reduced by a percentage to the amount of debt incurred to purchase the stock. This applies to stock whose holding period began after July 18, 1984.

Dividends in property. When a corporation receives a dividend from another domestic corporation in the form of property other than cash, the dividend is included in income in an amount equal to the **lesser** of the property's fair market value or the adjusted basis of the property in the hands of the distributing corporation, increased by any gain recognized by the distributing corporation on the distribution.

No deduction is allowed for dividends received from:

1) A real estate investment trust.
2) A corporation exempt from taxes either for the tax year of the distribution or the preceding tax year.
3) A corporation whose stock has been held by the payee corporation for 445 days or less.
4) A corporation whose stock has been held by the payee corporation for 90 days or less, if the stock has preference as to dividends and the dividends received on it for period or periods totaling more than 366 days.
5) Any corporation if the payee corporation is under an obligation, pursuant to a short sale or otherwise, to make related payments for positions in substantially similar or related property.

So-called *dividends on deposits* or *withdrawable accounts* in domestic building and loan associations, mutual savings banks, cooperative banks, and similar organizations are *interest* and do not qualify for the deduction.

Limit on deduction for dividends. Generally, the total deduction for dividends received or accrued is limited to:

1) 80% of the difference between taxable income and the 100% deduction allowed for dividends received from affiliated corporations or by a small business investment company, for dividends received or accrued from 20%-owned corporations.
2) 70% of the difference between taxable income and the 100% deduction allowed for dividends received from affiliated corporations or by a small business investment company, for dividends received or accrued from less than 20%-owned corporations, reducing taxable income by the total dividends received from 20%-owned corporations.

In figuring the limit, taxable income is determined without allowance for the net operating loss deduction or the deduction of dividends received and without any adjustment due to the nontaxable part of an extraordinary dividend. Taxable income is also determined without any capital loss carryback to the tax year.

If a corporation has a *net operating loss* for a tax year, the limitation of 80% or 70% of taxable income does not apply. To determine whether or not a corporation has a net operating loss, the dividends received deduction is figured with the 80% or 70% of taxable income limitation.

If a corporation received an *extraordinary dividend* on a share of stock held two years or less before the dividend announcement date, its basis in the stock is reduced (not below zero) by the nontaxed part of the dividend. The total of the nontaxed parts of dividends on a share of stock that did not reduce the basis of the stock due to the limit on reducing bases below zero, is treated as gain from the sale or exchange of the stock for the tax year the stock is sold or exchanged.

If a corporation establishes, to the satisfaction of IRS, the fair market value of a share of stock as of the day before the ex-dividend date, the corporation may elect to determine whether the dividend is extraordinary by using the fair value of the stock rather than its adjusted basis.

The nontaxed part is the amount of any dividends-received deduction allowable for the dividends. The dividend announcement date is the date the corporation declares, announces, or agrees to either the amount or the payment of the dividend, whichever is earliest.

The rules apply to an extraordinary dividend on *disqualified preferred stock* without regard to the period the corporation held the stock. Disqualified preferred stock is any stock that is preferred as to dividends if:

1) The stock, when issued, has a dividend rate that declines or can reasonably be expected to decline in the future.
2) The issue price of the stock exceeds its liquidation rights or stated redemption price.
3) The stock is otherwise structured to avoid the rules for extraordinary dividends and to enable corporate shareholders to reduce tax through a combination of dividends-received deductions and loss on the disposition of the stock.

These rules apply to stock issued after July 10, 1989, unless issued under a written binding contract in effect on that date and thereafter before the stock is issued.

A corporation can claim a deduction, with certain limits, for any *charitable contributions made in cash or other property.* To be deductible, the contribution generally must be made to, or for the use of, community chests, funds, foundations, corporations; or trusts organized and operated exclusively for religious, charitable, scientific, literary, or educational purposes; or to foster national or international amateur sports competition; or for the prevention of cruelty to children or animals; or other charitable organizations.

A deduction is not allowed if any of the net earnings of an organization that receives the contribution are used for the benefit of any private shareholder or individual. A corporation using the *cash method* of accounting can deduct contributions only in the year paid.

A corporation using the *accrual method of accounting* can choose to deduct contributions for the tax year authorized by the board of directors, but not paid during that year, if payment is made within months after the close of that year. The choice is made by reporting the contribution on the corporation return for the tax year. A copy of the resolution authorizing the contribution and a declaration stating the resolution was adopted by the board of directors during the tax year must accompany the return. The president or other principal officer must sign the declaration.

A corporation cannot deduct contributions that total more than 10% of its taxable income. Taxable income for this purpose is figured without taking into account the following:

1) Deductions for contributions.
2) Deductions for dividends received and dividends paid.
3) Any net operating loss carryback to the tax year.
4) Any capital loss carryback to the tax year.

Carryover of excess contributions. Any charitable contributions made during the year that are more than the 10% limit can, with certain restrictions, be carried over to each of the following 5 years. Any excess not used up within that period is lost. Thus, if a corporation has a carryover of excess contributions paid in 1990 and the excess is not completely used up in filing its return for 1991, it can be carried over to 1992, 1993, 1994, and 1995. A carryover of excess contributions is not deducted in the carryover year until after any contributions made in that year, subject to the 10% limit, have been deducted. A carryover of excess contributions is not allowed to the extent that it increases a net operating loss carryover in a succeeding tax year.

A corporation, other than an S corporation, can deduct *capital losses* only up to its capital gains. If a corporation has a net capital loss, the loss cannot be deducted in the current tax year. Instead, it is carried to other tax years and deducted from capital gains that occur in those years.

A net capital loss is first carried back 3 years. It is deducted from any total net capital gain which occurred in that year. If the loss is not completely used up, it is carried forward 1 year (2 years back) and then 1 more year (1 year back). If it is still not used up, it is carried over to future tax years, 1 year at a time, up to 5 years. When a net capital loss is carried to another tax year, it is treated as a short-term loss. It does not retain its original identity as long- or short-term.

When carrying a capital loss from 1 year to another, the following rules apply:

1) When figuring this year's net capital loss, no capital loss carried from another year can be used. Capital losses can only be carried to years that would otherwise have a total net capital gain.

2) If capital losses from 2 or more years are carried to the same year, the loss from the earliest year is deducted first. When that loss is completely used up, the loss from the next earliest year is deducted, and so on.

3) A capital loss carried from another year cannot be used to produce or increase a net operating loss in the year it is carried to.

Estimated tax payments. Every corporation whose tax is expected to be $500 or more must make estimated tax payments. A corporation's estimated tax is its expected tax liability, including alternative minimum tax, less its allowable tax credits. The payments are quarterly, and the estimated tax payments must equal 25% of the required annual estimated amount. If, after figuring and making payments of estimated tax, a corporation determines that its estimated tax is substantially larger or smaller than originally estimated, it should refigure the tax before the next installment to determine the amount of its remaining installment payments.

A corporation that fails to pay-in-full a correct installment of estimated tax by the due date is generally subject to a penalty. The penalty rate is applied to the period of underpayment for any installment. The penalty is figured at a rate of interest published quarterly by the IRS. The underpayment of any installment is the amount required to be paid minus the amount paid by the due date. The amount required to be paid in installments is the lesser of:

1) 93% of the tax shown on the return, or if no return is filed, 93% of the tax for the year.

2) 100% of the tax on the return for the preceding year, if that year was a 12-month tax year and a return for that year was filed showing a tax liability.

A large corporation, (at least $1 million of taxable income in any of the last 3 years) can use 1) or 2) if applicable, only for determining the amount of its first installment in any tax year. If the installment determined under 1) is greater than that determined and paid under 2) the difference is added to the next required installment.

If an installment is based on 93% of the current year's tax that would be due if income were annualized, **no penalty** is imposed. Annualized income is the total income for the tax year determined as if an amount actually received over a specified period in the tax year were received at the same rate over the full 12-month year. Any reduction in a required installment from using the annualized exception is added to the amount of the following required installments if not taken into account in earlier installments.

If a corporation's income tax return is not filed by the due date, and if it cannot show reasonable cause, a delinquency penalty of 5% of the tax due will apply if the delinquency is for 1 month or less. An additional 5% is imposed for each additional month or part of a month the delinquency continues, not exceeding a total of 25%.

REVENUE RECONCILIATION BILL OF 1990

The 1990 *Reconciliation Bill* contains a number of changes in the tax law. The review that follows contains the important changes for business. In addition, the following section summarizes the significant portions of the 1986–1989 tax laws which apply primarily to domestic corporations and which were not included in the *Accounting Desk Book.*

Tax Changes for Business

The new legislation affects the reporting of *cash payments* of over $10,000 received in a trade or business.

The IRS charges *user fees* for written responses to corporations which relate to the tax status or the effects of specific transactions for tax purposes. The IRS responses are in the form of letter rulings, determination letters, and opinion letters. A fee is charged for most of these requests. The new law extends the fee program for 5 years; that is, fees will generally apply to requests made before October 1, 1995, and must be collected in advance.

The income exclusion for *employer-provided education assistance payments* is extended through December 31, 1991. In 1991 graduate level courses can be included as part of an educational assistance program. Also, the exclusion from employees' income for employer-provided *group legal services plans* is extended through December 31, 1991. For each year, the exclusion is limited to $70 of the value of the insurance against legal costs.

Any *cellular telephones* or similar telecommunications equipment placed in service in tax years beginning after December 31, 1989, fall under the rules for listed property. If listed property is not used more than 50% for qualified business use during any tax year, the section 179 deduction is not allowable and the property must be depreciated using the alternate MACRS method over the class life of the property. In particular, an employee may not take any credit or deduction unless the use of the property is for the convenience of the employer and required as a condition of employment.

If listed property placed in service after June 18, 1984, is not used **predominantly** (more than 50%) in a qualified business use, no deduction on the property is allowed and the property must be depreciated using the straight-line method. For listed property placed in service after 1986, or after July 31, 1986 if MACRS elected, that is not used predominantly in a qualified business use, the depreciation is figured using the straight-line method over the alternate MACRS recovery period. For listed property placed in service before 1987, the property should be depreciated over the following periods:

Property Class	Listed Property Recovery Period
3-year property	5 years
5-year property	12 years
10-year property	25 years
18-year real property	40 years
19-year real property	40 years

The property placed in service after June 18, 1984, to which the predominant use rules apply, includes the following:

1) Any passenger automobile. A passenger automobile is any vehicle manufactured primarily for use on public streets, roads, and highways and rated at 6,000 pounds or less of unloaded gross vehicle weight, or rated at 6,000 pounds or less of gross vehicle weight for trucks and vans. A passenger automobile does **not** include:

   a) An ambulance, hearse, or combination ambulance-hearse used by the taxpayer directly in a trade or business.

   b) A vehicle used by the taxpayer directly in the trade or business of transporting persons or property for compensation or hire.

2) Any other property used as a means of transportation.

3) Any property of a type generally used for entertainment, recreation, or amusement, including property such as photographic, phonographic, communication, and video recording equipment.

4) Any computer and related peripheral equipment except for any computer used only at a regular business establishment and owned or leased by the person operating the establishment. A regular business establishment includes a portion of a dwelling unit if, and only if, that portion is used both regularly and exclusively for business.

   A *computer* is a programmable electronically activated device that:

   a) Is capable of accepting information, applying prescribed processes to the information, and supplying the results of these processes with or without human intervention.

   b) Consists of a central processing unit containing extensive storage, logic, arithmetic, and control capabilities.

   Related peripheral equipment is any auxiliary machine, whether on- or off-line, which is designed to be placed under the control of the central processing unit of a computer. Related or peripheral equipment does **not** include:

   a) Any equipment which is an integral part of other property which is not a computer.

b) Typewriters, calculators, adding machines, copiers, duplicating equipment, and similar equipment.

c) Equipment of a kind used primarily for amusement or entertainment of the user.

Any **improvements** made to listed property that must be capitalized are treated as new items of depreciable property. The period and method that apply to the listed property as a whole also apply to the improvements—if the listed property must be depreciated using the straight-line method, the improvements must also be depreciated using the straight-line method.

Qualified business use.   A qualified business use is any use in a trade or business. Qualified business use does **not** include:

a) Use of property held merely for the production of income or investment use.

b) The leasing of property to any 5% owner or related person, to the extent that the use of the property is by a 5% owner or person related to the owner or lessee of the property.

c) The use of property as compensation for the performance of services by a 5% owner or related persons.

d) The use of property as compensation for the performance of services by any person other than a 5% owner or related person, unless an amount is included in that person's gross income for the use of the property and, where required, there has been withholding of income tax on that amount.

If at least 25% of the total use of any aircraft during the tax year is for a qualified business use, the leasing or compensatory use of the aircraft by a 5% owner or related person is considered a qualified business use.

A 5% owner of a corporation is any person who owns, or is considered to own, **more than** 5% of the outstanding stock of the corporation. For a business other than a corporation, a 5% owner is any person who owns **more than** 5% of the capital or profits interest in the business. A *related person* is any person related to a taxpayer (see *related parties transactions*). The percentage of ownership for the listed property rules is **more than** 50%.

For example, assume John Doe is the proprietor of a heating contracting business. John's brother, James, is employed by John's company. As part of James' compensation, he is allowed to use one of the company automobiles for personal use. James includes the value of the use of the automobile in gross income, and John properly withholds tax on this compensation. The use of the automobile by James, who is a related person, is not a qualified business use. If James uses the automobile 60% in connection with John's business and 40% for personal purposes, the 40% is included in James' income and subject to withholding. The company's total business use is 100% and the company's qualified business use is 60%.

Suppose John in the example allows employees unrelated to him to use company automobiles as part of their compensation. The employees, however, do not include the value of these automobiles in their gross income and John does not withhold the appropriate taxes. The use of company automobiles by the employees is **not** a qualified business use.

Assume John owns several automobiles which the employees use for business purposes. The employees are also allowed to take the automobiles home at night. However, the fair market value of the use of the automobile for any personal purpose, such as commuting to work, is reported by John as income to the employee and the tax is withheld by John. The use of the automobile by the employee, even for personal purposes, is a qualified business use for the company.

Investment use.   The use of listed property in the production of income is not a qualified business use. Whether the use of the straight-line method is required for listed property is determined by reference to the qualified business use in a trade or business rather than by reference to business/investment use. The use of listed property for entertainment, recreation, or amusement purposes is treated as a qualified business use only to the extent that expenses, other than interest and property tax expenses, attributable to the use are deductible as ordinary and necessary business expenses.

Employees.   Any use by an employee of his own listed property, or listed property that the employee rents, in the performance of services as an employee is not business/investment use unless that use is for the convenience of the employer and required as a condition of employment.

Whether the use of listed property is for the convenience of the employer must be determined from all the facts. The use is considered for the employer's convenience if it is for a substantial business reason of the employer. The use of listed property during the employee's regular working hours in carrying on the employer's business will generally be considered for the employer's convenience. The use of property must be required for the employee to perform employee duties properly. The employer need not explicitly require the employee to use the property. A mere statement by the employer that the use of the property is a condition of employment is not sufficient.

For example, Harry is employed by ABC Company as an errand boy. Harry owns and uses his motorcycle to deliver packages to the downtown offices of ABC. All delivery persons are explicitly required to own a small car or motorcycle for use in their employment with the company. The company reimburses delivery persons for their costs. Harry's use of the motorcycle for delivery purposes for the convenience of the Company is required as a condition of employment.

Assume that ABC Company makes a car available to Harry, but he would rather use his own car and receive reimbursement. The use of his own car is not for the convenience of the Company and is not required as a condition of employment.

Predominant use test.   Listed property is predominantly used in a qualified business use for any year if the business use is more than 50% of the total use of the property. The taxpayer must allocate the use of the listed property that is used for more than one purpose during the tax year to the various uses of the property. The percentage of investment use of listed property is not part of the percentage of qualified business use for purposes of the more than 50% test. The combined total business and investment use is taken into account to figure the depreciation deductions for the property. Property does not cease to be used predominantly in a qualified business use because of a transfer at death.

Example: John Smith uses a home computer 50% of the time to manage his investments. He also uses the computer 40% of the time in his part-time consumer research business. Because his business use of the computer **does not exceed 50%**, the computer is not predominantly used in the taxable year. His business/ investment use for determining his percent of the total allowable straight-line depreciation is 90%.

Assume that Smith uses the computer 30% of the time to manage his investments and 60% of the time in his consumer research business. His business use **exceeds 50%**. His business/investment use for determining the allowable depreciation deduction is 90%.

Method of allocating use.   For passenger automobiles and other means of transportation, allocate the use of the property on the basis of mileage. Determine the percentage of qualified business use by dividing the number of miles the vehicle is driven for business during the year by the annual total mileage.

For other listed property, its allocation of use is made on the basis of the most appropriate unit of time. Determine the percentage of use of a computer in a trade or business for a tax year by dividing the number of hours the computer is used for business purposes during the year by its total annual usage.

Meeting the predominant use test.   The predominant use test must be used each year of the recovery period for the item of listed property. For example, if an item of listed property is placed in service after June 18, 1984, and before 1987, such an item that is 5-year property must use the predominant use test each year for the 12 recovery years. If an item of listed property is placed in service after 1986, the predominant use test must be applied to the property each year of the alternate MACRS recovery period. If any listed property placed in service after 1986 is not used predominantly in a qualified business use in the year it is placed in service, calculate the depreciation deduction using the alternate MACRS method.

Example: On July 1, 1990, James Jones bought and placed in service a computer, which is 5-year property, for $4,000. In 1990 he uses the computer 40% in a qualified business use, 30% for the production of income, and 30% for personal use. Since the qualified business use is only 40%, Jones is not allowed any Section 179 deduction. He must also use the alternate MACRS method over a 5-year recovery period to figure his depreciation deduction for 1990. He takes 40% of $400 ($\frac{1}{2} \times 20\% \times \$4,000$) to determine the business use depreciation of $160. He uses 30% of $400 to figure investment use depreciation of $120. The other 30% personal use percentage is not deductible.

Any *excess depreciation* must be included in gross income and added to the property's adjusted basis for the first tax year the property is not predominantly used in a qualified business use. Excess depreciation is the excess of 1) the amount of the depreciation deductions for the property, including any Section 179 (ACRS deduction) elected for that purpose for tax years before the first tax year the property was not predominantly used in a qualified business use over 2) the amount of the depreciation which would have been allowable for those years if the property were not used predominantly in a qualified business use for the year it was placed in service.

Example: On June 25, 1986, John Doe purchased and placed in service a pickup truck with a gross vehicle weight of 7,000 pounds at a cost of $18,000. He used it only in a qualified business use for 1986, 1987, and 1988. Since the truck weighs over 6,000 pounds, it is not a passenger automobile for the limits set forth in *Passenger Automobiles*. Using the Section 179 deduction and the regular ACRS percentages for 3-year property, he recovers the $18,000 cost in full. During 1990 he uses the truck 50% for business and 50% for personal purposes. He must include in gross income for 1990 his excess depreciation of $5,400, computed as follows:

Total depreciation claimed	$18,000	
Total listed property, depreciation allowable		
1986—10% of $18,000	$ 1,800	
1987—20% of $18,000	$ 3,600	
1988—20% of $18,000	$ 3,600	
1989—20% of $18,000	$ 3,600	12,600
Excess Depreciation		$ 5,400

In 1990 Doe must include $5,400 in gross income. His adjusted basis for the property is increased by $5,400. His 1990 depreciation deduction is $1,800 (20%, the fifth-year percentage) $18,000 × 50%, the business use percentage.

Assume that Doe in 1991 uses the truck only in business. His 1991 depreciation deduction for the truck will be $1,800, (the sixth-year percentage of 10% × $18,000). No depreciation can be deducted in 1992.

The predominant use rules generally apply to the rental of listed property by the *lessor*. The mandatory use of the listed property recovery periods generally does not apply to any listed property leased, or held for leasing, by any person regularly engaged in the business of leasing listed property. It does apply to any listed property that is rented, or held for rent, by a lessor not regularly engaged in the business of leasing listed property. The mandatory use of the listed property recovery periods applies to any listed property used for personal purposes by the lessor, even though the lessor is regularly engaged in the business of holding listed property for lease.

A person is considered *regularly engaged in the business of leasing* listed property only if contracts for the leasing of listed property are entered into with some frequency over a continuous period of time. This determination is made on the basis of the facts and circumstances in each case and takes into account the nature of the person's business in its entirety. Occasional or incidental leasing activity is insufficient. For example, a person leasing only one passenger automobile during a tax year is not regularly engaged in the business of leasing automobiles. In addition, an employer who allows an employee to use the employer's property for personal purposes and charges the employee for the use of the property is not regularly engaged in the business of leasing the property used by the employee.

For listed property (other than passenger automobiles leased after June 18, 1984) the *lessee* must include an amount in gross income for the first tax year the property is not used predominantly in a qualified business use.

The inclusion amount for listed property leased after 1986 is the sum of Amount X and Amount Y:

> Amount X is 1) the product of the fair market value of the property times 2) the business/investment use for the first tax year the business use percentage is 50% or less times 3) the applicable percentage provided by the IRS. Amount Y is the product of 1) the fair market value of the product times 2) the average of the business/investment use for all tax years the property is leased that precede the first tax year the business use is 50%, or less, times 3) the applicable percentage provided by IRS.

Record Keeping for Listed Property

No deduction is allowed for the use of any listed property unless the use is substantiated by adequate records or sufficient evidence corroborating a taxpayer's own statement. For listed property placed in service after June 18, 1984, the records must be kept for any tax year for which excess depreciation can be recaptured. Recapture can occur for property placed in service before 1987 in any tax year for which a percentage is provided. For example, for 3-year recovery property, adequate records must be kept for 6 years even if the property is fully depreciated in the 3 years of the regular recovery period. For property placed in service after 1986, recapture can occur in any tax year of the alternate MACRS recovery period.

To meet the adequate records requirement a taxpayer must maintain an account book, diary, log, statement of expense, trip sheet, or similar record and documentary evidence that, in combination, are sufficient to establish each element of an expenditure or use. It is not necessary to record information in an account book, diary, log, statement of expense, or similar record that duplicates information reflected on a receipt so long as the records and receipt complement each other in an orderly manner.

Substantiation of Business Use

An adequate record contains sufficient information on each element of every business/investment use. The level of detail required to substantiate the use depends on the facts and circumstances. For example, a taxpayer whose only business use of a truck is to make deliveries to customers on an established route can satisfy the requirement by recording the length of the delivery route once, the total number of miles driven during the tax year, and the date of each trip at or near the time of the trips.

An adequate record generally must be written. However, a record of the business use of listed property, such as a computer or automobile, prepared in a computer memory device with the aid of a logging program, is an adequate record.

Separate or Aggregate Business Uses

Each use by the taxpayer is ordinarily considered to be a separate use. However, repetitious uses can be substantiated as a single item.

Each expenditure is recorded as a separate item and not aggregated. However, at the taxpayer's option, amounts expended in the use of listed property during a tax year, such as for gasoline or automobile repairs, can be aggregated. If these expenses are aggregated, the taxpayer need not prove the business purpose of each expense, but can pro rate the expenses based on the total business use of the listed property.

Uses which can be considered part of a single use, such as a round trip or uninterrupted business use, can be accounted for by a single record. For example, use of a truck to make deliveries at several different locations, a trip which begins and ends at the business premises and which can include a stop at the business premises in between two deliveries, can be accounted for by a single record of miles driven. Use of a passenger automobile by a salesman for a business trip away from home over a period of time can be accounted for by a single record of miles traveled. Personal use, such as a stop for lunch on the way between two business stops, is not an interruption of business use.

Loss of Records

When taxpayers establish that the failure to produce adequate records is due to their loss through circumstances beyond control, such as destruction by fire, flood, earthquake, or other casualty, the taxpayer has the right to substantiate a deduction by reasonable reconstruction of expenditures and use.

Business Use of Passenger Automobiles and Other Vehicles

Employers who provide more than 5 vehicles to their employees need not include any information on their returns. The employers, instead, must obtain the information from their employees, indicate on their returns that they have obtained the information, and retain the information received.

REVENUE RECONCILIATION ACT OF 1989

This section of the *Supplement* covers the 1989 tax act (the New Act). It also includes an update of significant tax accounting methods and policies as they pertain to important business topics in the 1989 editions of the Code and IRS regulations. These topics were included in the *Accounting Desk Book* either briefly or not at all because of space limitations as the book totals nearly 800 pages. Therefore, the objective of this *Supplement* is to provide applicable, detailed updates of the significant accounting rules (FASB Statements) and of the business tax requirements of the 1986, 1987, 1988, and 1989 tax reform bills.

BUSINESS TAXES

Accounting Policies (Methods and Periods)

This section explains the IRS rules for accounting procedures, periods, and methods, used to determine when and how income and expenses are reported. **Every** taxpayer, business or individual, must calculate income on the basis of an annual accounting period, which is the taxpayer's taxable year. It is important that a consistent accounting method be used.

The two most commonly used *accounting methods* are the *cash method* and the *accrual method.* Under the cash method, income is reported in the tax year received, and expenses are deducted in the tax year in which paid. Under the accrual method, income is reported in the tax year earned regardless of when payment is received, and expenses are deducted in the tax year incurred, *regardless of when payment is made.*

The most common *accounting period* is the calendar year. A fiscal year may also be used, and under certain conditions a short tax year is permitted.

Taxable income must be figured on the basis of a *tax year.* The term *tax year* is the annual accounting period used for keeping records and reporting income and expenses. The tax year is adopted when the first income tax return is filed. The first tax year must be filed by the due date of the adoption year (not including extensions). The due date for filing returns for corporations and S corporations is the 15th day of the 3rd month after the end of the tax year. If the 15th day of the month falls on a Saturday, Sunday, or legal holiday, the due date is the next day that is not a Saturday, Sunday, or legal holiday. A calendar year must be adopted if (1) adequate records are not maintained, (2) there is no annual accounting period specified, (3) the present tax year does not qualify as a fiscal year. If a fiscal tax year is adopted, books and records must be kept and income and expenses must be reported using the same tax year, unless permission to change is obtained.

A 52–53 week tax year can be used if books and records and income and expenses are reported on that basis. A 52–53 week tax year is a fiscal year which (1) varies from 52–53 weeks, (2) always ends on the same day of the week, (3) always ends on:

a. The date that day last falls in a particular calendar month.

b. The date that day falls nearest to the last day of a particular calendar month.

Example: If a tax year always ends on the last Monday in March, then for the tax year ending in 1990, the tax year will end on March 26, 1990. If a tax year is elected ending on the Monday nearest to the end of March, the 1990 tax year will end on April 2, 1990.

With certain exceptions, approval of IRS is required to change a tax year. *An Application for Change in Accounting Period* (Form 1128) must be filed with IRS on the 15th day of the 2nd calendar month after the close of a short tax year (a tax year of less than 12 months). In some cases it is possible to get an extension of time to change a tax year. In no case should the tax year be changed until the IRS has approved the request.

A *partnership* is required to conform its tax year to the partners' tax years, unless the partnership can establish a business purpose for a different period or makes a section 444 election. The rules for the required tax year for partnerships are:

1) If one or more partners owns an interest in partnership profit and capital of more than 50% (a majority interest), the partnership must adopt the tax years of those partners.

2) If there are no partners who own a majority interest or if the partners who do own a majority interest do not have the same tax year, the partnership is required to change to the tax year of its principal partners (one who has a 5% or more interest in the profits *or* capital of the partnership).

3) If no tax year is established by either the majority partners or the principal partners, the partnership must adopt a tax year that results in the least aggregate deferral of income to the partners.

The tax year that results in the **least** *aggregate deferral of income* is the tax year of one or more of the partners that results in the **smallest** deferral to all the partners. The deferral is the number of months from the end of the partnership's tax year to the end of each partner's tax year that ends on or after the date the partnership's tax year ends. Multiply the number of months by the partner's interest in partnership profits and add each partner's deferral to determine the total deferral. The partner's tax year that produces the smallest deferral is the partnership's tax year.

A small business corporation can elect to be an *S corporation.* All S corporations, regardless of when they became S corporations, are required to use a calendar tax year or any other tax year for which the corporation establishes a business purpose (defined below) for a different period, or makes a Section 444 election. (S corporations are discussed below.)

Personal service corporation must use a calendar tax year unless it can establish a business purpose for a different period, or make a Section 444 election. For this purpose, a personal service corporation is a corporation in which the principal activity, during the testing period, is the performance of personal services that are substantially performed by employee-owners. Employee-owners must own more than 10% of the fair market value of the corporation's stock on the last day of the testing period. Generally, the testing period for a tax year is the prior tax year.

Example 1: Corporation A has been in existence since 1980, and has always used a January 31 fiscal year for its accounting period. To determine if A is a personal service corporation for its tax year beginning February 1, 1990, the testing period is A's tax year ending January 31, 1990. For a new corporation, the testing period for its first tax year starts with the first day of the tax year and ends on the earlier of the last day of its tax year, or the last day of the calendar year in which the tax year begins.

Example 2: B Corporation's first tax year begins June 1, 1990. B wants to use a September 30 fiscal year for its accounting period. B's testing period for its first tax year is June 1, 1990, through September 30, 1990. If B chooses to use a March 31 fiscal year, the testing period is June 1, 1990, through December 31, 1990.

Any activity that involves the performance of services in the fields of health, law, engineering, architecture, accounting, actuarial science, performing arts, or consulting is considered to be the performance of personal services. The principal activity of a corporation is considered to be the performance of personal services if, during the testing period, the corporation's compensation costs for personal service activities is more than 50% of its total compensation costs. A person is an employee-owner of a corporation if the person is an employee of the corporation on any day of the test period, and owns any outstanding stock of the corporation on any day of the test period.

Partnerships, S corporations, and personal service corporations can elect to use a tax year that is different from the required tax year. Certain restrictions apply to this election, which is called a Section 444 election. This election does not apply to any partnership, S corporation, or personal service corporation that establishes a business purpose for a different period. A Section 444 election can be made if:

1) It is not a member of a tiered structure.
2) It has not previously had a section 444 election in effect.
3) It elects a year that meets the deferral period requirement.

Generally, a partnership, S corporation, or personal service corporation may make a Section 444 election only if the tax year election results in a *deferral period* of 3 months or less. An election to change a tax year will be allowed only if the deferral period of the elected tax year is not longer than the shorter of three months or the deferral period of the tax year being changed.

For a partnership, S corporation, or personal service corporation that wants to adopt or change its tax year by making a Section 444 election, the deferral period is the number of months between the end of the elected tax year and the close of the required tax year. If the current tax year is the required tax year, the deferral period is zero.

Example 1: X Partnership used a calendar tax year which is also its required tax year. Because X's deferral period is zero, X is not able to make a Section 444 election.

Example 2: Y, a newly formed partnership, began operations on December 1, 1989. Y is owned by calendar year partners, and wants to make a Section 444 election to adopt a September 30 tax year. Y's deferral period for the tax year beginning December 1, 1989, is 3 months (September 30 to December 31, 1990).

The Section 444 election remains in effect until it is terminated. The election ends when the partnership, S corporation, or personal service corporation:

- Changes to its required tax year
- Liquidates.
- Willfully fails to comply with the required payments or distributions.
- Becomes a member of a tiered structure.
- If an S corporation's election is terminated, or a personal service corporation ceases to be a personal service corporation.

If a personal service corporation that has a Section 444 election in effect elects to be an S corporation, the S corporation may continue the 444 election of the personal service corporation. Or, if an S corporation terminates its S election and immediately becomes a personal service corporation, the personal service corporation can continue the Section 444 election of the S corporation.

If a 444 election is terminated, another Section 444 election cannot be made for *any* tax year.

A *business purpose* is defined as an accounting period that has a substantial business purpose for its existence. Both tax and nontax factors must be considered in determining if there is a substantial business purpose for a requested tax year.

A nontax factor that may be sufficient to establish a business purpose is the annual cycle of business activity, called a *natural tax year.* The accounting period of a natural business year includes all related income and expenses. A natural business year exists when a business has a peak period and a nonpeak period. The natural business year is considered to end at or soon after the end of the peak period.

Other nontax factors usually will not be sufficient to establish that a business purpose exists for a particular tax year. Some of these nontax factors are:

- The use of a particular year for regulatory or financial accounting purposes.
- The hiring patterns of a particular business such as the fact that a firm typically hires staff during certain times of the year.
- The use of a particular year for administrative purposes, such as the admission or retirement of partners or shareholders, promotion of staff, and compensation or retirement arrangements with staff, partners, or shareholders.
- The fact that a particular business involves the use of price lists, a model year, or other items that change on an annual basis.

In considering whether there is a business purpose for a tax year, significant weight is given to tax factors. An important consideration is whether the change should create a substantial distortion of income. Examples of distortion of income:

- The deferral of a substantial portion of income, or a substantial portion of deductions from one year to another so as to reduce tax liability.
- Causing a similar deferral or shifting for any other person, such as a partner or shareholder.
- Creating a short period in which there is a substantial operating loss.

Any deferral of income to partners or shareholders is not a business purpose.

A new corporation establishes its tax year when it files its first tax return. A newly reactivated corporation, which has been inactive for a number of years, is treated as a new taxpayer for the purpose of adopting a tax year.

A corporation may **change** its tax year without first getting the approval of the IRS if the following conditions are met:

1) It must not have changed its tax year within the 10 calendar years ending with the calendar year in which the short tax year resulting from the change begins.

2) Its short tax year must not be a tax year in which it has a net operating loss.

3) Its taxable income for the short tax year must be (when annualized) 80% or more of its taxable income for the tax year before the short tax year.

4) If it is a personal holding company, foreign personal holding company, an exempt organization, foreign corporation not engaged in a trade or business within the United States, either for the short tax year or for the tax year before the short tax year, it must have the same status for both the short tax year and the tax year before.

5) It must not try to become an S corporation for the tax year that would immediately follow the short tax year required to effect the change.

A statement on behalf of the corporation must be filed with the IRS office where the corporation files its tax returns by the time for filing its return for the short tax year required by the change. The statement must indicate that the corporation is changing its annual accounting period and must show that all preceding conditions have been met. If, on examination, the corporation does not meet all the conditions because of later adjustments in establishing tax liability, the statement will be considered a timely application for permission to change the corporation's annual accounting period to the tax year indicated in the statement.

If the corporation's records are not adequate or the corporation has an accounting period that does not qualify as a fiscal year, the tax year is the calendar year. In this case, if a fiscal year is adopted, it will be treated as a change in the annual accounting period, and the corporation will have to get the approval of IRS. A procedure is provided whereby certain corporations may expeditiously obtain approval to change their tax year.

Accounting methods.   An *accounting method* is a set of rules used to determine when and how income and expenses are reported. The term *accounting method* includes not only the overall method of accounting used, but also the accounting treatment applied for specific items. An accounting method is chosen when the first tax return is filed.

No single accounting method is required of all taxpayers. The significant factor is to choose a method that clearly shows income and expenses, and records must be maintained that enable a taxpayer to file a correct return. In addition to permanent books of account, other records must be kept that are necessary to support the entries on the books and on tax returns.

The same method must be used from year to year, and taxable income is calculated by the same accounting method that is used to keep the books. This method must clearly show income and expenses. Any accounting method that shows the consistent use of generally accepted accounting principles for the particular trade or business, generally is considered to clearly show income only if all items of gross income and all expenses are treated the same from year to year. If an accounting method does not clearly show income and expenses, they will be computed under the method which in the opinion of IRS clearly shows income and expenses.

Subject to specific tax rules, the following accounting methods are permissible.

1) Cash method.
2) Accrual method.
3) Special methods of accounting for certain items of income and expenses.
4) Combination (hybrid) methods using elements of 1), 2), and 3).

Any combination (hybrid) method of cash, accrual, and special methods of accounting can be used if the combination clearly shows income and expenses and is consistently used. For example, the accrual method for purchases and sales and the cash method for all other items of income and expenses can be used, with the following two restrictions:

1) If the cash method is used for reporting income, the cash method must be used for reporting expenses.
2) If the accrual method is used for reporting expenses, the accrual method must be used for reporting income.

Any combination that includes the cash method is treated as the cash method.

Business and personal items can be accounted under different accounting methods. Income from a business can be under an accrual method, and the cash method can be used to figure personal items. If more than one business is operated, a different accounting method for each separate and distinct business can be used, if the method used shows income and expenses clearly. No business will be considered separate and distinct if a complete and separable set of books and records for that business is not kept.

Cash method. *The cash basis* of accounting is used by many small businesses with **no inventories**. The accrual method for sales and purchases must be used if inventories are necessary in accounting for income. With the cash method, gross income includes all items of income actually or constructively received during the year. *Constructive receipt* is defined as the receipt of income when an amount is credited to the account or made available to the business without restriction. Possession of the amount is not necessary. If someone is authorized as an agent and receives income for the business, it is a constructive receipt when the agent receives it.

Example 1: Interest is credited to a bank account in December 1990. The amount must be included in gross income for 1990, not in 1991.

Example 2: A check is received in December in payment for merchandise, but is not cashed until the following January. The amount must be included in income in the year the check was received, not in the following year. Income cannot be postponed from one year to another to avoid paying tax on the income. Income must be reported in the year the property is received, or made available without restriction.

Under the cash method, expenses usually must be deducted in the tax year in which they are actually paid. Expenses paid in advance can be deducted only in the year to which they apply; certain costs have to be capitalized.

The cash method, including any combination of methods that includes the cash method, cannot be used by corporations, other than S corporations, partnerships having a corporation (other than an S corporation) as a partner, and tax shelters.

Accrual method. Under the accrual method of accounting, income is reported in the year earned, and expenses are deducted (or capitalized) in the year incurred. The objective of the accrual method is to match income and expenses in the correct taxable year.

All items of income are generally included in the gross income when the items are earned, even though payment may be received in another year. All events that establish the right to receive income must have happened and the amount must be calculable with reasonable accuracy.

Example: A calendar year taxpayer sold a radio on November 28, 1990, and billed the customer 3 days later. Payment was not received until February 1991. The amount of the sale must be included in 1990 income because the income was earned in 1990.

When gross income includes an amount that was estimated on the basis of a reasonable estimate, and the exact amount determined later, the difference, if any, is taken into account in the year in which the determination is made.

In what is termed the *nonaccrual experience method* (based on an experience factor), the accounts receivable that will not be collected need not be accrued.

Discounting notes receivable is a common business practice in some businesses. Many dealers receive the notes of customers as part payment for articles sold, the notes payable over a fixed period. The dealer then sells the notes to a finance company at a discount. The dealer and the finance company often agree that a part of the discount price will be held by the finance company in a *dealer's reserve* or similar account until collections are made or the reserve reaches a specified total, at which time it will be paid over or credited to the dealer. In these cases, amounts held in the reserve are treated as income. Under an accrual method of accounting the full amount of the *discount price,* not reduced by the reserve held by the finance company, is included in income when the notes are sold.

Advance payments cannot be postponed if, under the agreement 1) any part of the services is to be performed after the end of the tax year immediately following the year the advance payment is received, and 2) any part of the services is to be performed at any unspecified future date that may be after the end of the tax year immediately following the year the advance payments are received.

Any advance payment that is included in gross receipts in the tax year the payment is received may not be less than the amount of the payment included as gross receipts in the books and records and all reports (including consolidated financial statements) to shareholders, partners, other proprietors or beneficiaries, and for credit purposes.

In the following examples, assume the calendar year and the accrual method of accounting are used.

Example 1: X Company manufactures, sells, and services television sets. In 1990 payment was received for a one-year contingent service contract on a television set that was sold. Payments into income can be postponed if, in the normal course of business, television sets are offered for sale without the contingent service contracts.

Example 2: X Company is in the television repair business. In 1990 payments are received for one-year contracts under which X Company agrees to repair or replace certain parts that fail to function properly in television sets that were sold by an unrelated party. The payments are included in gross income as they are earned by performing the services. If some services are not performed by the end of the following tax year (1991), gross income for 1990 must include the amount of the advance that is for the unperformed services.

Example 3: Company X is a service company. On November 4, 1990, payment is received for a one-year contract beginning on that date and providing for services into 1991. One sixth (2/12) of the payment must be included in income for 1990, and five-sixths of the payment included in income for 1991, even if all of the services are not performed by the end of 1991.

Expenses. Business expenses are deducted or capitalized when the business becomes liable for them, whether or not they are paid in the same year as incurred. All events that set the amount of the liability must have happened, and the amount must be calculated with reasonable accuracy.

Example: X Company is a calendar year taxpayer and in December 1990 buys office supplies. The supplies are received and the bill for them in December, but the company does not pay for the supplies until January 1991. The expense can be deducted in 1990 because all events that set the amount of liability and economic performance occurred in that year.

Matching Principle. To determine whether the accrual of an item in a particular year results in a better matching of the item with the income to which it relates, generally accepted accounting principles are an important factor. Costs directly associated with the revenue of a period are properly allocable to that period.

For example, a sales commission agreement may require certain payments to be made in a year subsequent to when sales income is reported. In this situation, economic performance for part of the commission expense may not occur until the following year. Nevertheless, if the expense is deducted in the year the sales income is reported, it will result in a better matching of the commission expense with the sales income. In addition, if sales income is recognized in 1 year, but the goods are not shipped until the following year, the shipping costs are more properly matched to income in the year the goods are sold than in the year the goods are shipped.

Expenses such as insurance and rent are generally allocable to a period of time. Thus, if a calendar year taxpayer enters into a 12-month insurance contract on July 1, 1990, half of the expense is allocated to 1990 and half to 1991. If the amount of the expense is immaterial, the expense can be entirely accruable in 1990. Any expenses, such as advertising costs, that cannot be practically associated with income of a particular period, should be assigned to the period in which the costs are incurred. The matching requirement is satisfied for advertising expenses if the period to which the expenses are assigned is the same for tax and financial reporting purposes.

Inventories. If a business is required to account for inventories, the accrual method of accounting for purchases and sales must be used. The most common kinds of inventories are:

- Merchandise or stock in trade.
- Raw materials.
- Work in process.
- Finished products.
- Supplies that become a part of the item intended for sale.

The value of inventories at the beginning and end of each tax year is required to determine taxable income. To determine the value of inventory, a method is needed for identifying the items in inventory and a method for valuing those items.

Inventory valuation rules are not the same for all kinds of businesses. The method used must conform to generally accepted accounting practices used for similar businesses, and it must clearly show income. To clearly show income the same inventory method must be used consistently from year to year.

Merchandise is included in inventory only when the business has title to it. Merchandise should be included if purchased, if title to it has passed to the business, even though it is in transit or the business does not have physical possession of it for whatever reason. The following should be included in inventory:

- Goods under contract for sale that a business has not yet segregated and applied to the contract.
- Goods out on consignment.
- Goods that are in display rooms, merchandise mart rooms, or booths that are located away from the place of business.

In calculating gross income, business can account for a sale of a product when the goods are shipped, when the product is delivered or accepted, or when title to the goods passes to the customer, whether or not billed, depending upon the method used for keeping the books. Do not include goods sold in an inventory.

Cost identification. There are three methods of identifying items in inventory—specific identification, first-in, first-out (FIFO), and last-in, first-out (LIFO).

The *specific identification method* is used to identify the cost of each inventoried item by matching the item with its cost of acquisition in addition to other allocable costs, such as labor and transportation.

If there is no specific identification of items with their costs, an assumption must be made to decide which items were sold and which remain in inventory. Make this identification by either the FIFO or LIFO method.

The *FIFO method* assumes that the items purchased or produced first are the first items sold, consumed, or otherwise disposed of. The items in inventory at the end of the tax year are valued as the items most recently purchased or produced. If there is intermingling of the same type of goods in the inventory so that they cannot be identified with specific invoices, the FIFO method to value these items must be used, unless the LIFO method is elected.

The *LIFO method* assumes that the items of inventory that were purchased or produced last are sold or removed from inventory first. Items included in the closing inventory are considered to be those from the opening inventory plus those items that must be filed according to the form's instructions, or a statement that has all the information required in the form. The information must be filed with the timely filed tax return for the year in which LIFO is first used.

There are very complex rules involved in using the LIFO method. The following discusses two of the rules:

1) Dollar-value method.

2) Simplified dollar-value method.

Dollar-Value Method. Under the dollar-value method of pricing LIFO inventories, goods and products have to be grouped into one or more pools (classes of items), depending on the kinds of goods or products in the inventory.

The dollar-value method of valuing LIFO inventories is a method of determining cost by using "base-year" cost expressed in terms of total dollars rather than the quantity and price of specific goods as the unit of measurement. Under this method the goods contained in the inventory are grouped into a pool or pools. The term "base-year cost" is the aggregate of the cost (determined as of the beginning of the taxable year for which the LIFO method is first adopted, i.e., the base date) of all items in a pool. The taxable year for which the LIFO method is first adopted with respect to any item in the pool is the "base year" for that pool. Liquidations and increments of items contained in the pool shall be reflected only in terms of a net liquidation or increment for the pool as a whole. Fluctuations may occur in quantities of various items within the pool, new items which properly fall within the pool may be added, and old items may disappear from the pool, all without necessarily affecting a change in the dollar value of the pool as a whole. An increment in the LIFO inventory occurs when the end of the year inventory for any pool expressed in terms of base-year cost is in excess of the beginning of the year inventory for that pool expressed in terms of base-year cost. In determining the inventory value for a pool, the increment, if any, is adjusted for changing unit costs or values by reference to a percentage, relative to base-year cost, determined for the pool as a whole.

A *pool* consists of all items entering into the entire inventory investment for a business unit of a business enterprise. The taxpayer may elect to use the multiple pooling method. Each pool in a multiple pooling will consist of a group of inventory items which are substantially similar. For example, inventories of raw materials of an unlike nature would have to be multiple-pooled, even though the materials become part of identical finished products.

Simplified Dollar-Value Method. The simplified dollar value method can be used by eligible small businesses with average annual gross receipts of $5,000,000 or less for the 3 preceding tax years. This method establishes multiple inventory pools in accordance with general categories of inventory items set forth in applicable government price indexes and uses the change in those published indexes to estimate the annual changes in prices for inventory items in the pools.

Valuing Inventory. Since valuing inventory is a major factor in calculating income, the way the inventory is valued is very important. If the FIFO method is used, the two common ways to value inventory are the *specific cost identification method* and the *lower of cost or market method*. For a new business using FIFO, the specific cost method or the lower of cost or market method can be used to value inventory. The same method must be used to value the entire inventory and the method cannot be changed without IRS permission.

Several pricing methods are recognized for tax purposes which can be used to figure the correct cost basis of inventory. The dollar value that results is the cost basis of the inventory.

Specific Cost Identification Method. The cost of merchandise purchased during the year is the cost of acquisition in addition to costs allocable to the merchandise. If the specific cost identification method is used to figure the inventory value of merchandise materials or supplies, *cost* means:

1) The inventory price of goods on hand at the beginning of the tax year.
2) The invoice price, and the indirect costs allocable to the goods, less appropriate discounts for goods purchased during the year.

Discounts. The inventory cost must be reduced by trade or quantity discounts. Discounts usually are for volume or quantity purchases, and a discount that is allowed regardless of time of payment is a *trade* discount.

Whether or not the buyer deducts cash discounts is the buyer's option, but the discounts must be treated the same from year to year. If the cash discounts are not included in inventory costs, they must be included in the business income. Transportation and other necessary charges in acquiring goods are added to the net invoice price.

Lower of cost or market means that the market value of each item on hand at the inventory date is compared with the cost of each item with the lower value being the inventory value. The lower of cost or market rule applies to goods purchased and on hand, and to basic elements of cost (direct materials, direct labor, and an allocable share of indirect costs) of goods in process of manufacture and finished goods on hand. It does not apply to goods on hand or in process of manufacture for delivery at fixed prices on a firm sales contract. These goods must be inventoried at cost.

When, in the regular course of business, merchandise is offered for sale at prices lower than market, the inventory can be valued at these prices, less the direct cost of disposition. These prices are figured from the actual sales for a reasonable period before and after the date of the inventory. Prices significantly different from the actual prices determined are **not acceptable.**

If no market exists, or if quotations are given without reference to actual conditions because of an inactive market, whatever evidence of a fair market price is available, at the dates nearest to the inventory date, must be used.

Unsalable goods are goods in inventory that cannot be sold at normal prices or in the usual way because of damage, imperfections, shop wear, changes of style, odd or broken lots, or other similar causes including secondhand goods taken in exchange. These goods should be valued at selling prices minus direct cost of disposition, no matter what method is used to value the rest of the inventory. If these goods consist of raw materials or partly finished goods held for use or consumption, they must be valued on a reasonable basis, considering the usability and condition of the goods. They cannot be valued for less than the scrap value.

It is acceptable to calculate the cost of goods on hand by *perpetual or book inventories* if they are kept by following sound accounting practices. Inventory accounts, however, must be charged with the actual cost of goods purchased or produced, and credited with the value of goods used, transferred, or sold. Credits must be figured on the basis of the actual cost of goods acquired during the year and the inventory value at the beginning of the year.

Physical inventories must be taken at reasonable intervals and the book figure for inventory must be adjusted to agree with the actual inventory.

The following are some of the inventory practices that are not recognized for tax purposes:

1) Deducting a reserve for price changes or an estimated amount for depreciation in the inventory valuation.

2) Taking work in process or other parts of the inventory at a nominal price or less than the full value.

3) Omitting part of the stock on hand.

4) Using a constant price or nominal value for so-called normal quantity of materials or goods in stock.

5) Including stock in transit, shipped either to or by the business, the title to which is not held by the business.

6) Dividing indirect production costs into fixed and variable production cost classifications and then allocating only the variable costs to cost of goods produced while treating fixed costs as period costs that are currently deductible (the *direct cost* method).

7) Treating all or almost all indirect production costs (whether fixed or variable) as period costs that are currently deductible (the *prime cost* method).

Damage from fire or other casualty, or theft of items included in inventory, can result in a casualty or theft loss. Any loss from casualty or theft is reflected in the cost of goods sold.

The total amount of the sale of the entire inventory must be included in the tax return as ordinary income.

Uniform Capitalization Rules. Under the uniform capitalization rules, direct costs must be *capitalized.* Also, an allocable portion of most indirect costs that benefit or are incurred because of production or resale activities. This means that certain expenses incurred during the year will be included in the basis of property produced or in inventory costs, rather than taken as a current deduction. These costs will be recovered through depreciation, amortization, or cost of goods sold when used, sold, or the property is otherwise disposed of.

The uniform capitalization rules apply if the business:

1) Produces real or tangible personal property for use in a trade or business or an activity engaged in for profit.

2) Produces real or tangible personal property for sale to customers.

3) Acquires property for resale, but not personal property if the average annual gross receipts are not more than $10,000,000.

A business produces if it constructs, builds, installs, manufactures, develops, improves, creates, raises, or grows the property. Property produced for a business under a contract is treated as produced by the business to the extent that payments are made or costs are incurred in connection with the property.

Tangible personal property includes films, sound recordings, videotapes, books, artwork, photographs, or similar property. However, freelance authors, photographers, and artists are exempt from the uniform capitalization rules if they qualify under the property excluded from the rules.

Property Excluded from the Rules. The uniform capitalization rules do not apply to the following types of property:

1) Property used for personal or nonbusiness purposes, or for purposes not connected with a trade or business or an activity conducted for profit.

2) Costs paid or incurred by a freelance writer, photographer, or artist, or a qualified employee owner of a personal service corporation in the business of being a writer, photographer, or artist.

3) Property produced under a long-term contract.

4) Personal property purchased for resale if average annual gross receipts are $10,000,000 or less.

5) Property produced for personal use if substantial construction had occurred before March 1, 1986.

6) Certain intangible drilling and development costs of oil and gas, or geothermal wells, or other mineral property.

Direct material costs and direct labor costs incurred for production or resale property must be capitalized. All other costs are *indirect costs*. Direct material costs include the cost of materials that become an integral part of the asset plus the cost of materials that are used in the ordinary course of the production of the asset. Direct labor costs include the cost of labor that can be identified or associated with a particular activity. Labor costs include all types of compensation, e.g., basic, overtime, sick, vacation, etc. plus payroll taxes and payments to a supplemental unemployment benefit plan.

Indirect costs. Certain types of costs may directly benefit or be incurred because of a particular activity even though the same costs also benefit other activities. Therefore, these costs require a reasonable allocation to determine the portion that is attributable to each activity.

Indirect costs that must be capitalized for production or resale activities include amounts incurred for:

1) Repair and maintenance of equipment and facilities.

2) Utilities relating to equipment and facilities.

3) Rent of equipment, land, and facilities.

4) Indirect labor and contract supervisory wages, including payroll taxes and payments to supplemental unemployment benefit plans.

5) Indirect materials and supplies.

6) Tools and equipment that are not otherwise capitalized.

7) Quality control and inspection.

8) Taxes (other than state, local, and foreign income taxes) that relate to labor, materials, supplies, equipment, land, and facilities. This does not include taxes that are treated as part of the cost of property.

9) Depreciation, amortization, and cost recovery allowances on equipment and facilities.

10) Depletion (whether or not in excess of cost) is not capitalized until such property is sold.

11) Administrative costs, whether or not performed on a job site, but not including any cost of selling, or any return on capital.

12) Direct and indirect costs incurred by any administrative, service, or support function or department, to the extent such costs are allocable to particular activities.

13) Compensation paid to officers attributable to services performed in connection with particular activities, but not including any cost of selling.

14) Insurance on plant, machinery and equipment, or insurance on a particular activity.

15) Deductible contributions paid to or under a stock bonus, pension, profit sharing, or annuity plan.

16) Rework, labor, scrap, and spoilage.

17) Bidding costs incurred in the solicitation of contracts that the business is awarded.

18) Engineering and design costs.

19) Storage and warehousing costs, purchasing costs, handling, processing, assembly, and repackaging costs, and a part of general and administrative costs.

Current deductions can be taken for certain costs. These costs are not required to be capitalized with respect to production or resale activities. They include amounts for:

1) Marketing, selling, advertising, and distribution costs.

2) Bidding expenses incurred in the solicitation of contracts not awarded to the business.

3) General and administrative (other than those determined to be indirect expenses) and compensation paid to officers attributable to the performance of services that do not directly benefit or are not incurred by reason of a particular production activity.

4) Research and experimental costs allowable as a deduction.

5) Income taxes.

6) Costs attributable to strikes.

7) Depreciation, amortization, and cost recovery allowances on equipment and facilities that are temporarily idle.

8) Repair expenses that do not relate to production.

Allocation methods.   More than one method can be used to allocate costs.

Direct labor costs incurred during the tax year are generally allocated to or among activities using a specific identification or tracing method. However, direct labor costs can be allocated to or among particular activities using any method, provided that the method used reasonably allocates direct labor costs among such activities. For the purpose of allocating elements of direct labor cost (other than basis compensation) to particular activities, all such cost elements can be grouped together and then allocated to or among activities in proportion to the charge for basis compensation.

All direct costs must be capitalized. However, an incorrect method of accounting is allowable if it treats any direct costs as indirect costs, provided the costs are capitalized to the extent discussed below under *indirect costs.*

The *indirect costs* which must be allocated to or among production or resale activities are allocated to particular activities using either a specific identification or tracing method, the standard cost method, or a method using burden rates (such as ratios based on direct costs, hours, or other items, or similar formulas), provided the method used for the allocation reasonably allocates indirect costs among production or resale activities. Usually, indirect costs can be allocated to production and resale activities on the basis of direct labor and material costs, direct labor hours, or any other basis that results in a reasonable allocation of the indirect costs.

Administrative, service, and support costs are allocated to activities by consistently applying any reasonable method of cost allocation. Service department costs can be allocated using reasonable methods, such as the direct allocation method. A method is not considered reasonable if it effectively allocates service department costs to other service departments in a way that avoids the eventual reallocation of such costs to production and resale activities, if such reallocation would otherwise be required.

A *simplified production method* can be used to account for the additional costs that must be allocated. The method can be used for:

1) Stock in trade or other property included in the ending inventory.

2) Property held primarily for sale to customers in the course of the trade or business.

3) Property that is constructed for use in the trade or business if the business also produces property and the property constructed is substantially identical to and produced in the same manner as the inventory property or other allowable property.

4) Property constructed for use in a trade or business which normally produces this property on a routine and repetitive basis.

The simplified production method is designed to lessen the burdens of complying with the capitalization rules in situations where mass production of assets occurs on a repetitive and routine basis, with a typically high turnover rate for the produced assets. The method is not appropriate for use in accounting for casual or occasional production of property.

The simplified method cannot be used for property acquired for resale or property produced under a long-term contract. If a single trade or business consists of operations that include both the production of property and the acquisition of property for resale, the simplified method must be applied to operations of the particular trade or business.

Simplified Service Cost Method. A simplified method is also available for figuring the amount of certain indirect costs that producers must allocate to inventory production. This method provides for allocating administrative support, and service costs that directly benefit or are not incurred because of the performance of production activities, but also benefit other activities of the producer.

A producer can use the simplified service cost method whether or not the simplified production method is used. The inventoriable service costs can be determined under the simplified service cost method, and then the costs can be allocated to the production activities under the general provisions of the uniform capitalization rules. However, if the simplified production method is used, then the inventoriable service costs are allocated under that method. The simplified service cost method can be used only for the type of properties for which the simplified production method can be used.

Change in Accounting Method. When the first return for a business is filed, any appropriate accounting method can be chosen without the consent of the IRS. The method must clearly show the income and the same method must be used from year to year.

After the first return is filed, the consent of the IRS must first be obtained before an accounting method can be changed. The IRS will consider the need for consistency in the accounting method against the reason for wanting to change when the method from which the business wants to change clearly shows income. The absence of IRS consent to a change in the method of accounting because the taxpayer did not request a change (such as a change from an improper method of accounting to a proper method) does not prevent the IRS from imposing any penalty or addition to tax, nor lessen the amount of the penalty or the addition to the tax.

A change in an accounting method includes a change not only in the overall system of accounting, but also the treatment of any material item. Although an accounting method may exist without having a pattern of treating an item the same way all the time, in most cases, an accounting method is not established for an item unless the item is treated the same way every time.

Examples of changes that require consent:

1) A change from the cash method to the accrual method or vice versa, unless there **must** be a change to the accrual method and the change is made automatically.

2) A change in the method or basis used to value inventories.

3) A change in the method of figuring depreciation.

Some changes that are not changes in accounting methods and do not require consent are:

1) A correction of mathematical or posting errors.

2) An adjustment of any item of income or deduction that does not involve the proper time for including it in income or deducting it.

3) An adjustment in the useful life of a depreciable asset.

If the same taxpayer operates two or more separate and distinct trades or businesses, a different accounting method for each can be used, provided the methods used clearly reflect the income of each trade or business. A business is separate and distinct if books and records are maintained for each trade or business.

When the use of different methods of accounting results in the creation or shifting of profits or losses and there is not a clear reflection of income, the businesses will not be considered separate and distinct.

If the uniform capitalization rules require a change in accounting method, the change is made by revaluing the items or costs included in the *beginning inventory* for the year of change as if the capitalization rules had been in effect in all prior periods. In revaluing inventory costs, the capitalization rules apply to all inventory costs accumulated in prior periods. The difference between the inventory as originally valued and the inventory as revalued is equal to the amount of the adjustment required. If this change is required, the change is treated as though initiated by the taxpayer and with the consent of the IRS. The adjustment arising from the change in method is taken into account over a period not to exceed 4 years. The timing of the adjustment is made according to the regulations except that the maximum number of years over which the adjustment is to be spread is the number of tax years (not to exceed 4) that the taxpayer has engaged in the particular trade or business of producing property or acquiring property for resale to which the adjustment applies.

To determine estimated tax payments an adjustment is recognized ratably throughout the tax year of the adjustment. Any net operating loss and tax credit carryforwards are allowed to offset any positive net adjustment.

In revaluing the costs of inventory, the direct and indirect costs that are assigned to items of inventory under the capitalization rules must be determined, based on all the facts and circumstances (termed the *facts and circumstances revaluation*). The revaluation is required for every prior period that is relevant in determining the total restated balance as of the year of change. Under the facts and circumstances of the revaluation, the capitalization rules must be applied to production and resale activities, with the same degree of specificity as required of inventory manufacturers. Reasonable estimates and procedures in valuing inventory costs can be used if:

1) The taxpayer is unable to reconstruct from the books and records actual financial and accounting data required to apply the capitalization rules to the relevant facts and circumstances surrounding a particular item of inventory, or cost.

2) The total amount of costs, for which reasonable estimates and procedures are used, is not significant in comparison to the total restated value, including costs previously capitalized or costs.

If a change in the accounting method is required under the capitalization rules, the taxpayer can automatically change such method. A change is required under the capitalization rules if the change is necessary to properly allocate and capitalize costs for production and resale activities. An automatic change in method of accounting under the uniform capitalization rules includes:

1) A change in method of accounting in which certain costs are properly expensed under the capitalization rules that were previously capitalized under the prior method of accounting.

2) A change in method of accounting in which certain costs are properly capitalized under the capitalization rules that the taxpayer previously expensed under the prior method of accounting, regardless of whether such prior methods of accounting were correct or erroneous methods under the law in effect at that time.

A change is required if it relates to factors other than those described above. A change in method of accounting is considered to be all methods of complying with the Internal Revenue Code (including simplified methods), formulas, allocation methods, and inventory value procedures. If a change in accounting method is required and the change is not made, the taxpayer will be considered to be using an improper method of accounting.

Rule of 78's. The Rule of 78's cannot be used to figure interest income or expense, unless the loan qualifies as a short-term consumer loan. A short-term consumer loan is self-amortizing and requires level payments at regular intervals at least annually over a period of not more than 5 years, with no balloon payment at the end of the loan term. If the taxpayer has short-term consumer loans, the Rule of 78's method can be used for these loans to change the method of accounting for interest income or expense.

THE TECHNICAL AND MISCELLANEOUS REVENUE
ACT OF 1988

The *Technical and Miscellaneous Revenue Act of 1988* made numerous changes in the tax laws. Many IRS publications were sent to the press before the bill was enacted into law, and therefore contained only warnings about the pending legislation. All subjects that were finalized by Congress are in this update, *Supplement to the Accounting Desk Book, Ninth Edition.*

Also included in this *Supplement* are highlights from other prior enacted legislation, i.e., the *1986 Tax Reform Act* and the *1987 Technical Corrections Act.* Additional needed detail helpful to the accounting practitioner has been provided, with numerous examples the substance of which can be applied to specific tax accounting problems.

The tax changes starting with the 1986 Act and those in 1987 which affect business have been extensive and have necessitated this supplement providing rather exhaustive coverage.

The major topics in the three Acts are shown in the Table of Contents. For the location of specific subjects, see the Index in the back pages.

A feature of the 1988 law is the *Taxpayer Bill of Rights.* It is a part of Publication 1, *Your Rights as a Taxpayer.*

Taxpayer Bill of Rights

The new law gives the taxpayer certain rights when dealing with the Internal Revenue Service. These include the right to:

1) Receive an explanation of the examination and collection processes and the rights under these processes before or at the initial interview for the determination or collection of tax.

2) Have representation at any time during these processes by a person who may practice before the IRS, except in certain criminal investigations.

3) Make an audio recording or receive a copy of such recording of any interview for the determination or collection of tax.

4) Reasonably rely on written advice of the IRS that was provided in response to the taxpayer's specific written request.

5) File an application for relief with the IRS Ombudsman in a situation where the taxpayer is suffering or about to suffer a significant hardship as a result of the manner in which the IRS is administering the tax laws.

6) Receive a written notice of levy, no less than 30 days prior to enforcement, which explains in nontechnical terms the levy procedures and the administrative appeals and alternatives to levy which are available to the taxpayer.

Changes in the law define the costs that may be awarded in court proceedings when the taxpayer has prevailed in court and exhausted all administrative remedies available within the IRS. Also, the taxpayer may bring suit against the IRS for civil damages for certain unauthorized collection actions.

Accounting Methods and Periods

Tax year of partnership, S corporations, and personal service corporations. Generally, partnerships, S corporations, and personal service corporations must use *required tax years,* unless they can establish a business purpose for a tax year.

Section 444 election. Partnerships, S corporations, and personal service corporations may elect to use a tax year that is different from the required tax year. Certain restrictions apply to this election which is termed a *Section 444 election.* This election does not apply to any partnership, S corporation, or personal service corporation that establishes a business purpose for its tax year.

A partnership, S corporation, or personal service corporation may make a Section 444 election if:

1) It is not a member of a tiered structure.

2) It has not previously had a Section 444 election in effect.

3) It elects a year that meets the deferral period requirement.

Tiered structures. For tax years beginning after December 31, 1986, the election of a tax year other than the required tax year (Section 444 election) is prohibited by an entity that is part of a tiered structure, other than a tiered structure made up of one or more partnerships or S corporations, all of which have the same tax year. This exception applies whether all the entities are partnerships, or S corporations, or a combination of both, as long as all the entities have the same tax year. This exception does not apply to any other type of tiered structure.

This rule applies during the entire period an entity desires to have a Section 444 election in effect. Any Section 444 election is terminated if the entity becomes part of a tiered structure, other than one made up of partnerships, S corporations, or both.

Deferral period.   Generally, a partnership, S corporation, or personal service corporation may make a Section 444 election only if the tax year elected results in a deferral period of 3 months or less.

An election to change a tax year will be allowed only if the deferral period of the elected tax year is not longer than the **shorter** of:

1) 3 months.

2) The deferral period of the tax year being changed.

For a partnership, S corporation, or personal service corporation that wants to adopt or change its tax year by making a Section 444 election, the deferral period is the number of months between the end of the elected tax year and the close of the required tax year. If the current tax year is the required tax year, the deferral period is zero.

Example 1: X Partnership uses a calendar tax year which is also its required tax year. Because X's deferral period is zero, X cannot make a Section 444 election.

Example 2: X, a newly formed partnership, began operations on December 1, 1988. X is owned by calendar year partners. X wants to make a Section 444 election to adopt a September 30 tax year. X's deferral period for the tax year beginning December 1, 1988, is 3 months (September 30 to December 1, 1989).

The Section 444 election applies to tax years beginning after December 31, 1986.

Bad Debts

A new system (periodic) is provided for applying the nonaccrual-experience method of accounting for bad debts. The nonaccrual-experience method may be applied under either a separate receivable system or a periodic system. Under the separate receivable system the nonaccrual-experience method is separately applied to each account receivable. Under the periodic system, the nonaccrual-experience method is applied to total qualified accounts receivable at the end of the year.

Installment Sales

An *installment* is a sale of property where one or more payments is received after the close of the tax year. If a seller finances the buyer's purchase of seller's property instead of the buyer getting a loan or mortgage, the sale is usually an installment sale. The sale is not an installment sale if the buyer borrows the money from a third party and then pays the seller the total price of the property. If a sale qualifies as an installment sale, it must be reported on the installment method unless the seller elects to recognize a gain on the sale. Under the installment method, a gain is reported on a sale only as payments are received. It does not matter whether the seller uses the cash or accrual method of accounting.

A buyer's installment obligation to make future payments to the seller might be in the form of a deed of trust, note, land contract, mortgage, or other evidence of the buyer's indebtedness to the buyer. The tax rules apply regardless of the form of installment obligation.

Sales of personal property by a *dealer* or anyone who regularly sells property on the installment plan cannot be reported on the installment method for federal income tax purposes. This is any property in which substantially all of the use of which by the taxpayer is not in a trade or business or investment activity. Imputed interest affects the selling price and the contract price. It also affects the amount of gain on the sale, whether or not the installment method is used. If the installment method is used to report gain on the sale, both the selling price and the contract price must be reduced by any imputed interest. If a sale results in a loss, the installment method cannot be used. If the loss is on an installment sale of business assets, it can be deducted only in the tax year of the sale. A loss cannot be deducted on the sale of property owned for personal use. If a sale calls for payments in a later year, and there is little or no interest provided for in the contract of sale, unstated interest may have to be figured even though there is a loss.

In *figuring installment income,* each payment on the installment usually consists of three parts:

1) Return of an investment (basis) in the property sold.
2) Gain on the sale.
3) Interest.

Each year that payment is received, the interest part of the payment, as well as the part of the payment that is a gain, must be included in income. While interest is not included in a down payment, a part of each late payment must be treated as interest, even if it is not called interest in the agreement with the buyer.

Unstated interest. If an installment sale with some or all payments due more than one year after the date of sale does not provide for interest, part of each payment due more than 6 months after the date of sale will be treated as interest. The amount treated as interest is referred to as *unstated interest* or *imputed interest*. When the stated interest in the contract is under the applicable federal rate, the unstated interest is the difference between the federal rate of interest and any interest specified in the sales contract. The unstated interest rules do not apply to the borrower for a debt given in consideration for a sale or exchange of personal-use property. *Personal-use property* is any property substantially all of the use of which by the taxpayer is not in a trade or business or investment activity. Imputed interest affects the selling price and the contract price. It also affects the amount of gain on the sale, whether or not the installment method is used. If the installment method is used to report gain on the sale, both the selling price and the contract price must be reduced by any imputed interest. All other rules relating to installment sales apply as if there were no imputed interest.

If a sale is not reported using the installment method, the entire year of gain should be reported in the year of sale. If the payments received include imputed interest, the selling price must be reduced by the total amount of imputed interest before a gain or loss can be determined. The amount of interest to be reported is the sum of the imputed interest plus any interest specified under the contract.

Rules for imputing interest. If the unstated interest rules apply, both the buyer and the seller must treat part of the installment sales price as interest. The unstated interest rules require a part of each payment to be treated as interest, even though it is not called interest in an agreement with the buyer. The amount of unstated interest reduces the stated selling price of the property and increases both the seller's interest income and the buyer's interest expense.

A debt instrument must provide for adequate stated interest. If a debt instrument does not provide for adequate stated interest, interest is imputed on the debt. Generally, a debt instrument provides for adequate stated interest if it calls for interest at a rate no lower than the test rate of interest applicable to the debt instrument. The test rate of interest is the lower of the applicable federal rate of interest, or 9%, compounded semiannually.

Imputed principle. The issue price of a debt instrument has to be determined. Where there is adequate stated interest, the *issue price* is the stated principal amount. If the debt instrument does not provide for adequate stated interest, the issue price of the instrument is the imputed principal amount of the debt instrument. The issue price of a debt instrument is generally used to determine the sale price, in whole or in part, of any property acquired for the debt instrument. If an existing debt instrument is assumed, or property is acquired subject to a debt instrument, then determining whether the imputed interest rules apply to the debt instrument, the assumption, or acquisition, is not taken into account unless the terms or conditions of the debt instrument are modified or the nature of the transaction is changed.

The imputed interest rules do not apply in the following circumstances:

Publicly Traded Debt Instruments or Property. Transactions involving publicly traded debt instruments or any debt instrument issued in consideration for the sale or exchange of publicly traded property are not subject to the imputed interest rules. A publicly traded instrument is one that is traded on an established securities market.

Treatment of Obligors. An obligor or borrower (issuer) under a debt instrument given in consideration for the sale or exchange of property that is personal-use property in the hands of the issuer is not subject to the imputed interest rules. Personal-use property is any property in which substantially all of the use by the taxpayer is not in a trade or business or an investment activity.

Patents. When all substantial rights to a patent or an undivided interest in property that includes part or all substantial rights to a patent are sold or exchanged, the seller need not figure unstated interest or imputed principal on any amount contingent on the productivity, use, or disposition of the property transferred. This rule applies only if the seller is the inventor or a buyer who purchased the patent or right to the patent from the inventor before the invention was reduced to practice.

Disposition of Installment Obligations. A disposition includes a sale, exchange, cancellation, bequest, distribution, or transmission of an installment obligation. An installment obligation is the buyer's note, deed of trust, or other evidence that the buyer will make future payments to the seller. There is usually a gain or loss associated with an installment obligation. The gain or loss is considered to be gain or loss on the sale of the property for which the installment obligation was received. If the original installment sale of the property produced ordinary income, the disposition of the obligation will result in ordinary income or loss. If the original sale resulted in a capital gain, the disposition of the obligation also results in a capital gain or loss.

If an obligation is sold or exchanged, or if the seller accepts less than face value in satisfaction of the obligation, the gain or loss is the difference between the seller's basis in the obligation and the amount realized. If an obligation is disposed of in any other way, the gain or loss is the difference between the seller's basis in the obligation and its fair market value at the time of the disposition. This rule applies when the holder of the installment obligation gives it to someone else or cancels the buyer's debt.

No gain or loss is recognized on the transfer of an installment obligation between a husband and wife or a former husband and wife incident to a divorce. A transfer is incident to a divorce if it occurs within 1 year after the date on which the marriage ends, or is related to the end of the marriage. The same tax treatment for the transferred obligation applies to the spouse or former spouse receiving it as it applied to the transferor spouse or former spouse. The basis of the obligation to the transferee spouse, or former spouse, is the adjusted basis of the transferor spouse.

Adjusted basis is a way of measuring an investment in property that the owner is selling. The way the basis is figured depends on how the owner first acquired the property. The basis of property that was bought is usually its cost to the buyer. The basis of property inherited, received as a gift, built by the owner, or received in a tax-free exchange is figured differently. Various events can change the basis of an owner's personal-use property. Additions or permanent improvements increase the basis. Deductible casualty losses decrease the basis. The result of changes to the original basis of property is the *adjusted basis*.

The adjusted basis plus selling expenses and depreciation recapture income is the *installment sale basis*. *Selling expenses* are those that relate to the sale of the property. They include commissions, attorney fees, and any other expenses paid on the sale. Add the selling expenses to the basis of the sold property in determining the gross profit on the sale. For an installment sale, *gross profit* is the amount of gain reported using the installment method. To figure the gross profit, the seller must know the adjusted basis on the property sold and the selling price. Add the commissions and other expenses paid on the sale to the adjusted basis for the property. Then subtract the adjusted basis as increased from the selling price to determine the gross profit. If the property sold was the seller's home, subtract from the gross profit any gain that can be postponed or excluded. The result is the gross profit from the sale.

The *contract price* is the total of all principal payments the seller is to receive on the installment sale. It includes payments the seller is considered to receive, even though the seller has not been paid anything directly. If the selling price is partly payable in cash with the remainder secured by a mortgage payable from the buyer to the seller, the contract price equals the selling price. The profit has to be figured each year on the payments received, or are treated as receiving, from an installment sale including the downpayment and each later payment of principal on the buyer's debt. The seller is considered to have received a payment, even though the buyer does not pay the seller directly. These situations arise if the buyer takes over or pays off any of the seller's debt, such as a loan, or pays any of the seller's expenses, such as a sales commission.

The buyers note is not considered payment on the sale, unless it is payable on demand. Its full face value is included when figuring both selling price and contract price. Payments received by the buyer on the note are reported on the installment method. If the buyer assumes and pays the seller's expenses from selling the property, it is considered a payment in the year of sale. These expenses are included in both the selling and contract prices when figuring the gross profit percentage. A certain percentage of each payment, subtracting interest, is reported as gain from the sale. The percentage usually remains the same for each payment the buyer receives. It is called the *gross profit percentage* and is figured by dividing the gross profit from the sale by the contract price.

If the buyer sells property for which depreciation deductions have been taken, any depreciation recapture income in the year of sale is reported as ordinary income. If the amount of a gain equals or is less than the recapture, the buyer does not have an installment sale. Any gain that is more than the recapture income can be reported on the installment method. To figure the gross profit on the installment sale, add the selling expenses paid on the sale and the depreciation recapture income reported in the year of sale to the buyer's adjusted basis. Then subtract the adjusted bases as increased from the selling price to determine the gross profit on the sale.

Installment Obligation Used as Security

If an installment obligation from a $150,000 or more sale of nonfarm property is used to secure any debt, the net proceeds from the debt are treated as a payment on the obligation. This does not apply if the debt is incurred after December 17, 1987, to refinance a debt that was:

1) Outstanding on December 17, 1987.
2) Secured by that installment sale obligation on that date and at all times thereafter until the refinancing.

A refinancing as a result of the creditor's calling of the debt is treated as a continuation of the original debt if the refinancing is provided by a person other than the creditor or a person related to the creditor.

If the principal amount of the debt resulting from the refinancing exceeds the principal amount of the original debt immediately before the refinancing, the excess is treated as a payment on the installment obligation and will be subject to tax.

Personal service corporations. For tax years beginning after 1986, a personal service corporation can use the cash method of accounting if it meets a function test and an ownership test. For purposes of determining if a corporation meets the ownership test, indirect ownership is generally taken into account if the stock is owned indirectly through one or more partnerships, S corporations, or qualified personal service corporations. Stock owned by such an entity is considered owned by the entity's owners in proportion to their ownership interest in that entity. Other forms of indirect stock ownership, such as stock owned by family members, are generally not considered in determining if the ownership test is met.

Uniform Capitalization Rules

Freelance writers, artists, and photographers. The uniform capitalization rules do not apply to the deductible costs of writers, artists, and photographers incurred in producing creative property. The exception to the rules applies to the expenses of an individual (other than as an employee) and to a personal service corporation for expenses of a qualified employee-owner. The exception does not apply to any expense related to printing, photographic plates, motion picture films, videotapes, or similar items.

The exception is effective for costs incurred after December 31, 1986. If the uniform capitalization rules are applied using the 3-year safe harbor for qualified creative costs to tax years ending before November 10, 1988, the exception can be applied to those years by filing amended returns. The return for the first tax year ending after November 10, 1988, can be filed without applying the uniform capitalization rules.

Uniform capitalization checklist.   A uniform capitalization checklist must be attached to Form 3115, *Application for Change in Accounting Method*. Most taxpayers subject to the uniform capitalization rules must submit this checklist. Taxpayers who produce the following property do not have to submit the list:

1) Property produced in a farming business, **and**

2) Self-constructed property if the taxpayer's average annual gross receipts for the prior 3-year period are $10,000,000 or less.

If Form 3115 was filed before October 22, 1988, without a checklist, attach a Form 3115 (or copy of the previously filed form) with the checklist to the first income tax return filed after that date.

Depreciation

Change in use of real property.   All real property acquired before 1987 that is changed after 1986 from personal use to a business or income-producing use must be depreciated under the modified accelerated cost recovery system (MACRS).

Midquarter convention.   For tax years beginning after March 31, 1988, do not count property that is placed in service and disposed of in the same tax year to determine if the midquarter convention must be used instead of the half-year convention to compute depreciation. The taxpayer may elect in such a manner as prescribed by the Treasury Department to have this provision apply to tax years beginning before April 1, 1988.

Election to use the 150% declining balance method.   The 150% declining balance method may be used for property, other than residential rental and nonresidential real property, that is placed in service after 1986. The recovery period for property for which the 150% declining balance method is used is the property's class life. If the property does not have a class life assigned to it, the recovery period is 12 years.

The election to use the 150% declining balance method for a class of property applies to all property in that class that is placed in service during the tax year of the election. Once made the election cannot be changed. The election can be indicated by entering "150% DB" and "1/2" for the half-year convention, or "1/4" for the midquarter convention in column (e) of Section B, Part 1 of Form 4562.

Credits

Targeted jobs credit.   The deduction for the targeted jobs credit has been extended through 1989 for the wages of qualified employees who begin work before January 1, 1990.

An economically disadvantaged youth who begins work after December 31, 1988, must be at least age 18 but under age 23 rather than under age 25 on the hiring date. For a qualified summer youth employee who begins work after December 31, 1988, the credit percentage has been reduced from 85% to 40%, the same percentage as for all other qualified employees.

Research credit.   The research credit has been extended through 1989. However, for tax years beginning after 1988, if credit is taken, any deduction for research costs must be reduced by 50% of the amount of the credit. A similar rule applies if the qualified research expenses are capitalized, rather than expensed. To avoid this reduction, the choice not to take the credit can be made.

Business energy credits.   The following three business energy credits have been extended through 1989. The percentages for 1989 are 10% for solar energy and geothermal property and 15% for ocean thermal property.

General business credit ordering rules.   Tax credits must be deducted in the current tax year, or in any carryback or carryover year, in the following order:

1) Investment tax credit.
   a) Regular investment tax credit.
   b) Business energy investment tax credit.
   c) Former employee plan percentage investment tax credit which was in effect before the Tax Reform Act of 1954 was passed.
   d) Rehabilitation investment tax credit.
2) Targeted jobs tax credit.
3) Alcohol fuels credit.
4) Research credit.
5) Low-income housing credit.
6) Former WIN credit.
7) Former employee stock ownership credit.

An unused low-income housing credit cannot be carried back to tax years ending before 1987.

The credit ordering rules affect only the order in which credits arising in a single year are used. These rules do not affect the rule that requires that credit from the earliest years be used first.

These ordering rules apply to tax years beginning after 1983, and to carry-overs from these years.

General business credit limitations. The general business credit for tax years beginning after 1986 is limited to the taxpayer's net tax liability reduced by:

1) The tentative minimum tax.

2) 25% of the tax liability over $25,000, if this amount is larger.

The taxpayer's new limit can be calculated on:

1) Form 3438, *Computation of Investment Credit.*

2) Form 5884, *Jobs Credit.*

3) Form 6478, *Credit for Alcohol Used as Fuel.*

4) Form 6765, *Credit for Increasing Research Activities.*

5) Form 8586, *Low-Income Housing Credit.*

6) Form 3800, *General Business Credit,* if more than one of these credits can be used, or a carryback or carryover of any of these credits.

The special limit for **corporations** that applies to the investment credit part of the general business credit has also changed for tax years beginning after 1986. Form 3468 has instructions for information on how to figure this new limit.

Corporations: Corporate Tax Rates

Corporate taxable income is subject to tax under the following three-bracket graduated rate system:

TAXABLE INCOME	TAX RATE
Not over $50,000	15%
Over $50,000 but not over $75,000	25%
Over $75,000	34%

An additional 5% tax, up to $11,750, is imposed on corporate taxable income over $100,000. Corporations with taxable income of at least $335,000 pay a flat rate of 34%.

Estimated tax. Any shortfall of estimated taxes caused by the use of the annualized income or the adjusted seasonal income methods must be made up in the subsequent payment, if these methods are not used in figuring that subsequent payment. The *shortfall* is the difference between the amount required to be paid and the amount actually paid when using the annualized income or the adjusted seasonal income methods.

For payments made before 1989, if the subsequent payment made up at least 90% of the earlier shortfall, no penalty was imposed. However, for payments required to be made after 1988, a corporation that uses the annualized income or the adjusted seasonal income methods for a prior estimated tax payment must make up the entire shortfall (rather than 90% of the shortfall) in the subsequent payment in order to avoid an estimated tax penalty.

Waiver of tax penalty. A corporation is not subject to the estimated tax penalty for any period before March 16, 1989, for any underpayment caused by the provisions of Title I and II (Technical Corrections) of the Technical and Miscellaneous Revenue Act of 1988.

Alternative Minimum Tax

For tax years beginning after 1986, the following changes have been made to the minimum tax rules.

The Possessions Tax Credit must be used to reduce the corporation's regular tax.

Taxable Income. A corporation subject to the regular tax is also subject to the alternative minimum tax if the tentative minimum tax exceeds the regular tax; and where the corporation's tax base is measured by something other than taxable income (such as real estate investment trust taxable income or life insurance company taxable income), alternative minimum taxable income is determined using that tax base.

For Long-Term Small Construction Contracts, the percentage of the contract completed is determined by using the simplified procedures for allocation of costs.

The Alternative Tax Net Operating Loss is determined by reducing the regular tax net operating loss by tax preference items only to the extent they increased the amount of the net operating loss.

For Adjustments to Book Income, the definition of an "applicable financial statement" has been changed with regard to one that is filed with a federal, state, or local government in that it must be an income statement filed for a substantial nontax purpose.

The Alcohol Fuel Credit Does Not Apply to Alternative Minimum Tax. Therefore, regular taxable income, which includes the amount of the alcohol fuel tax credit, is reduced by the amount of that credit when figuring alternative minimum taxable income.

The Tax Credit for Bond Interest applies to tax-exempt bonds, and the exception for refunding bonds includes both current and advance refundings.

General Business Credit. The total amount of the general business credit allowable for a tax year in which the regular tax exceeds the tentative minimum tax is determined as if the portion of the general business credit not attributable to the regular investment tax credit first offset the regular tax, and then the regular investment credit (to the extent otherwise available) then reduced the net tax to 75% of the tentative minimum tax.

However, the regular investment tax credit cannot be used in a tax year to the extent that it results in the corporation's income tax (net of all nonrefundable credits) being less than an amount equal to 10% of the tentative minimum tax (figures without regard to the alternative net operating loss deduction and the foreign tax credit).

Accumulated Earnings Tax. For tax years beginning after 1987, the rate of the accumulated earnings tax has changed from 27.5% (38.5% of accumulated taxable income over $100,000) to 28%.

Dividends-Received Deduction. The dividends-received deduction was reduced from 80% to 70% for shareholders that own less than 20% of the voting power and value of the stock of a distributing corporation. The 20%-or-more corporate shareholders remain eligible for an 80% dividends- received deduction.

There is a new effective date that applies to the rule for dividends received by 20%-or-more corporate shareholders. The rule is effective for dividends received or accrued after 1987, in tax years ending after that date. Therefore, fiscal-year corporations who own 20% or more of a domestic corporation can deduct 80% of dividends received or accrued in 1987 and 1988.

Extraordinary Dividends. Effective for purposes of determining if a corporation must reduce its basis in stock after receiving certain extraordinary dividends declared after July 18, 1986, the definition of the dividend announcement date has been clarified. The dividend announcement date is the date on which the corporation declares, announces, or agrees to either the amount or the payment of the dividend, whichever is earliest.

Distributions to Shareholder. For tax years beginning after 1986, the amount of a distribution to a corporate or noncorporate shareholder from a corporation is determined by the amount of money received and the fair market value of all other property received.

Controlled Group of Corporations. For tax years beginning after November 10, 1988, in determining whether a corporation is a member of a parent-subsidiary controlled group of corporations, the attribution rules for partnerships, trusts, and estates must be applied.

Losses on Transactions Between Related Parties. The disallowance of losses from the sale or exchange of property between related parties does not apply either to any loss of a distributing corporation or to any loss of a distributee in the case of a distribution in complete liquidation. This rule is effective for tax years beginning after 1986.

Recapture of Mining Exploration Expenses. Previously expensed mining exploration costs that have been included in income upon reaching the producing state are not taken into account in determining the amount of recapture.

S Corporations

Effective for tax years beginning after 1986, the tax on built-in gains is modified to properly measure the net built-in gain when a C corporation converts to an S corporation under an election made after 1986.

Tax on Built-In Gains. Generally, the amount of tax is figured by applying the highest rate of tax (34%) to the net recognized built-in gain of the S corporation for the tax year less net operating and capital loss carryforwards allowed to be taken into account (the "amount subject to tax").

Net Recognized Built-In Gain. Generally, the term "net recognized built-in gain" for any tax year is the amount that would be the S corporation's taxable income if only recognized built-in gains less the recognized built-in losses were taken into account. However, the corporation's amount subject to tax for any year cannot exceed the taxable income for the year not taking into account net operating or capital loss carryforwards.

Carryover. If, for any tax year, the amount subject to tax is more than the corporation's taxable income, as described above, the excess is treated as a recognized built-in gain in the following tax year. This applies only to a corporation that made an election to be treated as an S corporation after March 30, 1988.

Net Operating Loss Carryforwards. Any net operating loss carryforward that arose in a tax year when the corporation was a C corporation is allowed as a deduction against the net recognized built-in gain of the S corporation for the tax year. To determine the amount of the loss that may be carried to later tax years, the amount of the net recognized built-in gain is treated as taxable income. The same rule applies for a capital loss carryforward arising in a tax year when the corporation was a C corporation.

Limitation on Amount of Net Recognized Built-In Gain. The amount of the net recognized built-in gains taken into account for any tax year cannot be more than the excess of:

1) The net unrealized built-in gain, **over**
2) The net unrecognized built-in gains for prior tax years beginning in the recognition period.

Recognized Built-In Gain. The term "recognized built-in gain" means any gain recognized during the recognition period on the disposition of any asset, except to the extent that the S corporation establishes that:

1) The asset **was not held** by the S corporation at the beginning of the first tax year for which it was an S corporation, or
2) The gain is more than the fair market value of the asset at the beginning of the first tax year, minus the adjusted basis of the asset at the beginning of that year.

Recognized Built-In Losses. The term "recognized built-in losses" means any loss recognized during the recognition period on the disposition of any asset to the extent that the S corporation establishes the following:

1) The asset **was not held** by the S corporation at the beginning of the first tax year for which it was an S corporation.
2) The loss is not more than the adjusted basis of the asset at the beginning of the first tax year for which it was an S corporation, minus the fair market value of the asset at the beginning of that year.

Treatment of Certain Property. If the adjusted basis of any asset is determined (fully or partly) by the adjusted basis of another asset held by the S corporation at the beginning of the first tax year for which it was an S corporation:

1) The asset is treated as held by the S corporation at the beginning of the first tax year, and
2) Recognized built-in gain or loss is determined by the fair market value and adjusted basis of the other asset at the beginning of that first tax year.

Recognition Period. The term "recognition period" means the 10-year period beginning with the first day of the first tax year for which the corporation was an S corporation.

Transfer of Assets From a C Corporation to an S Corporation. Generally, if an S corporation acquires an asset, and the S corporation's basis in the asset is determined (fully or partly) by the basis of the asset (or any other property) in the hands of a C corporation, then a tax is imposed on any net recognized built-in gain due to these assets for any tax year beginning in the recognition period.

However, when figuring the tax, the day on which the assets were acquired by the S corporation must be taken into account rather than the beginning of the first tax year for which the corporation was an S corporation.

First Tax Year. The "first tax year" for which a corporation is treated as an S corporation is determined by its most recent election to be an S corporation.

Capital Gains Tax Rate for S Corporations Not Subject to Built-In Gains. For tax years beginning after December 31, 1986, an S corporation not subject to the tax on built-in gains is still subject to prior law regarding the special tax on capital gains. However, for tax years beginning after 1986, the capital gains tax rate is 34% (not 28%, as under prior law).

LIFO

LIFO recapture tax.   If a C corporation made its election to be an S corporation after December 17, 1987, and used the LIFO inventory pricing method for its last tax year before its S election became effective, the C corporation may be liable for LIFO recapture.

The LIFO recapture tax is figured for the last year the corporation was a C corporation. The LIFO tax is paid in 4 equal installments. The first installment is due with the corporation's Form 1120 or Form 1120A for the corporation's last tax year as a C corporation, and the 3 remaining deferral installments are paid with the corporation's Form 1120S for the next 3 years. Include each year's installment in the total amount to be entered on line 22c, page 1 of Form 1120S. Write to the left of the line 22c total, the installment amount and the words "LIFO tax."

Adjusted Tax Attributes

Adjusted tax attributes means the sum of the following:

1) Any net operating loss (NOL) for the year of the discharge and any NOL carryovers to that year.
2) Any general business credit carryover to or from the year of discharge, multiplied by 3.
3) Any net capital loss for the year of the discharge and any capital loss carryovers to that year.
4) Any foreign tax credit carryovers to or from the year of discharge, multiplied by 3.

After adjusted tax attributes 1, 2, and 3 are reduced by the excluded amount, but before reducing tax attribute 4, any remaining excluded amount must apply to reduce the basis of "qualified property" in the following order:

1) Depreciable property.
2) Land used in a farming business.
3) Other qualified property.

Qualified property is any property used in a business or for the production of income.

Self-Employment Tax

Net earnings and tax rate. The maximum net earnings subject to self-employment tax for 1988 is $45,000. This amount increases to $48,000 in 1989. The net tax rate for 1988 and 1989 is 13.02%.

Corporate director's earnings. For services performed in tax years beginning after 1987, for purposes of both the self-employment tax and the social security earnings test, a corporate director's earnings are treated as received when the services are performed, regardless of when paid or received (unless it was actually paid or received prior to that year).

Religious exemption time limit. Members of certain religious faiths may file an application for an exemption from self-employment tax. The application previously had to be filed by the due date, including extensions, for the first year in which the individual had self-employment income. This time limit has been eliminated for applications filed after November 9, 1988.

Employment Taxes

The payment of *uniformed reservists for inactive duty training* (generally weekend training and drills) is subject to social security taxes.

Wages paid to *children employed by parents,* over 18 years of age, and for services in the parent's trade or business are subject to social security taxes. Wages paid to parent's children under the age of 21 for service not in the parent's trade or business, however, such as domestic service in the parent's private home, are still exempt from social security taxes.

Wages paid to a spouse in the other spouse's trade or business are subject to social security taxes. Wages paid to one's spouse for service that is not in the other spouse's trade or business, however, such as domestic service in their private home, are still exempt from social security taxes.

Employee *cash tips* are subject to the employer portion of the social security tax.

A new *Form W-4* must be put into effect no later than the start of the first payroll period ending on or after the 30th day from the date that the employee receives the revised form. If wages are paid without regard to a payroll period, the employer must put the new Form W-4 into effect no later than the first payment of wages on or after the 30th day from the date that the employer receives the new Form W-4.

The gross *federal unemployment* (FUTA) tax rate will remain at 6.2% through 1990.

The maximum wages subject to the social *security tax increase* from $45,000 to $48,000 is effective in calendar year 1989. The *tax rate* in 1989 remains at 7.51% for the employee and the employer.

The exclusion from employment taxes of *employer-provided group legal plans* has been extended and modified for tax years ending after 1987 and before 1989. If an employer contributed to a qualified group legal services plan for employees (including spouses and dependents), up to $70 of the annual premium paid for the plan can be excluded from the gross income of each employee. The excluded amount is not subject to social security taxes, federal unemployment tax, or income tax withholding.

After 1987, the cost of *group-term life insurance* provided to an employee that is includible in the employee's gross income is subject to social security taxes, as well as income taxes. However, under the new law, if the employee quit or retired before 1989, that cost is not subject to social security taxes with regard to coverage provided for the employee after the employee quit or retired, unless he or she later returns to work for the employer. The cost of group-term life insurance includible in gross income of an employee who quits or retires after 1988 is subject to social security taxes.

The provision that allows *self-employed members of religious sects that are conscientiously opposed to acceptance of public or private insurance benefits* to claim an exemption from social security coverage has been extended to include the employees of such members. Both the employer and employee must be members of a qualifying religious sect.

The exemption applies to both the employer and employee portions of the tax. Both the employer and the employee must receive approved applications for exemption from social security coverage before the exemption can take effect. This provision is effective for tax years beginning after 1988.

Federal, state, and local governments may treat an individual *who provides dependent care or similar services* as other than an employee for employment tax purposes after 1983 and before 1991 if:

1) He or she does not provide any dependent care or similar services in a facility owned or operated by the government.

2) He or she is paid out of funds provided under the Family Security Act of 1988.

3) The government does not treat the individual as an employee for employment tax purposes.

4) The government files all required federal income tax returns, treating the individual as other than an employee, and

5) No more than 10% of the employees of the government are covered by social security under voluntary agreements with the Department of Health and Human Services.

Reimbursement or allowances for meals, entertainment, and lodging. Under the *Family Support Act of 1988,* an employer will have to withhold federal income tax and social security taxes and pay the federal unemployment tax on any reimbursement or other expense allowable if the employer either:

1) Does not require employees to adequately account for their expenses.

2) Allows employees to keep any excess reimbursement or allowance over the expenses adequately accounted for.

If an employee is given a per diem or other fixed allowance, the employee is considered to have adequately accounted to the employer for the amount of the expenses covered by this arrangement up to the amounts that have been specified by IRS. Other than the amount of these expenses, your employee's business expenses (for example, the business purpose of the travel or the number of business miles driven) must be substantiated.

These new rules apply to tax years beginning after 1988.

Fringe benefit-air transportation. The value of fringe benefits provided by an employer to employees is generally includible in their income as wages. Certain classes of fringe benefits, however, are excludable from income, and one of them is the "no-additional-cost service." To qualify as an excludable no-additional-cost service, the service provided to an employee must be the same service sold to customers in the ordinary course of the employer's business.

New law change. For determining whether a fringe benefit qualifies as an excludable no-additional-cost service, transportation of passengers by air and transportation of cargo by air are treated as the same service. Thus, an air freight company that does not transport passengers by air in the ordinary course of its business can exclude from its employees' income, as a no-additional-cost service, the value of transporting them by air. This also includes passenger travel provided through reciprocal agreements with other airlines. This rule is effective for transportation furnished after 1987.

Excessive termination payments (golden parachutes). A corporation that makes excess golden parachute payments cannot deduct them. However, payments to key personnel of a corporation that, immediately before a change in control, has no stock that is readily tradable on an established securities market (or otherwise) are exempt from the golden parachute rules if:

1) The payments are approved by a vote of shareholders owning more than 75% of the voting power of the outstanding stocks.
2) There was adequate disclosure of all material facts concerning such payments.

New law clarifies that for purposes of the above the term *stock* does not include any stock:

1) That is not entitled to vote.
2) That has limited and preferred dividends and does not participate significantly in corporate growth.
3) That has redemption and liquidation rights not exceeding its issue price.
4) That cannot be converted into another class of stock.
5) That has no rights adversely affected by the parachute payments.

Excise Taxes

Windfall profits tax repealed. The repeal of the windfall profit tax applies to crude oil removed from the premises after August 22, 1988. All requirements, including filing returns, remain in effect for the portion of the year before August 23, 1988.

The requirement that Form 6248, *Annual Information Return of Windfall Profit Tax,* be furnished or filed for calendar year 1988 is waived for crude oil removed (or deemed removed) from the premises on or after January 1, 1988, if:

1) The person otherwise subject to the requirement reasonably believes that no windfall profit tax accrued during 1988 for such crude oil (disregarding the net income limitation), and
2) There must have been no windfall profit tax withholding for such crude oil.

Imported substances. After 1988, a new tax applies to certain imported substances made from taxable chemicals. Form 6627, *Environmental Taxes,* and its instructions list these substances and the tax rates. The tax is based on the rate of tax on the taxable chemicals used as materials in the manufacture or production of each listed substance.

Tax on certain vaccines. After 1987, an excise tax is imposed on certain prescribed vaccines sold in the United States. The use by a manufacturer, producer, or importer will be treated as a sale. The taxable vaccines are those prescribed for:

1) Diphtheria, pertussis, and tetanus (DPT).
2) Diphtheria and tetanus (DT).
3) Measles, mumps, and rubella (MMR).
4) Polio.

Liable for the tax are the manufacturer, producer, or importer. The tax is reported on Form 720, *Quarterly Federal Excise Tax Return,* which shows the specific tax rates. The tax does not apply to vaccines shipped to a United States possession.

1988 Tax Changes for Pensions and Annuities

Simplified general rule for recovering pension contributions. If the retiree's annuity starting date is after July 1, 1986, he or she may be able to use a new simple computation to figure the taxable and nontaxable parts of an annuity. This simple method can be used only if:

1) The annuity payments are for either:
   a) The retiree's life.
   b) The retiree's life and that of his/her beneficiary.
2) The annuity payments are from a qualified employee plan, an employee annuity, or a tax-sheltered annuity.

3) As of the annuity starting date, either the retiree was under age 75, or if 75 or older, the number of years of guaranteed payments was fewer than 5. Publication 575, *Pension and Annuity Income,* gives complete instructions for recovering pension contributions.

Simplified employee pensions (SEPs).   New law made changes to the rules on SEPs. Generally, for plan years beginning after December 31, 1987, a SEP cannot include a salary reduction arrangement (permitting elective deferrals) unless the plan provides that the total amount a participant can defer under that plan and any other plans, arrangements, or contracts of the employer may not exceed the deferral limit.

Effective for years after December 31, 1986, plan provisions must ensure the distribution of deferrals made by highly compensated employees that exceed the limit under a salary reduction SEP.

Under prior law, SEPs could include a salary reduction arrangement if at least 50% of the employees chose to have amounts taken out of their pay and contributed to their SEP-IRAs. New law makes it clear that the reference is to employees who are eligible to participate. Also, prior law provides that the employer must have no more than 25 employees during the preceding year. New law clarifies that this refers to employees who were eligible to participate in the SEP (or would have been required to be eligible to participate if a SEP were maintained). This clarification applies to years beginning after December 31, 1986.

Excise tax increase on plan reversions.   The excise tax on any reversion of qualified plan assets to an employer upon plan termination is increased from 10% to 15%. The tax increase applies, with certain exceptions, to reversions occurring on or after October 21, 1988.

Also, for reversions received after December 31, 1988, the time for paying the tax has been reduced. Payment is due by the last day of the month following the month in which the employer reversion occurs.

Individual Retirement Arrangements (IRAs)

Coverage by an employer plan—married person filing a separate return.   If contributions to an IRA are covered by an employer retirement plan or if the employee is married filing a joint return and the spouse is covered, the IRA deduction is subject to the phaseout rule, which may reduce or eliminate the deduction. Under prior law, if the employee were married, filed a separate return, and was **not** covered by an employee retirement plan, the employee's IRA deduction was not subject to the phaseout rule, even if the spouse was covered by an employer's retirement plan. Therefore, the full deduction of up to $2,000 or 100% of the compensation, whichever was less, could be taken.

Generally, beginning in 1988, the treatment in the preceding paragraph applies to the employee only if he/she did not live with the spouse at any time during the year. In this case, under the phaseout rule, the employee is treated as an unmarried person. The IRA deduction is not reduced or eliminated even if the spouse is covered by an employer retirement plan. The spouse is also treated as unmarried. Therefore, if the spouse is covered by an employer retirement plan, he or she can have up to $25,000 of modified adjusted gross income before his or her IRA deduction is reduced or eliminated.

Penalty for failure to file Form 8606. For tax years beginning after 1986, a taxpayer who made nondeductible IRA contributions has to pay a penalty if he or she does not file Form 8606, *Nondeductible IRA Contributions, IRA Basis, and Nontaxable IRA Distributions.* The penalty is $50 for each failure to file the form, unless the taxpayer can prove that the failure was due to reasonable cause.

Withdrawal of contributions before due date. New law provides that a taxpayer can make tax-free withdrawals of any contributions made to an IRA for a year, provided:

1) The contributions were received before the due date (including extensions) of the return for that year.
2) A deduction is not claimed for them.
3) Earnings on them have been received. These earnings are includible in the gross income in the year that contributions were made.

Under prior law, tax-free treatment applied only to the extent that the withdrawn contributions were more than the amount allowable as a deduction. The new rule applies to the receipt of contributions for tax years beginning after 1986.

Lump-sum distributions. New law has made corrections to the rules on the special averaging and capital gains treatment of lump-sum distribution.

Under prior law, *5-year averaging* applied to a taxpayer who reached at least age 59 at the time of the distribution. New law clarifies that this averaging applies to distributions with respect to an employee who was at least age 59 at the time of the distribution.

The law provides that only one *special averaging election* can be made with regard to any one employee. The election for phased-out capital gains treatment of, or having the 20% tax rate apply to, a portion of the lump-sum distribution is treated as an averaging election. New law makes it clear that such an election is treated as a **special averaging election** for all purposes of the law, and not just to determine whether a later distribution can be averaged.

For **individuals born before January 2, 1936,** prior law said that special 10-year averaging or capital gains treatment (at a 20% rate) is available to "individuals" who were born before January 2, 1936. New law makes it clear that this special treatment applies to employees born before January 2, 1936, who receive lump-sum distributions, or to individuals, estates, or trusts for distributions made with respect to such employees.

Publication 590, *Individual Retirement Arrangements (IRAs)*, covers the details for IRA distributions.

Withholding.   The rule that income tax will be withheld from pension, annuity, or similar payments received unless the choice is made not to have tax withheld has been clarified. A taxpayer can choose not to have tax withheld on these payments if the taxpayer:

1) Gives the payer the taxpayer's home address in the United States, or
2) Certifies to the payer that the taxpayer is not a U.S. citizen, a resident alien of the United States, or a tax-avoidance expatriate.

III

The 1987 and 1986
Tax Legislation

REVENUE ACT OF 1987

The Omnibus Budget Reconciliation Act of 1987, which includes the Revenue Act of 1987, changed the tax law to increase revenues by:

1) Curbing certain abuses under prior law.
2) Setting new restrictions.

The 1987 law primarily affects business taxpayers, i.e., corporations, partnerships, proprietorships, and tax-exempt organizations.

This section of the Supplement discusses these tax changes to show how the changes in prior laws apply to current business tax problems.

New Rules for Deductible Home Mortgage Interest

The Tax Reform Act of 1986 preserved the deduction for home mortgage interest while phasing out deductions for other personal interest. But certain limits apply to some homeowners having mortgage interest. These limits are figured differently for 1988 and later years than they were for 1987. However, under the rules for either year, most homeowners who take out mortgages only to buy or improve their main or second homes can still deduct all the interest on those mortgages.

For 1987 all the interest on debt secured by the main or second home could be deducted provided the debt was not more than the cost of the home plus the cost of improvements. Generally, all of the interest for additional debt secured by a home to pay for medical or educational expenses was deductible. If the total debt was more than the total cost of the home including improvements and medical and educational expenses, only part of the interest was deductible.

Interest that is secured by the main or second home is deductible in any one of the following situations:

1) The debt, regardless of amount, was incurred on or before October 13, 1987, and was not increased after that date.
2) The debt is not more than $1 million ($500,000 if married but filing separately), provided the debt proceeds are used to buy, build, or substantially improve the home.
3) The debt was not used for the purpose in 2), but is equal to or less than $100,000, or $50,000 if married but filing separately.

Under the rules for 1988, therefore, interest is fully deductible that was not fully deductible for 1987. For example, home equity debt can be used up to $100,000 in excess of the home's cost for any purpose, not just for medical or educational expenses. If the taxpayer's situation is not described in the above list, only part of the interest on the home debt is fully deductible as home mortgage interest. However, the remainder of the interest may be claimed as personal interest (40%) deductible for 1988.

The maximum amount of home mortgage debt incurred after October 13, 1987, on which all of the interest is deductible, depends on how the debt is used, as in situations 2 and 3. If the debt is secured by a main or second home and is used to buy, build, or substantially improve that home, it is called *acquisition debt*. If it is secured by the home but is not used for those purposes, it is called home equity debt.

Acquisition debt also includes debt from the refinancing of previous acquisition debt, up to the amount of the refinanced debt. Total acquisition debt is generally limited to $1 million, $500,000 if married and filing separately.

Debt that is incurred before October 14, 1987, is treated as acquisition debt regardless of the purpose for which the funds are used. To qualify, the debt must have been secured by a main or second home on October 13, 1987, and must be secured continuously by that home for the whole time the interest is paid or accrued. This pre-October 14, 1987 debt is not subject to the $1 million or $500,000 limit. However, if additional debt is taken out after October 13, 1987, to improve a home, the new debt is subject to the limit. Subtract the total outstanding pre-October 14, 1987 debt from the limit to figure the amount of the new debt that qualifies as acquisition debt.

Pre-October 14, 1987 debt includes debt that is incurred after October 13, 1987 to refinance pre-October 14 debt, if the replacement debt is secured by a main or second home. The replacement debt qualifies as pre-October 14 debt, but only up to the principal amount of the refinanced debt at the time of the refinancing, and only over a limited term which is:

1) The remaining term of the original debt, if the original debt was to be repaid over its term.
2) If the original debt was not to be repaid over its term, the term of the first refinancing (but not more than 30 years after the first refinancing).

Debt that is secured by a main or second home, but that does not qualify as acquisition debt, is treated as *home equity debt*. Generally, home equity debt is limited to the lesser of:

1) The fair market value of that home minus the total acquisition debt on that home.
2) $100,000, or $50,000 if married filing separately.

If the borrower has a main home and a second home, the total home equity debt on both homes cannot be more than the dollar limit in (2) for any year. There is no restriction on the uses of the proceeds of home equity debt.

The following three examples will clarify the application of these requirements for the accountant and taxpayer.

Example 1: Pre-October 14, 1987 Debt. Taxpayer bought the main home 10 years ago for $75,000. The fair market value of the home rose to more than $120,000, so that in January 1987, the original mortgage was refinanced to obtain a new loan, which had an average balance of $120,000 for the year. None of the proceeds of the loan were used for any improvements on the home, nor were any of the proceeds from the refinancing used for medical or educational expenses. Since the average balance of the mortgage debt in 1987 was more than the cost of the home, the interest on the $120,000 debt was not fully deductible under the rules applicable for 1987. Form 8598, *Home Mortgage Interest,* showing the part of total interest expense that was fully deductible and the part that was not must be filed.

For 1988, all of the interest expense on the new mortgage is fully deductible if the mortgage was secured by the main home on October 13, 1987, and continuously thereafter. The new mortgage is considered *acquisition debt* even though it is more than the cost of the home.

Example 2: Refinancing of Acquisition Debt. Assume the same facts as in Example 1, except that the new loan to refinance the original loan was taken out in January 1988, instead of in January 1987. By that time the principal balance of the original mortgage had been reduced to $50,000. In this situation, only $50,000 of the new mortgage balance qualifies as acquisition debt, because that was the refinanced debt amount, e.g., the remaining principal of the original debt. The remaining $70,000 average balance of the new mortgage also qualifies for the full deduction of interest, but only as home equity debt.

Example 3: Home Equity Debt. The facts are the same as in Example 2. The fair market value of the home further increases to more than $160,000, and later in 1988 an additional home equity loan is taken out. The proceeds are used to take a trip around the world and to buy a new luxury car. The new debt has an average balance of $40,000 for the year.

When determining how much of the interest on the new debt is deductible as home mortgage interest, it does not matter what is done with the loan proceeds. However, the new debt is subject to the $100,000 limit on home equity debt. Since there is already a home equity debt of $70,000 (the excess of the January, 1988, mortgage average balance of $120,000 over the refinanced mortgage of $50,000), the unused limit is $30,000 ($100,000 minus $70,000). Therefore, only $30,000 of the average balance of the new debt qualifies for the full deduction of interest. The interest on the remaining $10,000 new debt average balance is personal interest that is only 40% deductible for 1988.

Employment Taxes

Inactive duty reservists. Before 1988, only the pay of uniformed reservists for full-time active duty or for active duty training (generally training duty for two weeks, or more) was subject to social security taxes. After 1987, the pay of uniformed reservists for inactive duty training (generally weekend training and drills) is also subject to social security taxes.

One spouse employed by another.   Before 1988, one spouse working for another was not subject to social security taxes. After 1987, wages paid by one spouse to another spouse for services in a trade or business are subject to social security taxes. Wages paid to a spouse for service that is not in the other spouse's trade or business, such as domestic service in the married couple's private home, are still exempt from social security taxes.

Children employed by parents.   Before 1988, if a child under the age of 21 worked for a parent in his/her trade or business, the child's wages were not subject to social security taxes. After 1987, wages paid to the child under the age of 18 for services in a parent's trade or business are not subject to social security taxes. Wages paid on or after the child's 18th birthday are subject to social security taxes. The wages paid to a child under the age of 21 for service that is not in a parent's trade or business, however, such as domestic service in the parent's private home, are still exempt from social security taxes.

Employers must pay social security tax on employees' tips.
Before 1988, the employer did not have to pay the employer portion of the social security tax on cash tips reported to the employer by the employees, unless the wages paid were less than the federal minimum wage. All cash tips received after 1987, however, are subject to the employer portion of the social security tax. The employer must pay the employer social security tax on the total amount of cash tips and wages up to the social security maximum of $45,000 for 1988.

Group-term insurance cost may be subject to social security taxes.   Before 1988, the cost of group-term life insurance provided to an employee for coverage over $50,000, or for coverage that discriminated in favor of the employee, was included in the employee's income and subject to income tax. The cost of the insurance, however, was not subject to social security taxes. After 1987, the cost of such group-life insurance that is included in income and subject to income tax is also subject to social security taxes.

Employers must make form W-4 effective promptly.   Before 1988, an effective date for a revised Form W-4, *Employee's Withholding Allowance Certificate,* was the first status determination date (January 1, May 1, July 1, October 1) that occurred at least 30 days after receipt of the Form W-4 from an employee. For a revised Form W-4 that is received after January 21, 1988, the period allowed for putting it into effect has been shortened to no later than the start of the first payroll period ending on or after the 30th day from the date that the W-4 is received from the employee.

Federal Unemployment Tax (FUTA)

Beginning in 1988, the gross FUTA tax rate under the prior law was scheduled to decrease to 6.0% For wages paid beginning in 1988, the gross FUTA tax rate remains at 6.2% through 1990. Since the credit against the FUTA tax for payments to state unemployment funds stays at a maximum of 5.4%, the net FUTA tax rate remains at 0.8% (.008).

Corporate Directors

Before 1988 many corporate directors deferred receipt of directorship earnings until reaching age 70. In doing so, these directors were able to avoid social security benefit reductions because of the social security earnings test. The earnings test does not apply to recipients age 70 and older. The delay in receipt of these earnings also delayed payment of the self-employment tax.

Beginning in 1988 a corporate director's earnings are treated as received when the services are performed, regardless of when paid, for purposes of both the self-employment tax and the social security earnings test.

Business Expenses

- Accrual of certain vacation pay repealed.
- Past service pension costs capitalized.
- Employee benefit plan rules changed.

Repeal of vacation pay accrual account.   Prior to 1988, if the accrual method of accounting were used, a reasonable amount credited to a reserve account for vacation pay could be deducted. The amount must have been paid during the year or within 8½ months after the close of the year.

The new law repealed this vacation-pay rule for tax years beginning in 1988. If the employer's accounting method had to be changed because of the repeal of the vacation-pay rule, any change was treated as though it had been requested and had received permission from the IRS. No formal application for permission to make the change had to be filed with the IRS.

The amount of any adjustment to prevent income and expense items from being duplicated or omitted that results from the change in the law is reduced by the balance in the vacation pay suspense account (the nondeductible accrued vacation pay at the close of the last tax year beginning before 1988). Generally, the reduced adjustment in income over a 4-year period must be included, starting with the 1st tax year beginning after 1987 as follows:

For the	Percentage of adjustment included is
1st year	25%
2nd year	5%
3rd year	35%
4th year	35%

Capitalization of past service pension costs.   Uniform capitalization rules govern what costs must be included in inventory or capital accounts. These rules generally apply to the costs of producing (manufacturing, constructing, etc.) real or tangible personal property, or of acquiring property for resale. The property must be held for sale or used in a trade or business or in an activity that is conducted for profit.

The capitalization rules do not apply, however, to personal property acquired for resale if the amount of average annual gross receipts for the 3 preceding tax years is $10 million or less.

Before 1988 contributions to a pension plan for past service costs could be deducted because these costs were not subject to the uniform capitalization rules. After 1987, however, past service pension costs are subject to the rules. Therefore, an allocable portion of these costs must be added to the basis of property produced or acquired that is subject to the capitalization rules. These rules normally require a change in accounting method. The change in accounting method that may be required by a change in the rules is treated as initiated by the company with the consent of the IRS.

For years beginning in 1988 an allocable portion of past service pension costs must be included in inventory that is subject to the capitalization rules. Adjustments may be required under IRS Code section 481 to reflect the inclusion of these costs in inventory on hand at the start of the first tax year beginning in 1988. Also for tax years beginning in 1988, an allocable portion of past service pension costs must be added to the basis of property (except inventory) that is subject to the capitalization rules.

Employee benefit plans.   For plan years beginning in 1988, the new law changed the rules on minimum funding standards for certain defined benefit plans. The following summarizes many of the changes.

The full funding limitation, which limits the amount of deductible contributions an employer can make to a defined benefit plan, was previously the excess of accrued liability over the value of the plan assets. The limitation now is the excess of any, of 1) the lesser of the accrued liability (including current year cost) under the plan (using the formula for entry age normal if accrued liability cannot be figured under the plan), or 150% of current liabilities, over 2) the lesser of the fair market value of the plan's assets, or the value of assets as figured using the plan's assumptions.

The period for filing an application for a minimum funding waiver has been shortened. The waiver request must now be filed no later than 2 months after the plan year, and 5 months if the waiver request is for a plan year beginning in calendar 1988.

The number of minimum funding waivers that may be granted to a single-employer plan within 15 years is reduced from five to three. There is a transition rule which applies to certain waivers granted prior to December 18, 1987

Funding waiver applications submitted by a single-employer plan after December 17, 1987, must establish that the financial hardship supporting the waiver request is temporary. If the employer is a member of a controlled group, this requirement must be met on a controlled group basis.

For funding applications submitted by a single-employer plan after March 21, 1988, the requirement that an employer give advance notice to certain parties has been expanded. The applicant must now notify each employee organization, participant, beneficiary, and alternate payee, of the waiver request. In addition, the notice must describe the extent to which the benefits under the plan are funded.

For a funding waiver to be granted, an employer may have to provide security, if the total outstanding funding deficiencies along with certain other amounts equal or exceed one (previously two) million dollars.

IRS regulations permitting asset valuations to range between 85% and 115% of average value no longer apply to defined benefit plans other than multi-employer plans. As a result, bonds and other evidence of indebtedness are subject to general valuation rules.

Employer contributions to a single-employer defined benefit plan made within 8 months after the plan year are considered made on the last day of the plan year. For plan years beginning after 1988, and subject to a transition rule, the employer must make quarterly payments of estimated required contributions.

Unless a waiver request is pending, an employer who fails to make a required contribution within 60 days after its due date to a single-employer plan must notify each plan participant and beneficiary (including alternate payees) of the failure.

A lien will arise in favor of a defined benefit plan, other than a multi-employer plan, which has assets less than those necessary to fund all current liabilities, if a required employer installment or contribution is not made by the due date and the unpaid balance (including interest) exceeds one million dollars when added to the unpaid balance of all preceding unpaid contributions or payments. The lien is on all real and personal property and rights to property belonging to the employer and any other person who is a member of a controlled group that includes the employer.

Corporations

- Dividends-received deduction changed.
- Personal service corporations subject to flat tax rate.
- Worthless stock deduction limits NOL carryover.
- Estimated tax changed.

Dividends-received deduction. Before 1988, a domestic corporation could generally take a deduction for 80% of dividends received or accrued from taxable domestic corporations. Under the new law, the deduction is limited to 70% of the dividends received or accrued if the corporation owns less than 20% of the paying domestic corporation. This rule is effective beginning in 1988 for dividends received or accrued.

A corporation can take a deduction for 80% of dividends received or accrued if it owns 20% or more of the taxable domestic corporation. Ownership, for purposes of these rules, is determined by the amount of voting power and value of stock (other than certain preferred stock) the corporation owns.

For a *fiscal year* corporation that is a 20% or more owner and whose tax year begins in 1987 and ends in 1988 the following percentage deductions apply:

1) 80% of dividends received or accrued in 1987.
2) 70% of dividends received or accrued after 1987 and before the 1st day of the fiscal tax year beginning in 1988.
3) 80% of dividends received or accrued in fiscal tax years beginning after the year 1987.

Personal service corporations.   The tax on the taxable income of a corporation generally is computed using graduated tax rates. For tax years beginning in 1988 the taxable income of a qualified personal service corporation is taxed at a flat rate of 34%. These corporations cannot use the graduated tax rates that apply to other corporations.

A corporation is a qualified personal service corporation if its employees perform services at least 95% of the time in any of the following fields:

- Health
- Law
- Engineering
- Architecture
- Accounting
- Actuarial science
- Performing arts
- Consulting

In addition, at least 95% of the value of its stock must be held by employees, retired employees, or their estates or beneficiaries.

Net operating loss carryover limitation.   Corporate net operating loss carryovers are limited if there is an ownership change which occurs when there is a more than 50% change in the ownership of the corporation's stock during the testing period. The testing period is generally the 3-year period ending on the day of the change in ownership.

For tax years beginning in 1988, if a 50% shareholder claims a worthless stock deduction during its tax year, the stock for which the deduction was claimed is, for purposes of determining ownership change, considered transferred by the 50% shareholder on the earlier of the date it is actually transferred or on the first day of that shareholder's next tax year.

For example, if a 50% shareholder on a calendar year basis owns 60% of the corporation and treats all of its stock as becoming worthless on July 1, 1988, then, for purposes of determining ownership change, any of that stock not actually transferred before January 1, 1989, is considered transferred on that date.

A 50% shareholder is a person who at any time during the 3-year period ending with the year that the deduction is claimed owned 50% or more of the stock of the corporation.

Corporation Estimated Tax.

OLD LAW

A corporation that fails to pay an installment of estimated tax by the due date is subject to a penalty. The penalty is figured at a rate of interest published quarterly by the IRS. The penalty cannot be waived.

The amount of the underpayment with respect to an installment is the excess of the required installment payment over the payments made on that installment by the due date of the installment. To determine the required installment payment, divide 90% of the total tax shown on the return for the year that should have been made.

An estimated tax payment is first credited against the most recent installment due. Then, any part of the payment in excess of the amount due for that installment is credited against any previous unpaid installment.

The penalty does not apply if the estimated tax is less than $40.

NEW LAW

SAME

The underpayment of any installment is the amount required to be paid minus the amount paid by the due date of the installment.

The amount required to be paid is an installment based on:
1) The lesser of 90% of the tax shown on the return for the tax year (or 90% of the tax for the year).
2) 100% of the tax on the return for the preceding year, if that year was a 12-month tax year and a return for that year was filed showing a tax liability.

An estimated tax payment is credited against unpaid installments in the order in which they are required to be paid.

Tax shown on the return, or if no return is filed, the tax for the year

OLD LAW

The penalty on underpayments of estimated tax that are between 80% and 90% of the tax shown or due is imposed on ¾ of the full rate.

No penalty is imposed if the installment is based on the least of the following amounts:
1) 100% of last year's tax liability if a return for 12 months was filed showing the liability.
2) The tax based on facts shown on last year's return but using the current year's tax rates.
3) 90% of the current year's tax that would be due if income were annualized (what the total income for the tax year would have been if an amount of income actually received over a specific period within the tax year were received at the same rate over the full 12-month year).

NEW LAW

is less than $500. The reduced rate of the penalty for underpayments between 80% and 90% is eliminated.

If an installment is based on 90% of the current year's tax that would be due if income were annualized [old law's exception 3)], no penalty is imposed. Any reduction in a required installment from using the annualized exception must be added to the amount of the next required installment.

The old law's exception 2) is eliminated.

The new law is effective for tax years beginning January 1, 1988.

Accounting Periods and Methods

Before 1988, family farm corporations were allowed to use the cash method of accounting. A *family corporation* is one in which 50% or more of the stock is owned by members of the same family. Members of the same family include any individual's parents, grandparents, their ancestors and lineal descendants, and their spouses and estates.

For tax years beginning in 1988, family corporations (other than S corporations) that have over $25 million of gross receipts for a prior tax year beginning after 1985 must use the accrual method of accounting. Gross receipts for any tax year of less than 12 months must be annualized to determine if gross receipts exceed $25 million. (To annualize the corporation must figure what its gross receipts would be had it been operating for a full 12 months.)

For the gross receipts test, a special rule applies to a family corporation that is a member of a controlled group of corporations. A percentage of the gross receipts of each of the other members of the controlled group must be allocated to the family corporation in determining the amount of its gross receipts. The allocation percentage is generally equal to the family corporation's ownership percentage in each of the other members of the controlled group.

The Tax Reform Act of 1986 required partnerships, S corporations, and personal service corporations to use certain tax years called *required tax years.* A required tax year does not apply to any partnership, S corporation, or personal service corporation that has established a business purpose for a tax year.

The new law allows partnerships, S corporations, and personal service corporations to elect the use of a tax year that is different from the tax year they would otherwise be required to use (the required tax year). However, certain restrictions apply to this election. But this election, including its restrictions, does not apply to any partnership, S corporation, or personal service corporation that establishes a business purpose for its tax year. Both the required tax year and the election apply to tax years beginning in 1987.

An S corporation or personal service corporation is required to use the calendar tax year. A partnership is required to conform its tax year to the tax year of its majority partners, or if there are no majority partners, to the tax year of its principal partners. If a partnership is unable to determine its tax year by reference to either its majority partners or its principal partners, it must use a tax year that results in the least aggregate deferral of income to its partners.

For its first tax year beginning in 1987, a partnership, S corporation, or personal service corporation may elect to retain the last tax year it had beginning in 1986 and may continue the use of that year for all later years. If the entity does not want to retain its year, it may elect to change its tax year for any tax year beginning in 1987.

Generally, a partnership, S corporation, or personal service corporation may elect to change its tax year only if the year elected results in a deferral period of 3 months or less. The deferral period is the number of months between the beginning of the tax year elected and the close of the first required tax year ending within the elected year.

For example, if a tax year beginning 10/1/87 and ending 9/30/88 is elected and a calendar tax year is required, the deferral period of the elected tax year is 3 months (10/1/87 to 12/31/87). That election is allowable unless the deferral period of the tax year being changed is shorter than the elected year's deferral period. An election to change a tax year will be allowed only if the deferral period is the shorter of: 1) Three months. 2) The deferral period of the tax year being changed.

Example: An S corporation had a tax year beginning 11/1/86 and ending 10/31/87 when it was required to change to the calendar year. In this case, the deferral period of the tax year being changed is 2 months, 11/1/87 to 12/31/87. The S corporation may elect to retain the old tax year or change it to a tax year beginning 12/1/87 and ending 11/30/88. However, it may not elect a tax year beginning 10/1/87 and ending 9/30/88 because the deferral period of that elected year is 3 months (10/1/87 to 12/31/87), which is longer than the 2-month deferral period of the tax year being changed.

Electing partnerships and S corporations must make the *required payment* for any tax year that the election is in effect and the required payment amount is more than $500. This *required payment* represents the value of the tax deferral that the owners receive through the use of a tax year different from the required tax year. For an elected tax year beginning in 1987, the required amount should be reported for the period ending 6/30/88. If the required payment is more than $500, pay it when a Form 720 is filed. If $500 or less, payment does not have to be made until the total required payment amount for a current and all preceding election years is more than $500. However, Form 720 must be filed showing a zero amount if its payment is $500 or less.

Example: The required payment for Partnership X is $400 for its first election year and $450 for its second election. X does not make a required payment for its first election year, but does make a required payment of $850 for its second election year.

Installment Sales

The installment method is repealed for dealers. Dealers in personal or real property generally may not use the installment method to report income from sales occurring after 1987. The repeal does not apply to dealer sales of farm property, nor to dealer sales of certain time shares or residential lots if the dealer elects to pay interest on the deferred tax arising from the use of the installment method for these sales.

The allocable installment indebtedness rules provided by the Tax Reform Act of 1986 have been repealed for dispositions beginning in 1988. These rules, which applied to tax years ending after 1986, dealt with outstanding business debts arising from unrelated transactions as a payment received at the end of the tax year on certain installment sales. The amount treated as a payment was referred to as the allocable installment indebtedness. This amount was treated as a payment on the installment sale even though no actual payment on that sale had been received during the tax year. These rules applied to sales after February 28, 1986, by dealers in personal or real property, and to sales after August 16, 1986, of business or rental real property if the selling price was more than $150,000.

An election can be made for nondealer sales to have the repeal of the allocable installment indebtedness rules apply to tax years ending after 1986. The election applies only to the sale after August 16, 1986, of business or rental real property for more than $150,000. If the election and outstanding installment obligations at the end of the tax year exceed $5,000,000, interest must be paid on the tax deferred on the installment obligations.

If an election is made on an installment obligation from a sale of business or rental real property for more than $150,000 to secure any debt, the net proceeds from the debt are treated as a payment on the installment obligation. The amount treated as a payment is considered received on the later of the date the debt becomes secured, or the date the proceeds of the debt is received.

TAX REFORM ACT OF 1986

The Tax Reform Act of 1986 made numerous and significant changes to the U.S. tax system. Overall, it provided for a more equitable system by broadening the tax base and eliminating most tax shelters.

The law affects both individuals and businesses. This review for the *Supplement* covers those changes that apply to businesses since the *Accounting Desk Book* is oriented solely to business topics.

This review begins with an overview of how the major provisions of the new law differ from the old, and which provisions of the old law have been repealed. The overview is followed by discussions on the various tax law changes. Examples of the major changes are included in many of the discussions to show how the 1986 law applies in various circumstances.

It should be emphasized that the material in this *Supplement* covers changes that apply to businesses, and while the changes are explained to some extent, the material does not cover every situation nor in complete detail. Consequently, the *Supplement is not intended to be a substitute for the law itself.*

PASSIVE LOSSES AND CREDITS.

Old Law: Losses from an activity could be used to offset *income* from any other activity. Credit from an activity could be used to offset *tax* from any other activity.

New Law: After 1986, losses from passive activities may only be used to offset income from passive activities. Also, credits from passive activities may only be used to offset tax allocable to passive activities. Disallowed losses and credits carried forward; special phase-in rules apply to interest held in passive activities on October 22, 1986.

MEALS AND ENTERTAINMENT EXPENSES.

Old Law: Meals and entertainment expenses were generally deductible in full if ordinary and necessary. Business meals had to take place in an atmosphere conducive to business discussion.

New Law: Beginning in 1987, 80% of meals and entertainment expenses are deductible. Further, a substantial and bona fide business discussion must occur during, just before, or after the business meal.

TRAVEL EXPENSES.

Old Law: Travel expenses were generally deductible if ordinary and necessary.

New Law: Cruise ship travel deduction is limited. Investment seminar expenses are not deductible.

DEPRECIATION.

Old Law: Personal property was computed under ACRS. 3 classes, 3-, 5-, and 10-year recovery property. 150% declining balance.

New Law: Personal property has 6 classes, 200% declining balance for 3-, 5-, 7-, and 10-year recovery property; 150% declining balance for 15- and 20-year property.

Old Law: Real property was computed under ACRS. 3 classes, 15-, 18-, and 19-year recovery periods. 175% declining balance.

New Law: Real property has 2 classes. Residential rental, 27.5-year property. Nonresidential, 31.5-year property. Straight line.

Old Law: Section 179 expense. $5000 maximum deduction on personal property.

New Law: Section 179 expense. Beginning in 1987, $10,000 maximum deduction; limited to amount of business income; dollar-for-dollar reduction in maximum for investments over $200,000.

INVESTMENT CREDIT.

Old Law: 10% credit allowed when certain business property was placed in service.

New Law: Repealed for property placed in service after 1985.

REHABILITATION CREDIT.

Old Law: 15% or 20% credit for rehabilitating older nonresidential buildings. 25% credit for rehabilitating certified historic structures.

New Law: Beginning in 1987, the credit is 10% for nonresidential buildings first used before 1936; 20% for certified historic structures.

BUSINESS ENERGY CREDIT.

Old Law: The energy credit expired on December 31, 1985.

New Law: The credit is reinstated for 3 years for solar, geothermal, and ocean thermal property; 2 years for biomass property; 15% rate for 1986; varying rates for 1987 and 1988.

GENERAL BUSINESS CREDIT.

Old Law: Before 1986, the percentage was 85%.

New Law: After 1985, the maximum tax that can be offset by the credit is $25,000, plus 75% of tax over $25,000.

TARGETED JOBS CREDIT.

Old Law: The targeted jobs credit expired on December 31, 1985. The credit was 50% of qualified first-year wages and 25% of second-year wages.

New Law: The credit is reinstated for 3 years, through 1988. Credit is 40% of qualified first-year wages; no credit for second-year wages.

LOW INCOME HOUSING CREDIT.

Old Law: No provision.

New Law: New tax credit for owners of low-income residential rental housing placed in service after 1986; allowed each year for 10 years; 1987 rates, 9% for cost of new buildings not federally subsidized, and 4% for new federally subsidized buildings and existing buildings.

CORPORATIONS.

Old Law: 5 rate brackets ranging from 15% to 46%, plus additional tax.

New Law: 3 tax rate brackets, 15%, 25%, and 34%, plus a 5% additional tax for taxable income beginning on or after July 1, 1987; tax prorated for other tax years that include July 1, 1987.

Old Law: Alternative 28% tax on net capital gain.

New Law: Alternative rate for capital gains repealed for tax years in which the new corporate rates are fully in effect; 34% rate for 1987.

Old Law: Alternative minimum tax, 15% add-on minimum tax; exemption amount was greater of $10,000 or regular tax.

New Law: After 1986, 20% rate; $40,000 exemption amount with phase-out; adjustments and preference items added.

Old Law: 85% of dividends received from domestic corporations were deductible.

New Law: After 1986, 80% of dividends received from domestic corporations are deductible.

CASH OR DEFERRED ARRANGEMENTS (401K).

Old Law: $30,000 limit on elective deferrals.

New Law: $30,000 limit on elective deferrals reduced to $7,000 after 1986. $7,000 adjusted for increases to CPI after 1987.

SIMPLIFIED EMPLOYEE PENSION (SEP).

Old Law: Employer's contribution to SEP included in employee's income. Employee's deduction limited to lesser of $30,000 or 15% of compensation.

New Law: After 1986, certain contributions to SEP treated like elective deferrals to 401(K). Elective deferrals limited to $7,000.

ACCOUNTING PERIODS.

Old Law: Partnerships could retain existing tax year. When adopting or changing a tax year, generally had to use same tax year as principal partners. S corporations generally could retain existing tax year. New S corporations were required to use "permitted" tax year.

New Law: After 1986, partnerships are generally required to have the same tax year as that of partners holding a majority interest in the partnership. All S corporations after 1986 are generally required to use "permitted" tax year, usually a calendar year.

CASH METHOD OF ACCOUNTING.

Old Law: Generally available to taxpayers without inventories.

New Law: Generally, after 1986, cash method may not be used by C corporations, partnerships with a C corporation partner, or tax shelters.

Repealed Provisions

The 1986 Act repealed many provisions of prior law. Some of the repealed provisions are listed below with the effective date of repeal. (Some of these changes are reviewed in some detail later in this *Supplement.*)

- The investment credit, generally for property placed in service after 1985.
- The deduction for land clearing expenses of farmers, amounts paid or incurred after 1985.
- The 5-year amortization of trademark and tradename expenditures for amounts paid or incurred after 1986.
- The alternative tax on capital gains of corporations, generally after 1986.
- The 60% deduction for capital gains of individuals, after 1986. Gains will be taxed as ordinary income.
- The reserve method for figuring bad debt deductions of taxpayers other than financial institutions, after 1986.
- The employee stock ownership credit, compensation paid or accrued after 1986.

Gross Income

Election to reduce basis of depreciable property rather than recognize income from discharge of business indebtedness is repealed.

Capital gains deduction is retained for gains from the sale of certain dairy cattle.

Income from Discharge of Indebtedness

Generally, if a debt is cancelled or forgiven, other than as a gift, the debtor must include the cancelled amount in gross income. Under prior law, there were exceptions to this rule. The new law repealed the exclusion for discharges of qualified business indebtedness taking place after 1986. The exclusions for debt discharges in bankruptcy or insolvency still apply.

Example: At the beginning of 1987, the X Corporation's liabilities totaled $11,000 and the fair market value of its assets was $7,500. Since its liabilities were more than its assets, it was insolvent. Rather than declare bankruptcy, the corporation's management decided to negotiate with its creditors to have some of the debts forgiven. This would allow the corporation to remain in business and eventually pay off the remaining debts.

The X Corporation's creditors agreed to cancel $4,000 of its liabilities. Of this amount, $3,500 is excludable from income by the corporation under the insolvency exclusion; that is, the amount of cancelled debt that does not exceed the amount by which the corporation was insolvent (its total liabilities minus the fair market value of its assets). The corporation's tax attributes (if any) must be correspondingly reduced by the amount of the excluded debt cancellation. The remaining $500 debt cancellation must be included in gross income. It may not exclude the debt cancellation as qualified business indebtedness by reducing basis, as allowed in previous years.

Reduction of Tax Attributes

The indebtedness that is excluded from income because it is cancelled in a bankruptcy case or during insolvency must be used to reduce certain "tax attributes" of the debtor. By reducing these tax attributes, tax on the cancelled indebtedness is in part postponed instead of being entirely forgiven. The following tax attributes are reduced, generally in the order indicated:

1) Any net operating loss for the tax year of the debt cancellation, and any net operating loss carryover to that tax year.

2) Research credit and general business credit carryovers to or from the tax year of the debt cancellation.

3) Net capital loss for the tax year of the cancellation, and any capital loss carryover to that year.

4) Basis of the debtors property.

5) Foreign tax credit carryovers to or from the tax year of the debt cancellation.

Amount of Credit Carryover Reduction

Under prior law, the credit carryovers (items 2) and 5) above) were required to be reduced by 50 cents for each dollar of cancelled debt that was excluded from income. The new law provides that, for tax years beginning after 1986, these credit carryovers must be reduced by 33⅓ cents for each dollar of cancelled debt excluded from income.

Business Expenses

- Deduction for business-related meals and entertainment limited to 80%.
- Amount deductible for business travel on cruise ship or other luxury water transportation limited.
- Deduction for the business use of a home limited.
- Self-employed individual may deduct as business expense 25% of the amount paid for medical insurance.
- Deduction for interest on certain life insurance loans limited.
- Deduction for removal of barriers to handicapped and elderly reinstated.
- Certain costs must be capitalized or included in inventory rather than claimed as current deductions.
- Time period for presumption that business operated for profit modified.
- Losses and credits from passive activities limited.
- Real property subject to at-risk rules.
- Reserve method for bad debts disallowed.
- Conservation expenses restricted.
- Percentage depletion reduced.
- Deduction for prepaid farm expenses limited.
- Exclusion for educational assistance programs and group legal plans extended.
- Exclusion for dependent care assistance program limited.
- Requirements for employee achievement awards changed.

Meals and Entertainment Expenses

The 1986 Act made several changes to the law relating to the deduction of expenses for business meals and entertainment. The deductions for business meals and entertainment expenses are limited to 80%. Meal expenses are deductible only if the expenses are directly related to or associated with the active conduct of a trade or business. In addition, the amount that can be deducted for entertainment tickets, skyboxes, or other private luxury boxes is limited. An employer who reimburses an employee for these expenses is subject to the 80% limit. In this situation, the 80% limit does not apply to the employee.

Example: Peter Jones is a self-employed salesperson. On July 8, 1987, he pays $50 for a business meal with a client. The meal is directly related to the active conduct of his business. The amount Peter can deduct is $40 (80% of $50).

The 80% limit on meals and entertainment expenses does not apply to:

1) Expenses that are treated by the employer as compensation to the employee.

2) Expenses for recreation, social, or similar activities incurred primarily for the benefit of employees, other than certain highly compensated employees.

3) Expenses for meals and entertainment, including the use of facilities, made available by the taxpayer to the general public.

4) Expenses for goods, services, and facilities sold by the taxpayer in a bona fide transaction.

5) Expenses paid or incurred by the taxpayer to the extent that the expenses are includible in the gross income of a recipient who is not an employee of the taxpayer as compensation for services or as a prize or an award.

6) Expenses paid by the taxpayer for meals (but not entertainment) that are excludable from the gross income of the recipient because their value is so small as to make accounting for them impracticable.

7) Expenses for meals incurred before January 1, 1989, that are an integral part of a qualified meeting. A qualified meeting is a convention, seminar, annual meeting, or similar business program for which:

   a) The expense for meals is not separately stated.

   b) More than 50% of the participants are away from home.

   c) At least 40 individuals attend the program.

   d) The meal is part of a program that includes a speaker.

8) The price of tickets and other expenses included in a package that includes admission to a charitable sports event.

Meal and Beverage Expense

Before 1987 taxpayers could deduct ordinary and necessary meal and beverage expenses if they occurred in an atmosphere conducive to business discussions. There was no requirement that business be discussed before, during, or after the meal, or that the meal or beverage expenses be directly related to or associated with the active conduct of a trade or business.

Effective for tax years beginning after 1986, taxpayers are not allowed to deduct meal and beverage expenses unless they establish that the expenses were directly related to the active conduct of their trade or business, or, in the case of an expense directly preceding or following a substantial and bona fide business discussion, that the expense was associated with the active conduct of their trade or business.

No deduction for meal and beverage expenses is allowed unless business is discussed during, or directly before or after, the meal, except when an individual is traveling away from home on business and claims a deduction for his or her meal only. The exceptions to the business connection requirement that apply to other entertainment expenses also apply to expenses for business meals.

Example: Debby Smith is a salesperson representing her own company. She has lunch with a client and discusses business during the lunch. At the end of the discussion, she gets an order from her client. She may deduct the cost of the meal subject to the 80% limit.

Meal and beverage expenses, whether or not incurred while an individual is on business travel, are not deductible to the extent they are lavish or extravagant under the circumstances. In addition, no deduction for meal and beverage expenses is allowed unless the taxpayer, or his or her employee, is present at the meal.

Entertainment Expenses

As under previous law, taxpayers may be able to deduct ordinary and necessary entertainment expenses if they establish that the expenses were directly related to the active conduct of their trade or business. In the case of an expense directly preceding or following a substantial and bona fide business-related discussion, taxpayers must establish that the expense was associated with the active conduct of their trade or business.

Starting in 1987, the 80% limit applies to allowable entertainment expenses. In addition, the amount that may be deducted for entertainment tickets, skyboxes, or other private luxury boxes is limited.

In determining the deduction for a ticket, the amount subject to the 80% limit may not be more than the face value of the ticket. However, taxpayers may be able to deduct in full, even if more than face value, expenses for tickets to a sports event if all of the following conditions are met:

1) The event's main purpose is to benefit a qualified charitable organization.
2) The entire proceeds go to the charity.
3) The event uses volunteers to perform substantially all the event's work.

Any expense covered by a package deal involving a ticket to such a charitable sports event is deductible in full, if the expense is otherwise deductible.

Example: A football exhibition game is organized by the local volunteer fire company, with all proceeds from the event going toward the acquisition of new equipment. The volunteers will run the exhibition. All football players will be donating their time. Ticket costs, if otherwise qualified as an entertainment expense, will be fully deductible.

In determining the amount that is subject to the 80% limit, the allowable expenses for rentals of skyboxes and other private luxury boxes for more than one event at the same sports arena are restricted. In determining whether a skybox has been rented for more than one event, a single game or other performance counts as one event. Therefore, a rental of a skybox for a series of games, such as the World Series, counts as more than one event.

If a taxpayer rents a skybox for more than one event, the allowable expense for all such events cannot be more than the face value of nonluxury box seat tickets generally held for sale to the public multiplied by the number of seats in such box. The 80% limit applies to the amount of this allowable. This restriction is phased-in over a 3-year period. In 1987, the allowable expense is increased by $2/3$ of the excess of the skybox price over the regular nonluxury box price. In 1988, the allowable expense is increased by $1/3$ of the excess cost of the skybox seats over the regular nonluxury box price. For tax years beginning in 1989, no deduction is allowed for any cost above the price of regular nonluxury box seat tickets.

Example: Corporation X pays $3,000 in 1987 to rent a 10-seat skybox at Z Stadium for three baseball games. The cost of regular nonluxury box seats at each event is $20 a seat. X Corporation figures its deduction as follows:

Deduction for 10 nonluxury seats at $20 for 3 games		$ 600
Excess cost of skybox:		
Cost for 3 games	$3,000	
Less: Cost of nonluxury seat	600	
Excess cost	$2,400	
2/3 allowance for 1987 (2/3 of $2,400)		1,600
Allowable expense subject to 80% limit		$2,200
Deduction for 1987 (80% of $2,200)		$1,760

Travel Expenses

Beginning in 1987, the new law limits the amount of deductions for costs of cruise ship or other luxury water transportation and eliminates the deduction allowed for educational travel expenses. It also limits the deduction for transportation and other travel expenses while a taxpayer is away from home for a charitable organization. In addition, it eliminates the deduction allowed for travel or other costs of attending conventions or seminars for investment purposes.

Before 1987, taxpayers could deduct ordinary and necessary expenses for travel by cruise ship or other luxury water transportation while away from home conducting a trade or business, if the expenses were substantiated by adequate records or by sufficient evidence confirming the taxpayer's own statement. There were no limits on the amount allowed as a deduction, except that meals and lodging could not be lavish or extravagant, and certain limits applied to cruise ship conventions.

For tax years beginning in 1987, the new law limits the deduction allowed for expenses of travel by cruise ship or other luxury water transportation to twice the highest per diem generally allowed employees of the federal government for travel in the United States, times the number of days in transit.

Example: Peter Smith makes a business trip by ship from New York to England. Assuming that the voyage takes 4 days and that the highest per diem is $126, Peter's deduction cannot be more than $1,008 ($252 per day times 4 days).

Before 1987, a taxpayer could deduct expenses for travel as a form of education. The expenses had to be for a period of travel that was directly related to work or business duties. Also, a major part of the taxpayer's activities during the period of travel had to be directly related to maintaining or improving skills required at work or business.

Beginning in 1987, taxpayers cannot be allowed to deduct the cost of travel that in itself constitutes a form of education.

Example: A professor of Italian touring Italy to maintain general familiarity with the Italian language and culture cannot deduct expenses of the trip.

As under the previous law, taxpayers may still take a charitable deduction for travel expenses while away from home if they establish that the expenses were incurred in performing services for a qualified charitable organization, and if they kept records to prove the amount of the charitable deduction.

However, beginning in 1987, an additional restriction applies. A charitable deduction is allowed for transportation and other travel expenses (including expenses for meals and lodging) while the taxpayer is away from home only if there is no significant element of personal pleasure, recreation, or vacation in such travel. It does not matter whether the expenses are paid directly by the taxpayer or indirectly through a contribution to a qualified charitable organization.

Convention Expenses

Until 1987, taxpayers were able to deduct expenses of attending a convention, seminar, or similar meeting in connection with their income-producing (investment) activities. Beginning in 1987, no deduction is allowed for travel or other costs of attending a convention, seminar, or similar meeting unless the activity relates to a trade or business of the taxpayer. For example, expenses for registration fees, travel and transportation costs, meals and lodging expenses, etc., while attending an investment seminar or other activity not related to the taxpayer's trade or business, are not deductible.

In addition, no deduction is allowed for expenses of attending a trade or business-connected convention, seminar, or similar meeting unless the meeting offered significant business-related activities, such as meetings, workshops, lectures, or exhibits held during the day, and the taxpayer participated in the activities offered. Thus, the cost of attending a seminar would not be deductible if participants are merely furnished video tapes of business-related lectures to be viewed at their own convenience.

Business Use of Home

The new law further limits the expenses that may be deducted for the business use of a home. These expenses are those that are related to using a part of a home regularly and exclusively as either a principal place of a business or as a place to meet patients, clients, or customers.

Before 1987, the amount that could be deducted for these expenses was limited to the gross income from the business use of the home. Beginning in 1987, the deduction is limited to the gross income from that business use minus the sum of:

1) The business percentage of the mortgage interest, real estate taxes, and casualty losses.

2) The business expenses other than those related to the business use of a home.

Therefore, the deduction is limited to a modified net income from the business use of a home—the net income of the business without including the home expenses other than the business percentage of mortgage interest, real estate taxes, and casualty losses. Thus, deductions for the business use of a home will not create a business loss or increase a net loss from a business.

Deductions in excess of the limit may be carried forward to later years, subject to the income limits in those years.

Example:

Gross income		$12,000
Minus:		
Business percentage (20%) of mortgage		
interest and real estate taxes	$2,000	
Materials, supplies, etc.	$9,000	$11,000
Modified net income—deduction limit		$ 1,000
Business use of home expenses:		
Maintenance, insurance, utilities (20%)		$ 800
Depreciation (20%)		1,600
Total		$ 2,400
Deduction limited to modified net income		1,000
Carryover expenses to 1988, (subject to		
income limitations in 1988)		$ 1,400

In addition to deducting the $1,000 for home expenses in 1987, John can deduct his interest, taxes, materials, and supplies.

For tax years beginning after 1986 and before 1990, self-employed tax-payers may deduct, as an adjustment to income on Form 1040, 25% of the amount paid for medical insurance for themselves and their families. The deduction cannot exceed their net earnings from self-employment. This deduction may be taken even if the taxpayer does not itemize on Schedule A.

However, a self-employed taxpayer who is also an employee of another person may not deduct the medical insurance costs paid if he or she is eligible to participate in a subsidized plan maintained by his or her employer. This is true even if it is the taxpayer's spouse who is employed, and the taxpayer would be eligible to participate in the spouse's company plan.

The 1986 Act places a limit on the amount of interest that a taxpayer may deduct on loans against certain life insurance contracts that are purchased after June 20, 1986. This limit applies to contracts that insure the life of any officer, employee, or person who has a financial interest in any trade or business carried on by the taxpayer. If the total indebtedness is more than $50,000 for any person, the taxpayer cannot deduct the interest on the loans that exceed $50,000 for that person.

Capitalizing Costs of Property

Uniform capitalization rules apply to taxpayers in a trade or business who produce real or tangible personal property or acquire property for resale. Under these rules, certain expenses must be included in inventory costs or capitalized. These expenses include the direct costs of the property and the share of any indirect costs that are allocable to that property.

A taxpayer produces real or tangible personal property if the taxpayer constructs, builds, installs, manufactures, develops, creates, improves, raises, or grows the property. Therefore, the new rules apply to inventory, noninventory property produced for sale to customers, and assets constructed for use in a trade or business. Tangible personal property includes films, sound recordings, video tapes, books, or similar property.

For tax years beginning before 1987, accumulated *inventory costs* for all business taxpayers were generally deducted as the related goods were sold. All direct production costs, such as the costs of materials incorporated into the product or consumed during production, together with the cost of labor that was involved in manufacturing, were included in inventory. The treatment of indirect production costs varied according to the nature of the expense. Purchasers of goods for resale included the price of the goods, transportation, and other costs incurred in acquiring the goods in their inventory costs.

For tax years beginning in 1987, in addition to direct costs, producers of inventory property must also include a portion of certain indirect costs in their inventory costs. Purchasers of inventory property acquired for resale must also include in inventory a portion of certain indirect costs. This will apply to personal property acquired for resale only if the taxpayer's average annual gross receipts for the 3 prior tax years exceed $10,000,000.

Taxpayers will have to revalue their beginning inventories for tax years beginning in 1987 by including the additional indirect costs in their inventories. Indirect costs that must be included in inventory include those that benefit property produced by the taxpayer for sale to customers in a trade or business, or that are incurred in acquiring, storing, or processing property acquired for resale to others by the taxpayer. Examples include items such as depreciation, rent, taxes, interest, storage, purchasing (buyer's wages), processing, repackaging, handling, and general and administrative costs.

Direct costs incurred by taxpayers before 1987 in acquiring, constructing, or improving buildings, machinery, equipment, or other assets having a useful life of more than one year were capital expenditures. The direct cost of constructing an asset for the taxpayer's own use or a noninventory asset produced for sale were capitalized. The treatment of the related indirect costs of constructing an asset for use in a trade or business or producing a noninventory item for sale varied according to the nature of the expense of the property produced.

For costs incurred after December 31, 1986, in addition to the direct costs, a portion of the indirect costs that benefit real or tangible personal property constructed by a taxpayer for use in a trade or business, or noninventory property produced for sale to customers by a taxpayer, must also be capitalized. Indirect costs that benefit property include items such as depreciation, taxes, interest, and general and administrative costs.

The capitalization rule will not apply to property produced by taxpayers for their own use if substantial construction had occurred before March 1, 1986. **Exceptions** to the uniform capitalization rule include:

1) Personal use property produced by the taxpayer that is not for use in the taxpayer's trade or business or in an activity conducted for profit.

2) Certain research and experimental expenses allowable as a deduction.

3) Certain developmental and other intangible costs of oil and gas or geothermal wells or other mineral property allowable as a deduction.

4) Property produced under a long-term contract.

5) Trees raised, harvested, or grown by the taxpayer unless the trees are fruit, nut, or ornamental trees. Ornamental trees do not include evergreens that are more than 6 years old at the time of cutting.

6) Plants or animals produced by certain farmers if the preproductive period is not more than 2 years.

7) Certain taxpayers may elect not to apply the uniform capitalization rules to any plant or animal produced in any farming business run by the taxpayer. The farmer, however, will have to recapture these costs as ordinary income on the disposition of the plant or animal. In addition, the alternative depreciation rules apply to property placed in service in any tax year in which the election is in effect. This election must be made in the first tax year after 1986 during which the taxpayer engages in a farming business.

Not-for-Profit Business or Investment

If a business or investment is not carried on to make a profit, the deductions that may be claimed for expenses related to the business or investment are limited. Also, a loss from the business or investment may not be used to offset other income.

In determining whether the business or investment is carried on to make a profit, all the facts surrounding the activity are taken into account. There is, however, a presumption that the activity is carried on to make a profit if, beginning in 1987, it produces a profit in at least 3 out of 5 consecutive years. (Before 1987, the presumption was met if the activity produced a profit in 2 out of 5 years.)

Passive Activity Losses and Credits

Before the 1986 Act, taxpayers, with few exceptions, could use deductions from an activity to offset income from any other activity. Similarly, most tax credits could be used to offset tax on income from any of the taxpayer's activities. Often this was accomplished by investing in tax shelters.

Congress determined that extensive tax shelter activity contributed to public concerns that the tax system was unfair. In response to those concerns, Congress enacted the passive activity loss and credit rules discussed below.

Effective January 1, 1987, individuals and certain other taxpayers generally cannot offset income, other than income from passive activities, with losses from passive activities. Nor can they offset taxes on such income with credits resulting from passive activities. The new law does provide exceptions for certain activities, such as rental real estate activities, and it also contains phase-in rules for some losses.

Whether or not a loss or credit can be used to offset other income or tax depends on the nature of the activity that generated it; that is, whether or not the activity is a passive activity. A determination must be made each year the activity continues to operate.

A *passive activity* generally is any activity involving the conduct of any trade or business, including a research and experimentation activity, in which the taxpayer does **not** materially participate. A taxpayer *materially participates* in an activity if the taxpayer is involved on a regular, continuous, and substantial basis in the operations of the activity.

Example: Harold owns a 20% interest in a race horse. Harold does not perform any work nor does he participate in any of the decisions related to the race horse activity. For Harold, this is a passive activity because he does not materially participate.

Any *rental activity* is a passive activity regardless of whether the taxpayer materially participates. For this purpose, a rental activity generally is an activity the income from which consists of payments principally for the use of tangible property, rather than for the performance of substantial services.

Except as provided in regulations, an interest in an activity as a *limited partner* in a limited partnership is not an activity in which a taxpayer materially participates. However, if a taxpayer is paid to perform services for a partnership in which the taxpayer owns a limited partnership interest, the income for performing such services is not considered income from a passive activity. Similarly, portfolio income from a limited partnership is not considered income from a passive activity.

A *closely held corporation or personal service corporation* is treated as materially participating in an activity if one or more shareholders, who singly or together hold more than 50% by value of the outstanding stock of the corporation, materially participate in the activity.

A closely held corporation, for this purpose, is a corporation in which 5 or fewer individuals own, directly or indirectly, more than 50% by value of the outstanding stock at any time during the last half of the tax year. Individuals include certain trusts and private foundations.

The law specifically *excludes from the passive activity loss rules* any working interest in any oil and gas property that the taxpayer holds directly, or through an entity that does not limit the taxpayer's liability.

With respect to *nonpassive income,* generally only income from passive activities can be used to offset losses from passive activities. Consequently, a taxpayer generally cannot use passive activity losses to offset other income such as:

- Salaries, wages, or commissions.
- Self-employment income from a trade or business in which a taxpayer materially participates.
- Distributive shares of income (other than income from passive activities) from pass-through entities, such as S corporations.
- Portfolio income; that is, any gross income from interest, dividends, annuities, or royalties that is not derived in the ordinary course of a trade or business. Expenses, other than interest, which are clearly and directly allocable to such gross income and interest expense property allocable to such income do not enter into the computation of the taxpayer's passive activity income or loss. However, such interest and other expenses may be subject to other limits such as the investment interest limits and other itemized deduction limits. Portfolio income also includes gains or losses from the sale or disposition of property (other than an interest in a passive activity) producing portfolio income or held for investment.

Disallowance Rule

The passive activity loss and the passive activity credit for the tax year are disallowed. The *passive activity* loss is the amount by which the total losses (including any interest incurred to finance the investments in passive activities) from all passive activities for the tax year exceed the total income from all passive activities for that tax year. The *passive activity credit* is the amount by which the total credits from all passive activities exceed the portion of the regular tax liability of the taxpayer for the tax year that is the result of passive activities.

Example: Mack's income for the tax year was as follows:

Salary	$90,000
Dividends	5,000
Interest	3,000
Partnership income from	
B Limited Partnership	2,000

Mack also had a reportable loss of $3,000 from C Limited Partnership. Assuming neither limited partnership interest is an interest acquired before October 23, 1986 subject to the phase-in rules, Mack can use $2,000 of his passive activity loss to offset his $2,000 passive activity income from the B Limited Partnership. The remaining $1,000 loss is Mack's nondeductible passive activity loss for the tax year.

Mack will be able to carry the $1,000 disallowed passive activity loss forward to the next year. If, in that next year, Mack has at least $1,000 of income from passive activities, he can use the loss. If not, he will have to carry over the unused portion to the next tax year.

Losses from Former Passive Activities

If an activity was a passive activity in any prior tax year but is not a passive activity in a later tax year, any unused deduction or credit from the activity used in computing a passive activity loss or credit can be used to offset any income or tax from that same activity in the later year. Any remaining carryover deduction or credit will continue to be treated as arising from a passive activity, and will continue to be subject to the passive loss and credit limits.

Active Participation

Active participation should not be confused with *material participation.* The difference between active and material participation is that active participation can be satisfied without regular, continuous, and substantial involvement in operations. The *active participation standard* is satisfied so long as the taxpayer participates in a significant and bona fide sense such as by making management decisions or by arranging for others to provide services such as repairs. Relevant management decisions include approving capital or repair expenditures and other similar decisions.

Example: Mike, a bachelor, had the following income and losses during the tax year:

Salary	$42,300
Dividends	300
Interest	1,400
Rental Loss	4,000

The rental loss resulted from the rental of a house Mike owned. Mike had advertised and rented the house to the current tenant himself. He also collected the rents, which usually came by mail. All repairs were either done or contracted out by Mike. Even though the rental loss is a loss from a passive activity, if Mike is treated as actively participating, he can use the entire $4,000 loss to offset his other income.

Phase-out Rule

For rental real estate activities, other than low-income housing and rehabilitation activities, the special $25,000 offset for rental real estate activities is reduced by 50% of the amount that an individual's adjusted gross income exceeds $100,000 ($50,000 for married individuals filing separate returns and living apart at all times during the year). Thus, generally, there is no relief from the passive activity loss limitations for an individual with adjusted gross income that is more than $150,000 ($75,000 for married individuals filing separate returns and living apart at all times during the year).

Adjusted gross income for this purpose does **not** include the following:

- Taxable social security and railroad retirement benefits.
- Deductible contributions to individual retirement accounts.
- Any passive activity loss.

Example: During his entire 1987 tax year, John, a young executive, was an unmarried individual. For 1987, he had $120,000 in salary, $5,000 of distributable partnership income from a limited partnership in which he invested on December 31, 1986, and a $31,000 loss from his rental real estate activities in which he actively participated and that he acquired on November 30, 1986. When John files his 1987 return, he may deduct only $15,000 of his passive activity loss. He must carry over the remaining $11,000 passive activity loss to 1988.

John's deduction and carryover are computed as follows:

Adjusted gross income	$120,000
Less amount not subject to phase-out	$100,000
Amount subject to phase-out rule	$ 20,000
Multiplied by applicable %	$ × 50%
Required reduction to APRE* amount	$ 10,000
Maximum Offset	$ 25,000
Less required reduction	$ 10,000
Adjusted offset amount APRE activities	$ 15,000
Passive loss from rental real estate	$ 31,000
Less passive income	$ 5,000
Passive activity loss	$ 26,000
Deduction allowable/adjusted offset	15,000
Amount that must be carried forward	$ 11,000

*Active Participation Real Estate

Allowance of Unused Losses

Generally, any passive activity losses (but not credits) that have accumulated because of the annual limit will be allowed in the tax year in which the taxpayer disposes of the interest in the activity. However, for the losses to be allowed, a taxpayer must dispose of the entire interest in the activity, not just part of it, in a transaction in which all realized gain or loss is recognized. Furthermore, the person acquiring the interest from the taxpayer must not be related to the taxpayer.

In the year the interest is disposed of, the unused losses and any current year losses from the activity are allowed to offset income in the following order:

1) Income or gain, including any gain recognized upon disposition, for the tax year from the passive activity disposed of.
2) Net income or gain for the tax year from all other passive activities.
3) Any other income or gain.

If the taxpayer has a capital loss on the disposition of an interest in a passive activity, the loss is first limited, if necessary, by the limitation on capital losses before applying the above rule. Generally, the limitation is $3,000 for individuals.

Example: Ray, whose only other income during the year was his $60,000 salary, had a 5% interest in the B Limited Partnership, which had an adjusted loss of $42,000 at the date of sale. He had carried over $2,000 of passive activity losses from prior years and then sold his entire interest in the current tax year to an unrelated person for $50,000. Ray realized an $8,000 gain from the sale, and may offset $2,000 of that gain with his $2,000 carryover loss. Ray's $6,000 net gain is computed as follows:

Sales price	$50,000
Minus: adjusted basis	42,000
Gain	$ 8,000
Minus: carryover loss allowable	2,000
Net gain	$ 6,000

Ray will treat the $6,000 gain as income from a passive activity. If Ray sold his interest for $30,000, instead of $50,000, his deductible loss would be $5,000, computed as follows:

Sales price	$30,000
Minus: Adjusted basis	42,000
Capital loss	$12,000
Minus: Capital loss limitation	3,000
Capital loss carryover	$ 9,000
Allowable capital loss on sale	$ 3,000
Carryover losses allowable	2,000
Total current deductible loss	$ 5,000

The $5,000 total current deductible loss computed above is currently deductible because it is not treated as a passive activity loss. Nor is the $9,000 capital loss carryover treated as a passive activity loss.

Phase-in Rules for Interests Acquired before October 23, 1986

Interests in passive activities the taxpayer acquired before October 23, 1986 are eligible for a gradual phase-in of the passive activity loss and credit limitations. Because of the phase-in provision, a certain percentage of these passive activity losses and credits will be allowed to offset nonpassive income and taxes beginning in 1987 and continuing until the phase-in of the limitations is complete in 1991.

The percentage of loss allowed for each year in the phase-in period is as follows:

Year	Percentage Deductible
1987	65%
1988	40%
1989	20%
1990	10%
1991	0

Example: Mike has an interest in a race horse, *Neverontime,* purchased before October 23, 1986. He also has an interest in another race horse, *Your Pick,* purchased after that date. Each race horse is a separate activity. Mike does not materially participate in the business operations related to either horse. Mike's share of *Neverontime's* loss for 1987 is $4,000. His share of *Your Pick's* loss is $7,000.

Although both losses are losses from passive activities, the special phase-in rules apply only to *Neverontime's* loss. Consequently, $2,600 ($4,000 × 65%) of that loss is deductible from nonpassive income; that is, it is not subject to the passive loss limits. The remaining $1,400 is subject to the passive activity loss rules.

Mike's share of *Your Pick's* $7,000 loss, on the other hand, does not qualify for the phase-in rule relief and is, therefore, fully subject to the passive loss limits. That means the loss is only allowable as a deduction to the extent of any income from other passive activities during the tax year. Any remaining loss must be carried over to the next tax year.

At-Risk Rules Extended to Real Property

The at-risk rules have been extended to apply to the holding of real property. The at-risk rules place a limit on the amount of deductible losses from certain activities that are often described as tax shelters. Although often referred to as a tax shelter activity, the holding of real property (other than mineral property) was not previously subject to the at-risk rules.

The holding of personal property and the providing of services related to making real property available as living accommodations are part of the activity of holding real property. Therefore, businesses, such as hotels and motels, that may not have been subject to the at-risk rules before may now be subject to them.

The at-risk rules apply to losses incurred on real property the taxpayer placed in service after 1986. However, in the case of an interest in an S corporation, a partnership, or any other pass-through entity acquired after 1986, the extended rules apply regardless of when the entity placed the property in service.

Generally, any loss from an activity subject to the at-risk rules is allowed only to the extent of the total amount a taxpayer has at risk in the activity at the end of the tax year. A taxpayer is considered at risk in an activity to the extent of cash and the adjusted basis of other property the taxpayer contributed to the activity and certain amounts borrowed for use in the activity.

A taxpayer is not considered at risk for amounts protected against loss through nonrecourse financing. Nonrecourse financing is financing for which the taxpayer is not personally liable. However, an exception applies to qualified nonrecourse financing secured by real property used in an activity holding real property. Qualified nonrecourse financing is financing for which no one is personally liable for repayment that is:

- Borrowed by the taxpayer with respect to the activity of holding real property.
- Secured by real property used in the activity.
- Not convertible from a debt obligation to an ownership interest.
- Loaned or guaranteed by any federal, state, or local government, or borrowed by the taxpayer from a qualified person.

A *qualified person* is a person who actively and regularly engages in the business of lending money. The most common example is a bank.

A qualified person is **not**:

- A person related to the taxpayer.
- The seller of the property, or a person related to the seller.
- A person who receives a fee due to the taxpayer's investment in the real property, or a person related to that person.

A person related to the taxpayer may be a qualified person if the nonrecourse financing is commercially reasonable, and on substantially the same terms as loans involving unrelated persons.

Reserve Method for Deducting Bad Debts

Under prior law, taxpayers could use either the reserve method or the specific charge-off method to determine their deduction for bad debts. However, for tax years beginning after 1986, the reserve method may no longer be used by taxpayers other than certain financial institutions. This also applies to dealers who guarantee their customers' debts and who use the reserve method to deduct any bad debt losses that arise from these guarantees.

The specific charge-off method must now be used to account for losses from bad debts. Under this method, taxpayers are allowed a deduction when the debt is partially or totally worthless. If a reserve for bad debts was maintained for tax years beginning before 1987, a change must be made to the specific charge-off method. Any balance in the reserve is generally to be included in income in equal amounts over a 4-year period starting with the first tax year beginning after 1986.

A change from the reserve method is treated as a change initiated by the taxpayer with the consent of the Internal Revenue Service. Therefore, no formal consent is required.

Educational Assistance Programs and Group Legal Plans

The new law extends, generally, through 1987 the provisions that allow employers to exclude from an employee's income amounts paid under educational assistance programs or group legal plans.

One of these provisions allows employers to exclude amounts paid or expenses incurred for educational assistance provided to the employee if the educational assistance program meets certain requirements. The maximum amount of educational assistance benefits that may be excluded has been raised from $5,000 to $5,250.

The other provision allows employers to exclude amounts they contributed to a qualified group legal services plan for employees (or employees' spouses or dependents). The exclusion also applies to any services received by an employee or any amounts paid to an employee under the plan as reimbursement for the cost of legal services for the employee (or the employee's spouse or dependents).

These provisions generally are effective in the case of educational assistance benefits for tax years beginning on or before December 31, 1987, and in the case of group legal services benefits, for tax years ending on or before December 31, 1987.

Dependent Care Assistance Programs

Before 1987, an employee could exclude from income an amount of qualified dependent care assistance provided by an employer that did not exceed the lesser of the earned income of the employee or the employee's spouse.

Beginning in 1987, the amount an employee may exclude from income for dependent care assistance provided by an employer is limited to a maximum of $5,000 ($2,500 for married taxpayers filing separate returns). If the place where the dependent is cared for is at the employer's place of business, the amount that may be excluded from income will be based on the employee's use of the facility and the value of the services.

Employee Achievement Awards

The new law made several changes that affect whether or not an employer must include employee achievement awards in an employee's income. Before 1987, the employer did not include certain employee achievement awards in an employee's income because the award was considered a gift. The employer could deduct, as a business expense, the cost of tangible personal property given as awards to employees for length of service, productivity, or safety achievement, but only to the extent that:

1) The cost of each award did not exceed $400.

2) The award was a qualified plan award.

3) An award was a qualified plan award if:

    a) It was awarded as part of a permanent written plan of the employer that did not discriminate in favor of officers, shareholders, or highly compensated employees.

    b) The average cost of all items awarded under all plans did not exceed $400.

    c) The maximum cost deductible for any item awarded did not exceed $1,600.

After 1986, the employer may only exclude an employee achievement award from the employee's income if the employer may deduct the award. To be deductible, the award must:

1) Be made for length of service or safety achievement.

2) Be tangible personal property.

3) Be awarded as part of a meaningful presentation.

4) Be awarded under conditions and circumstances that do not create a significant likelihood of the payment of disguised compensation.

The total of all nonqualified awards made to any one employee during the tax year may not exceed $400. The total of all awards, both qualified and nonqualified plan awards, made to any one employee during the tax year may not exceed $1,600.

If the cost of the award is more than the amount the employer may deduct, the employer must include in the employee's income the greater of:

1) The amount the employer may not deduct, but not more than the value of the award.

2) The amount by which the value of the award exceeds the amount the employer is allowed to deduct.

If the employer is a tax-exempt organization, the same rules apply. That is, the employer may exclude the cost of the award from the employee's income to the extent that the employer would be allowed to deduct it if the employer was not a tax-exempt organization. If the employer is a partnership, the deduction limits apply to the partnership as well as to each partner.

A *qualified plan award* is one awarded as part of an established written plan by the employer that does not discriminate in favor of highly compensated employees. An award will not be considered a qualified plan award if the average cost of all employee achievement awards given by the employer during the tax year exceeds $400. In determining average cost, awards of very small value are not taken into account.

An award will not qualify as a *length-of-service award* if it is presented during an employee's first 5 years of employment, or if the employee received a length-of-service award during that year or any of the prior 4 years.

An award will not qualify as a *safety achievement award* if it is awarded to a manager, administrator, clerical employee, or other professional employee. Or, safety achievement awards are made to more than 10% of the employer's employees during the year.

Example: Dale Bran has 100 employees, not including managers and clerical employees. During the tax year, Dale presented the following qualified plan awards (none of which exceeded $1,600 in cost) to 15 different employees:

	Average Cost	Total Cost
10 Length-of-service awards	$350	$3,500
5 Safety achievement awards	500	$2,500
Total expenses for awards		$6,000

Since the average cost of all awards did not exceed $400 ($6,000 ÷ 15 = $400), Dale is allowed to deduct the entire expense and does not include awards in the employees' income.

Depreciation

- Modified accelerated cost recovery system applies to all tangible property placed in service after 1986.
- Section 179 deduction increased.

Modification of ACRS

The 1986 Act modified the accelerated cost recovery system (ACRS) of depreciation for all tangible property placed in service after December 31, 1986. Taxpayers were also permitted to make a property-by-property election to have the modified accelerated cost recovery system (MACRS) still apply to property that is already under construction, or under contract to be constructed, by March 1, 1986. This property is referred to as "transition property." *Transition property* is:

1) Property that is constructed, reconstructed, or acquired by the taxpayer under a written contract on March 1, 1986.

2) Property that is constructed or reconstructed by the taxpayer if:

   a) The lesser of $1,000,000, or 5% of the cost of the property had been incurred or committed by March 1, 1989.

   b) The construction or reconstruction of the property began by March 1, 1986.

3) An equipped building or plant facility if construction was started by March 1, 1986, under a written specific plan and more than one-half of the cost had been incurred or committed by March 1, 1986.

Also, the property must have a class life of at least 7 years or be residential rental or nonresidential real property that is placed in service before:

- 1989 if it has a class life of at least 7 but less than 20 years.
- 1991 if it has a class life of 20 years or more, or is residential rental or nonresidential real property.

A *plant facility* is a facility that does not include any building, or for which buildings are an insignificant part, and that is:

1) A self-contained single operating unit or processing operation.

2) Located on a single site.

3) Identified as a single unitary project as of March 1, 1986.

Sale and leaseback of transition property.   A taxpayer's property is treated as transition property if the taxpayer acquired the property from a person in whose hands the property was transition property. It is also considered transition property if it was acquired from a person who placed it in service before 1987 and the property is leased back by the taxpayer to that person no later than the earlier of the day that is 3 months after the property is placed in service or either 1989 or 1991 depending on the type of property.

Property classes under MACRS.   The new classes of property are 3-, 5-, 7-, 10-, 15-, and 20-year property. In addition, most real property is classified as residential rental or nonresidential real property. The class to which property is assigned is determined by the class life. The class life of an item of property determines the recovery period and the method of depreciation used.

Class life. The class life of an item of property is the asset guideline period that would apply to the property on January 1, 1986, if an election had been made to use the asset depreciation range (ADR) system.

Recovery periods. Under MACRS, property that is placed in service after 1986 falls into one of the following recovery classes:

1) *3-year property.* This class includes property with a class life of 4 years or less, such as tractor units for use over the road and, as designated, any race horse that is over 2 years old when placed in service, and any other horse that is over 12 years old when placed in service.
2) *5-year property.* This class includes property with a class life of more than 4 years but less than 10 years, such as heavy general purpose trucks (actual unloaded weight of 13,000 pounds or more), computers and peripheral equipment, and office machinery (typewriters and office machinery), and, as designated, any automobile, light general purpose truck (actual unloaded weight of under 13,000 pounds), and any property used in connection with research and experimentation.

Cars. Cars and light purpose trucks that were 3-year property under prior law have been designated by the Act as 5-year property for 1987 and later years. For a passenger automobile placed in service after December 31, 1986, the maximum depreciation deduction is limited. Depreciation deduction for an automobile may not exceed $2,560 for the first year of the recovery period. For the second and third years, the depreciation for an automobile is limited to $4,100 and $2,450, respectively. The maximum will be $1,475 in each succeeding tax year. These limits are further reduced if business use is less than 100%.

The *7-year property class* includes property with a class life of 10 or more but less than 16 years, such as office furniture and fixtures, and, as designated, any single purpose agricultural or horticultural structure. This class also includes any property that does not have a class life and that has not been designated by law as being in any other class.

10-year property class includes property with a class life of 16 years or more but less than 20 years. It includes vessels, barges, tugs, and similar water transportation equipment.

15-year property class includes property with a class life of 20 years or more but less than 25 years. It includes any municipal wastewater treatment plant.

20-year property class includes property with a class life of 25 years or more, such as farm buildings and any municipal sewers.

Nonresidential real property class includes any real property with a class life of 27.5 years or more that is not residential rental property. This property is depreciated over 31.5 years.

Residential Rental Property includes any real property that is a rental building or structure for which 80% or more of the gross rental income for the tax year is rental income from dwelling units. If any part of the building or structure is occupied by the taxpayer, the gross rental income includes the fair rental value of the part the taxpayer occupies. This property is depreciated over 27.5 years.

A dwelling unit is a house or an apartment used to provide living accommodations in a building or structure, but not a unit in a hotel, motel, inn, or other establishment where more than half of the units are used on a transient basis.

Depreciation methods.   For property in the 3-, 5-, 7-, or 10-year class, the 200% declining balance method over 3, 5, 7, or 10 years and a half-year convention is used. For property in the 15- or 20-year class, the 150% declining balance method over 15 or 20 years and a half-year convention is used. For these classes of property, there is a change to the straight line method for the first tax year for which that method, when applied to the adjusted basis at the beginning of the year, will yield a larger deduction. The straight line method and a midmonth convention are used for nonresidential real property and residential rental property.

Instead of using the declining balance method, an election may be made to use the straight-line method over the recovery period. The election to use the straight-line method for a class of property applies to all property in that class that is placed in service during the tax year of the election. Once made, the election to use the straight-line method over the recovery period may not be changed. For all classes and methods, salvage value is treated as zero.

Declining balance method.   The MACRS deduction under the declining balance method is determined by first figuring the rate of depreciation. This is done by dividing the number 1 by the recovery period. This basic rate is multiplied by the percentage allowed for the class of property being depreciated. For the 200% declining balance method, the basic rate is multiplied by 2, and for the 150% declining balance method, the basic rate is multiplied by 1.5.

Example: Larry Woods purchases for $10,000 an item of 7-year property that he places in service on August 11, 1987. He does not elect a section 179 deduction for this property; therefore, the adjusted basis of the property is $10,000. He divides 1 by 7 to get the basic rate of $1/7$ or 14.29%. Since this is 7-year property, he multiplies 14.29% by 2 to determine the declining balance rate of 28.58%.

He multiplies $10,000 by 28.58% to get $2,858. He then modifies this amount for the half-year convention, which requires him to take half of $2,858 to arrive at his depreciation for 1987 of $1,429 for this item of 7-year property.

For 1988, his depreciation is figured by subtracting $1,429 from $10,000 to get the adjusted basis of the property ($8,571). He multiplies $8,571 by 28.58% to get his depreciation deduction of $2,450 for 1988.

For 1989, following the same procedure, he multiplies $6,121 ($8,571–$2,450) by 28.58% to get his depreciation deduction of $1,749.

For 1990, he multiplies $4,372 ($6,121–$1,749) by 28.58% for a deduction of $1,250.

For 1991 he multiplies $3,122 ($4,372–$1,250) by 28.58% for a deduction of $892.

The remaining basis at the beginning of 1992 will be $2,230 and the declining balance deduction would be $637 ($2,230 × 28.58%). But by switching to the straight-line method, the deduction will be $892 ($2,230 divided by the 2.5 remaining years in the depreciation period) for both 1992 and 1993. For 1994 (final year) he can deduct $446 (a half-year of depreciation). The total depreciation Larry will have claimed for this property will be its cost of $10,000.

Straight-line method.   The straight-line deduction is figured by dividing the adjusted basis of the property by the number of years remaining in the recovery period. This gives the amount of depreciation that may be deducted each year. Generally, this amount remains the same each year. However, in the first year a taxpayer claims depreciation for residential rental and nonresidential real property, the taxpayer must prorate the depreciation deduction for the number of months the property is in use and apply the midmonth convention. Also, for the first year of depreciation under the alternate MACRS method, the deduction must be apportioned based on the applicable convention.

Example: Ellen Right purchases a building for $100,000 and land for $20,000 which is nonresidential real property that she places in service in her business on December 8, 1987. Ellen uses the calendar year as her tax year. She figures her depreciation for the building by dividing $100,000 by 31.5 years to get the straight-line depreciation for a full year of $3,175. She divides $3,175 by 12 to get $265, the depreciation for one month since she placed the property in service in December. She takes half of this to get her 1987 depreciation deduction of $132.50 for the building.

Conventions.   A half-year convention is used to figure the deduction for property other than nonresidential real and residential rental property. Under a special rule, a midquarter convention may have to be applied. For nonresidential real and residential rental property, midmonth convention is applied to all situations.

Under MACRS, the half-year convention treats all property placed in service, or disposed of, on the midpoint of that tax year. A half year of depreciation is allowed for the first year property is placed in service, regardless of when the property is placed in service during the tax year. For each of the remaining years of the recovery period, a full year of depreciation is allowed. If the property is held for the entire recovery period, a half year of depreciation is allowed for the year following the end of the recovery period. If the property is disposed of before the end of the recovery period, a half year of depreciation is allowed for the year of disposition.

Short-tax year.   The half-year convention treats property placed in service during a tax year as if it were placed in service at the midpoint of the number of months in that tax year. For example, if property is placed in service during a short tax year that consists of 8 months, the depreciation is determined for a full year. This amount is then multiplied by $8/12$ to get the depreciation for the full short year. The half-year convention is applied to determine the deduction for the short year.

Midquarter convention.   If during any tax year the total bases of property placed in service during the last 3 months of that tax year exceed 40% of the total bases of all property placed in service during that tax year (whether or not all of the property is subject to MACRS), a midquarter convention is applied to all property subject to MACRS instead of a half-year convention. In determining the total bases of property placed in service, neither residential rental property nor nonresidential real property is included.

Under a midquarter convention, all property placed in service, or disposed of, during any quarter of the tax year is treated as placed in service, or disposed of, at the midpoint of the quarter. The deduction for property subject to the midquarter convention is determined by first figuring the depreciation for a full tax year. This amount is multiplied by the following percentages for the quarter of the tax year the property is placed in service.

Quarter of Tax Year	Percentage
First	87.5%
Second	62.5%
Third	37.5%
Fourth	12.5%

Example: During 1987, John Joyce purchases a machine for $4,000, which he places in service in September, and a computer for $5,000, which he places in service in October. John uses the calendar year as his tax year. He does not elect to claim a section 179 deduction. The total bases of all property placed in service in 1987 are $10,000. Since the bases of the computer ($5,000), which was placed in service during the last 3 months of his tax year, exceed 40% of the total bases of all property ($10,000) placed in service during 1987, John must use the midquarter convention for all three items. The machine and office furniture are 7-year property, and the computer is 5-year property under MACRS.

The depreciation for the machine and furniture is figured by dividing 1 by 7 to get 14.29%. Since 7-year property is depreciated using the 200% declining balance method, John multiplies 14.29% by 2 to get the declining balance rate of 28.58%. He multiplies the basis of the machine, $4,000, by 28.58% to get the depreciation of $1,143 for a full year. Since the machine was placed in service in the first quarter of the tax year, John multiplies $1,143 by 87.5% (midquarter percentage for the first quarter) to get the deduction of $1,000 for the machine in 1987.

John follows the same procedure for the furniture. He multiplies the basis of the furniture, $1,000, by 28.58%, to get the depreciation of $286 for the full year. The furniture was placed in service in the third quarter of John's tax year; therefore, he multiplies the $286 by 37.5% (midquarter percentage for the third quarter) to get the deduction of $107 for the furniture for 1987.

The depreciation for the computer is figured by dividing 1 by 5 to get 20%. Since 5-year property is depreciated using the 200% declining balance method, John multiplies 20% by 2 to get the declining balance rate of 40%. He multiplies the basis of the computer, $5,000, by 40% to get the depreciation of $2,000 for a full year. The computer was placed in service in the fourth quarter of John's tax year; therefore, he multiplies the $2,000 by 12.5% (midquarter percentage for the fourth quarter) to get the deduction of $250 for the computer for 1987.

Under a midmonth convention all property placed in service or disposed of during any month is treated as placed in service or disposed of on the midpoint of that month.

Additions or improvements to property. The depreciation deduction for any additions to, or improvement of, any property is figured in the same manner as the deduction for the property would be figured as if the property has been placed in service at the same time as the addition or improvement. The MACRS class for the addition or improvement will be determined by the MACRS class of the property to which the addition or improvement is made. The period for figuring depreciation will begin on the date on which the addition or improvement is placed in service.

Example: Amy Long owns a residential rental house that she is depreciating under ACRS. If she puts an addition on the house in 1987, the addition would be depreciated as residential rental property under MACRS.

Alternate MACRS method. An election may be made to use an alternate MACRS method for most property. Under this method, depreciation is figured using the straight-line method of depreciation with no salvage value. For personal property with no class life, the straight line method is applied to a 12-year recovery period with a half-year convention. For nonresidential real and residential rental property, the straight-line method is applied to a 40-year recovery period with a mid-month convention. For any section 1245 property that is real property with no class life, the straight-line method is applied over 40 years with a half-year convention. For automobiles, light general purpose trucks, and any computer or peripheral equipment, the straight-line method is applied over a 5-year period with a half-year convention. For single purpose agricultural and horticultural structures, it is applied over a 15-year period with a half-year convention. For all other property, the straight line method is applied over the class life of the property with a half-year convention.

The election of the alternate MACRS method for a class of property applies to all property in that class that is placed in service during the tax year of the election. However, the election applies on a property-by-property basis for nonresidential real and residential rental property. Once made, the election to use the alternate MACRS method may not be changed.

The straight-line method of computing depreciation under MACRS **must** be used for any tangible property that is used during the tax year predominantly outside the United States, any tax-exempt use property, any property financed by an obligation the interest on which is exempt from federal tax, and certain imported property.

There are rules to prevent a person from using MACRS for certain property placed in service before 1987 but transferred after 1986. Property that does not come under MACRS must be depreciated under ACRS or one of the other methods of depreciation. In addition, an election may be made to exclude certain property from the application of MACRS.

A taxpayer may elect to **exclude** property from MACRS by using a method of depreciation that is not based on a term of years, such as the unit-of-production method. If a taxpayer uses the standard mileage rate for an automobile purchased and used for business, the taxpayer is considered to have elected to exclude the automobile from ACRS and MACRS.

There are special rules that prevent a taxpayer from using MACRS for property that was placed in service **before 1987**. These rules apply to both personal and real property, but the rules for personal property are more restrictive. Neither real nor personal property is treated as owned before it is placed in service. Therefore, if property is owned in 1986, but not placed in service until 1987, it is not treated as owned in 1986 for purposes of these rules.

A taxpayer may not use MACRS for personal property acquired after 1986 if:

1) The taxpayer or a party **related to** the taxpayer owned or used the property in 1986.

2) The property was acquired from a person who owned it in 1986 and, as part of the transaction, the user of the property does not change.

3) The taxpayer leases the property to a person (or a person related to this person) who owned or used the property in 1986.

4) The property is acquired in a transaction in which the user of the property does not change, and the property is not MACRS property in the hands of the person from whom the property was acquired due to 2) or 3).

MACRS does not apply to real or personal property used before 1987 and transferred in certain transfers after 1986 to a corporation or partnership, in which the basis of the property is determined by reference to the basis of the property in the hands of the transferor or distributor. The nontaxable transfers covered by this rule include:

1) A distribution in complete liquidation of a subsidiary.

2) A transfer to a corporation controlled by the transferor.

3) An exchange of property solely for corporate stock or securities in a reorganization.

4) A transfer of property solely in exchange for stock or securities under a reorganization as a result of bankruptcy proceedings.

5) A contribution of property to a partnership in exchange for a partnership interest.

6) A partnership distribution of property to a partner.

When figuring depreciation, the *transferee* (the person getting the property) is treated as the *transferor* (the person giving up the property) to the extent of the amount of the transferor's adjusted basis. The transferee may not use MACRS for the carried-over adjusted basis. However, MACRS does apply to that part of the new basis that is not represented by the carried-over adjusted basis.

The following list summarizes the method of depreciation to be used and examples of the type of assets included in each property class:

3-year (200% DB) property with a class life of 4 years or less, such as certain horses and tractor units for use over the road.

5-year (200% DB) property with a class life of more than 4 years but less than 10 years, such as autos, trucks, computers, typewriters, copiers.

7-year (200% DB) property with a class life of 10 years or more but less than 16 years, such as office furniture and fixtures, single purpose agricultural or horticultural structures, and any property that does not have a class life and that is not, by law, in any other class.

10-year (200% DB) property with a class life of 16 years or more but less than 20 years, such as vessels, barges, tugs, and similar water transportation equipment.

15-year (150% DB) property with a class life of 20 years or more but less than 25 years, such as any municipal wastewater treatment plant.

20-year (150% DB) property with a class life of 20 years or more, such as farm buildings and municipal sewers.

27.5-years (straight-line) residential rental property, such as rental houses and apartments.

31.5-years (straight-line) *real property* with a class life of 27.5 years or more that is *not* residential rental property, such as office buildings and warehouses.

Section 179 Deduction, Election to Expense Certain Depreciable Business Assets

The Section 179 deduction allows part of the cost of business property to be "expensed" in the year the property is put into use; that is, written off in that tax year, rather than depreciated over several years.

Under prior law, a taxpayer could elect to deduct up to $5,000 of the cost of certain depreciable property (described in Section 179) that was placed in service during a tax year in the taxpayer's trade or business. If the property was not used predominantly in the taxpayer's trade or business at any time before the end of the second tax year after the tax year in which the property was placed in service, the taxpayer had to include in income the benefit received from the deduction.

The benefit received from claiming the Section 179 deduction is the amount of the deduction that exceeds the total depreciation that would have been allowed on the part of the property's cost for which the deduction was claimed.

Example: Shirley Butler, a calendar year taxpayer, purchased and placed in service in her business on February 12, 1986, an item of 3-year property costing $5,000. She elected a Section 179 deduction of $5,000 for the property. Since Shirley deducted the full cost of the property in 1986, she may not claim any depreciation for this property.

For all of 1987, Shirley used the property exclusively for personal use. Because of this change from business to personal use, she must recapture the benefit she got from claiming the 179 deduction in 1986. Had she not elected to expense the $5,000 in 1986, she would have been entitled to a depreciation deduction of $1,250 (25% first year percentage for 3-year property of $5,000). Therefore, she must include in income for the 1987 tax year the excess of $5,000 (the amount claimed in 1986) over $1,250 (the depreciation that would have been allowed) or $3,750. Since Shirley did not use the property for business or investment purposes in 1987, she may not claim any depreciation in 1987.

For property placed in service after **1986,** the maximum cost of trade or business property that qualifies as Section 179 property that may be deducted has increased from $5,000 to $10,000. For each dollar of investment in 179 property in excess of $200,000 in a tax year, the $10,000 maximum is reduced (but not below zero) by one dollar. If the total investment is $210,000 or more in a tax year, there is no 179 deduction for that tax year.

Example: In 1987, JBK, Inc. places in service machinery with a cost of $207,000. Since the cost of the machinery exceeds $200,000 by $7,000, JBK is therefore entitled to a Section 179 deduction for 1987 of $3,000.

If Section 179 property is not used **predominantly** in the taxpayer's trade or business at any time before the end of the recovery period, the taxpayer must include in income the benefit received from the deduction.

There is a *taxable income limit* to the total cost that may be deducted in each tax year. The limit is the taxable income which is from the active conduct of the taxpayer's trade or business during the tax year. Taxable income is figured as usual, but without taking a deduction for the cost of any 179 property.

The cost of any 179 property that is not deductible in 1 year because of the limit may be carried to the next tax year and added to the cost of qualifying property placed in service in that tax year.

Example: Joyce, Inc. places in service in 1987 a machine that cost $8,000. Joyce's taxable income for 1987 (determined without regard to the cost of the machine) is $6,000. Joyce's deduction is limited to $6,000. The $2,000 cost that is not allowed because of the taxable income limit may be carried to 1988.

Tax Credits

- General business credit reduced and includes new credits.
- Business energy credit, targeted jobs credit, and research credit extended with changes in certain percentages.
- Low-income housing credit allowed for qualified buildings and certain rehabilitation expenses.
- Investment credit repealed.

The election to depreciate over 60 months expenses paid to rehabilitate low-income housing has been replaced with a new low-income housing tax credit. The credit is included as part of the general business and applies to qualified low-income housing constructed, rehabilitated, or purchased after 1986.

For buildings placed in service during 1987 that are new and are not federally subsidized, the credit is 9% of the qualified basis. For existing buildings and federally subsidized buildings, the credit is limited to 4% of the qualified basis.

The credit is taken annually over a 10-year period as long as the housing continues to qualify as low-income housing. If the building is sold or no longer qualifies for the credit within a 15-year period beginning with the first credit year, part or all of the credit must be recaptured.

Investment Tax Credit

The regular investment tax credit may no longer be claimed on most property placed in service after 1985. This credit, which was used to reduce the taxpayer's tax liability, was enacted to encourage taxpayers to invest in machinery and equipment for use in their trades or businesses, or in the production of income. The credit ranged from 4% to 10% of the cost of the property acquired and placed in service by a taxpayer during the tax year.

Although the investment credit was repealed for most property placed in service after 1985, it may still be claimed on transition property. Transition property is property placed in service after 1985 if the taxpayer had, on December 31, 1985, a written, binding contract to acquire, construct, or reconstruct the property. The taxpayer must also place the property in service by a specified date. The specified dates for acquired property are based on the (ADR) (asset depreciation range) midpoint life tables as follows:

ADR Midpoint Life	Must be Placed in Service Before
Less than 5 years	7/1/86
At least 5 but less than 7 years	1/1/87
At least 7 but less than 20 years	1/1/89
20 or more years	1/1/91

Property that a taxpayer constructs can qualify for the credit if construction began by December 31, 1985, and at least $1,000,000 or, if less, 5% of the cost was incurred or committed by that date. An equipped building or plant facility may also qualify for the credit if construction began by December 31, 1985, under a written, specific plan, and more than one-half of the cost of the project was incurred or committed by that date.

For tax years ending after July 1, 1987, any part of the general business credit and any carryover attributable to the regular investment credit must be **reduced** before they are used to offset tax liability.

The credit is reduced by a percentage. The percentage is figured by dividing the number of months in the tax year that fall after June 30, 1987, by the total number of months in the tax year. The resulting percentage is then multiplied by 35%. Thus, the credit is reduced by the full 35% for any tax year beginning after June 30, 1987.

The part of the general business credit this reduction applies to must be figured as if the investment credits are used before the other components of the general business credit. This reduction cannot be carried back and generally cannot be carried forward to the next tax year.

Corporations

- Corporate income tax rates reduced.
- Alternative tax on capital gains repealed.
- Alternative minimum tax replaces the minimum tax on corporations.
- New environmental tax.
- Dividends-received deduction reduced to 80%.
- Relief from estimated tax penalty.

For years beginning after June 30, 1987, *corporate taxable income* is subject to tax under the following three-bracket graduated rate system:

Taxable Income	Tax Rate
Not over $50,000	15%
Over $50,000 but not over $75,000	25%
Over $75,000	34%

An additional 5% tax, up to $11,750, is imposed on corporate taxable income over $100,000. Corporations with taxable income of at least $335,000 will pay a flat rate of 34%. Under prior law, corporations with taxable income of at least $1,405,000 paid a flat rate of 46%.

Corporations with tax years beginning before and including July 1, 1987, will use a **blend** of the old and the new rates. (See the tax computation worksheet in the *Instructions for Forms 1120 and 1120-A,* for information on how to figure the blended tax rate.)

Generally, for tax years beginning after December 31, 1986, the *28% alternative tax on capital gains is repealed.* An alternative tax at 34% is allowed until July 1, 1987, when the new lower tax rates go into effect. Capital losses are still deductible **only** against capital gains.

For corporations whose tax years begin after December 31, 1986, but before July 1, 1987, the alternative tax is figured as follows:

1) From corporate taxable income subtract the net capital gains (net long-term capital gain over net short-term capital loss).
2) Figure a partial tax on the remaining taxable income using the blended graduated tax rates.
3) Add to the partial tax 34% of net capital gains.

Fiscal-year corporations whose tax years begin in 1986 and end in 1987 figure alternative tax as follows:

1) From corporate taxable income, subtract the net capital gains.
2) Figure a partial tax on the remaining taxable income using the blended graduated tax rates.
3) Add to this partial tax 28% of the lesser of:
   a) The net capital gain that was subtracted from taxable income in 1), taking into account only gain or loss for the portion of the tax year before January 1, 1987, or
   b) The net capital gain for the entire tax year.
4) Add 34% of the net capital gain for the tax year over the net capital gain taken into account in 3).

For tax years beginning after 1986, corporations are subject to an *alternative minimum tax.* This tax helps ensure that all corporations with economic income will pay some amount of tax, despite their allowable use of exclusions, deductions, and credits. The AMT provides a formula for tax computation which, in effect, ignores certain preferential tax treatments that are allowed in figuring the regular tax. By eliminating these preferential deductions and credits, a tax liability is created for a corporation that would otherwise pay little or nothing.

The tax is figured by first adjusting certain items to eliminate the acceleration of deductions allowed in figuring the regular tax, and adding back corporate tax preference items. From this amount of income, called the *alternative minimum taxable income,* an exemption is subtracted. The maximum amount of this exemption is $40,000; however, it is reduced by $0.25 for every $1 by which the alternative minimum taxable income exceeds $150,000. After subtracting the exemption amount, the remaining income is taxed at a flat rate of 20%. The result is the *tentative minimum tax.* The alternative minimum tax is the amount by which the tentative minimum tax exceeds the corporation's regular tax.

Corporations must decide whether the alternative minimum tax applies when figuring estimated tax. Form 4626-W, *Estimated Alternative Minimum Tax Worksheet—Corporations,* may be used to compute the estimated alternative minimum tax. If it does apply, the AMT must be included in figuring the corporation's estimated tax payment.

A passive activity loss may not be used to reduce AMT income. The loss is reduced by the amount of any taxpayer insolvency. The passive loss rules apply for minimum tax purposes beginning in 1987. They are not phased in over several years as they are for certain passive activity losses for regular tax purposes.

Foreign tax credits are allowed against tentative minimum tax. However, these credits cannot exceed more than 90% of the tentative minimum tax liability figured without subtracting foreign tax credits and net operating losses.

Investment tax credits can be used either to reduce regular tax liability to 75% of tentative minimum tax liability or to offset 25% of the tentative minimum tax, whichever permits the use of the greater amount of such credits.

A *new minimum tax credit* will be allowed against regular tax liability in later years for part of the alternative minimum tax paid for tax years after 1986 that is attributable to certain preferences and adjustments. The amount of the credit allowable in any year may not exceed the excess of the regular tax liability (after other credits) over the tentative minimum tax for that year.

Environmental Tax

For tax years beginning after 1986 and before 1992, a corporation is liable for an excise tax equal to **.12%** of the excess of modified alternative minimum taxable income for the year over $2,000,000. The tax may apply even if the corporation is not liable for the alternative minimum tax. This tax must be included in the corporation's tax liability when determining its 1987 estimated tax.

Modified alternative minimum taxable income is alternative minimum taxable income determined without including the alternative tax net operating loss deduction and the deduction for the environmental tax.

No credits may be claimed against the new tax. However, the tax may be claimed as a deduction from income in arriving at the regular tax. Members of a controlled group of corporations are entitled to one $2,000 exemption.

Dividends-received deduction allowed for dividends received from domestic corporations has been reduced from 85% to 80% of the dividends received. This change applies to dividends received or accrued after 1986.

Relief from Underpayment of Estimated Tax Penalty

Corporations may not have to pay underpayment penalties for installment payments of corporate estimated tax that were due before July 1, 1987, for tax years beginning in 1987. The *safe harbor* is provided because many corporations found it hard to compute the payments necessary to satisfy the annualization exception frequently relied on to avoid an estimated tax underpayment penalty.

The annualization exception permits a corporation to compute its installment payments of estimated tax based on its taxable income for the first part of the year. Due to substantial changes made by the Tax Reform Act of 1986 and the Superfund Amendments and Reauthorization Act of 1986, corporations may have been uncertain about the proper tax treatment of items they were to take into account in computing their taxable income for purposes of estimated tax payments due before July 1, 1987.

A corporation that followed the requirements of the safe harbor is not subject to an underpayment penalty for an installment payment of estimated tax due before July 1, 1987. The *safe harbor* allows a corporation to compute any installment payment of estimated tax due before July 1, 1987 under the annualization exception. It assumes that the corporation's annualized income is at least 120% of the taxable income shown on its return for the preceding year. Under the safe harbor, the corporation is not required to include alternative minimum tax or environmental tax in an installment payment made before July 1, 1987.

To obtain the benefits of the safe harbor, the corporation must satisfy one of two conditions by the due date of the first installment payment after it ceases to use the safe harbor. The corporation may satisfy the usual requirements of the annualization exception by that date. Alternatively, the corporation may make a payment that, when added to earlier payments, is at least 67.5% of its tax for the year (45% if the first payment after the safe harbor ceases is the second payment).

If the subsequent installment payment is less than the amount required, the corporation loses the benefit of the safe harbor for any installment due before July 1, 1987. However, the underpayment penalty for prior installment payments will be limited to the underpayment penalty that would be charged on an underpayment equal to the amount of the shortfall in the subsequent payment. The shortfall is the amount by which the amount required to be paid exceeds the amount actually paid by the subsequent payment.

Example: Corporation M, which uses the calendar year as its tax year, relies on the safe harbor for its first two installment payments of estimated tax for 1987. M is required to make a timely subsequent installment payment of $1,000,000 by September 15, 1987, but M's actual installment payment by that date is only $990,000. Because of this shortfall, M loses the benefit of the safe harbor and is subject to underpayment penalties on the first two installments. The total penalties on those two installments, however, cannot exceed the amount of the underpayment penalty to which M would be subject if there were an underpayment of $10,000 on the September 15, 1987, installment payment. These penalties are independent of any penalty that may apply to M's third installment payment under the normal rules for an estimated tax underpayment penalty.

Employee Benefit Plans

- Salary reduction arrangements permit employer to make contributions to SEP on behalf of electing employee.
- New limit placed on elective deferrals.
- Maximum rate reduced for contributions for owner to certain Keogh plans.
- Distribution, coverage, nondiscrimination, and minimum participation requirements for tax-sheltered annuities similar to those for qualified retirement plans.
- New overall limits apply to contributions and benefits under qualified plans.
- Requirements for including leased employees in pension plans tightened.
- New excise tax on reversion of plan assets.
- Plan amendments not required until 1989 if certain conditions are met.
- Employer required to report on Form W-2 whether employee covered by retirement plan.

Simplified employee pensions (SEPs).   A simplified employee pension (SEP) provides an easy way for an employer to make contributions, within certain limits, to the individual retirement account or annuity (IRA) that is set up for an employee with a bank, insurance company, mutual fund, or other organization qualified to sponsor or trustee an IRA.

Under new law for years beginning after 1986, an employee who participates in certain SEPs has a choice. If the SEP includes a salary reduction arrangement, the employee may choose to have the employer make contributions to the SEP out of his or her salary, or the employee may choose to receive payment directly in cash.

If an employee chooses to have amounts taken out of his or her pay for employer contributions to a SEP, i.e., *elective deferrals,* certain conditions must be met:

1) At least 50% of the employees of the employer must choose to have amounts contributed to the SEP.
2) The employer must have no more than 25 employees at any time during the preceding year.

3) The amount deferred each year by each highly compensated employee as a percentage of pay (the *deferral percentage*) can be no more than 125% of the average deferral percentage of all other employees.

A *highly compensated employee* means an employee who during the year or preceding year:

1) Owns more than 5% of the capital or profits interest in the employer (if not a corporation); or more than 5% of the outstanding stock or more than 5% of the total voting power of all stock of the employer corporation.

2) Received annual compensation from the employer of more than $75,000.

3) Received annual compensation from the employer of more than $50,000 and was a member of the top-paid group of employees during the year.

4) Is an officer whose annual compensation exceeds 150% of the limit on the annual additions under a defined contribution plan.

Under a *participation requirement* an employer maintaining a SEP must allow each employee to participate who:

1) Has reached age 21 (previously age 25).

2) Has performed services for the employer during at least 3 of the immediately preceding 5 years.

3) Has received at least $300 in compensation from the employer for the year.

In general, the total amount an employee can defer from income under a SEP and certain other elective deferral arrangements is limited to $7,000, indexed to the rate of inflation. This $7,000 limit applies only to the amounts that represent a reduction from the employee's salary, not to any contributions from employer funds. Deferrals under an elective deferral arrangement are not included in the employee's income in the year of deferral.

Beginning in 1987, a U.S. citizen whose residence address is in a **foreign country** and who receives pension or annuity payments may not choose exemption from withholding on the payments. To choose exemption from withholding on pension or annuity benefits, a U.S. citizen or resident must give the payer of the benefits a residence address in the United States. Otherwise, the payer must withhold tax. For example, the payer would have to withhold tax if the recipient has provided a U.S. address for a nominee, trustee, or agent to whom the benefits are delivered, but has not provided his or her own U.S. residence address.

New Annual Limit on Elective Deferrals

Employees who are covered by certain kinds of retirement plans can choose to have part of their pay contributed by their employer to a retirement fund, rather than having it paid to them that year. These amounts are called *elective deferrals,* because the employee chooses (or elects) to set aside the money, and tax on the money deferred until it is taken out of the account.

Beginning in 1987, there are limits on the amount that an employee may defer each year under these plans. Generally, an employee may not defer more than a total of $7,000 each year for all plans by which he or she is covered. If the employee defers more than $7,000, the excess is included in the employee's gross income for that year.

Special limit for tax-sheltered annuities.   If an employee is covered by only one plan, and that plan is a tax-sheltered annuity, he or she may defer up to $9,500 each year. If he or she is covered by several different plans and at least one of the plans is a tax-sheltered annuity, then the basic $7,000 limit for all deferrals is increased by the amount deferred in the tax-sheltered annuity that year, up to an overall total of $9,500.

If an employee has completed at least 15 years of service with an educational organization, hospital, home health service agency, health and welfare service agency, church, or convention or association of churches (or associated organization), the $9,500 limit is increased each tax year. The limit is increased by the smallest of the following:

1) $3,000.
2) $15,000, reduced by increases to the $9,500 limit the employee was allowed in prior years because he or she was covered by a tax-sheltered annuity.
3) $5,000 times the number of the employee's years of service for the organization, minus the total elective deferrals under the plan for prior years.

Beginning in 1988, the basic $7,000 limit on elective deferrals is increased for inflation to reflect increases in the *Consumer Price Index.*

Amounts deferred under a *collective bargaining agreement* that was ratified before March 1, 1986, are not subject to the limits until tax years beginning after 1988 unless the agreement terminated before then.

Treatment of Excess Deferrals

If the total deferred by an employee is more than the limit for the year, the excess is included in the employee's gross income for the year. If the plan permits, the employee may receive the excess amount.

If only one plan is involved and it permits such distributions, the employee must notify the plan by March 1 after the end of the tax year that an excess was deferred. The plan must then pay the employee the amount of the excess, along with any income on that amount, by April 15.

If more than one plan is involved, the employee may have the excess paid out of any of the plans that permit such distributions. He or she must notify each plan by March 1 of the amount to be paid from that particular plan, and the plan must then pay the employee that amount by April 15.

Even if the employee takes out the excess, the amount still counts as having been contributed for purposes of satisfying or not satisfying the requirements the plan must meet regarding not discriminating against nonhighly compensated employees. If the excess is taken out, it is not again included in the employee's gross income, nor is it subject to the additional 10% tax on distributions before age 59. Any income on the excess taken out is taxable. However, it is treated as earned and received in the tax year in which it was set aside, rather than in the tax year in which it was taken out.

If the excess amount is **not** taken out, the amount included in the employee's gross income but not distributed may be left in the plan. But the excess amount is not included in the employee's investment in the contract for purposes of figuring the taxable amount of any eventual benefits or distributions under the plan. Thus, in effect, an excess deferral left in the plan would be taxed twice, once when contributed, and then again when distributed.

Keogh Plans

The Tax Reform Act of 1986 made several changes to the rules affecting Keogh plans. These plans, which are also known as H.R.10 plans, may be set up by self-employed persons or partnerships to provide retirement benefits for the owners of the business and their employees. In general, the limit on the deduction that a business may take for contributions to a Keogh plan that is a *profit-sharing plan* is limited to 15% of the participants' compensation from the business. For purposes of this limit, an owner's compensation is his or her net earnings from self-employment. However, for tax years beginning after 1984, these net earnings must take into account the deduction for contributions to the Keogh plan that are made on behalf of the owner.

Taking the contributions deduction into account in figuring the net earnings requires an adjustment to the net earnings. This adjustment presents a problem, however, because the amount of the deduction and the amount of the net earnings are dependent on each other. The adjustment is made to net earnings indirectly by **reducing** the rate for contributions for the owner. If this is done, the **maximum** contribution rate for an owner works out to 13.0435% of unadjusted net earnings.

If a contribution rate of less than the maximum 15% is specified in the plan, the reduced rate for owners may be determined by using the following worksheet:

1) Rate of contribution in plan . . . . _____ %

2) Rate in 1), shown as a decimal, plus 1 . . . . _____

3) Adjusted rate, divide 1) by 2) . . . . _____ %

Example: The Keogh plan of a sole proprietorship specifies a contribution rate of 12% of compensation for the owner and the employees. To determine the rate for the owner, the above worksheet is completed as follows:

1) Rate of contribution in plan 12%

2) Rate in 1), shown as a decimal, plus 1 .... 1.12

3) Adjusted rate, divide 1) by 2) 10.7143%

The owner in this example would be limited to a contribution deduction based on 10.7143% of the net earnings from self-employment. The deductible contributions for his or her employees would be limited under the plan to 12% of their compensation (no adjustment is made to the rate for contribution for these employees).

Under prior law, if the contributions under a profit-sharing plan for a tax year were less than the deductible limit for that year, the *unused limit amount* could be carried over and used in a later year. This carryover has been repealed for tax years beginning after 1986, except for unused limit carryovers accumulated for tax years beginning before 1987.

Generally, a *loan from a Keogh plan to an owner* is a prohibited transaction and, as such, is subject to certain penalty taxes. However, the penalty taxes will not be imposed on loans made after October 22, 1986, if the Department of Labor finds that an exemption from the penalty is administratively feasible, is in the interest of the plan and the participants and beneficiaries, and is protective of the rights of the participants and beneficiaries.

Tax-Sheltered Annuities

Tax-sheltered annuity programs (Section 403(b) plans) allow eligible employees of public schools and certain tax-exempt organizations to defer paying tax on the employers' qualified contributions toward their annuities.

New law requires that tax-sheltered annuity programs meet *distribution requirements* similar to those of qualified pension, profit-sharing, and stock bonus plans. Tax-sheltered annuity programs generally must require that distributions begin no later than April 1 of the year following the calendar year the employee reaches age 70. The new distributions requirements apply to benefits accruing after December 31, 1986, in tax years ending after that date.

New law generally provides that employer contributions, other than those made by churches, must satisfy the **coverage, nondiscrimination, and minimum participation requirements** as if the tax-sheltered annuity were a qualified retirement plan. These new rules generally require that tax-sheltered annuities plans may not discriminate in favor of highly compensated employees. Rules similar to those of qualified plans will now apply to integration of employer-provided amounts with social security benefits. In certain cases, a tax-sheltered annuity that does not meet the nondiscrimination and coverage requirements may be aggregated with certain qualified plans.

New limits apply to the amount that an employee may elect to **defer** under a salary reduction agreement. Generally, beginning in 1987, the limit on elective deferrals to tax-sheltered annuity plans is $9,500. Certain employees who have 15 years of service with qualified organizations are allowed to defer additional amounts as a "catch-up election." The amount of any elective deferral that is in excess of these limits will be included in the employee's income for the year to which the excess deferral relates.

Profit-Sharing Plans

A profit-sharing plan of an employer may qualify for favorable tax treatment if it meets certain requirements for employee retirement plans. For years beginning after 1985, an employer, including a tax-exempt organization, need not have actual profits (either current or accumulated) for its plan to qualify as a profit-sharing plan.

Limits on Contributions and Benefits

There are new limits on the amount of the annual addition for each employee to a qualified defined contribution plan, and on the amount of benefits that can be paid under a qualified benefit plan each year.

Defined contribution plans. Defined contribution plans are plans that provide for a separate account for each person covered by the plan. Benefits are based only on amounts contributed to or allocated to each account. Types of defined contribution plans include profit-sharing plans, stock bonus plans, and money purchase pension plans.

For years before 1987, the annual addition under a defined contribution plan was limited to the lesser of 25% of compensation for the year, or $30,000. The annual addition includes items such as employer contributions and certain employee contributions. For years beginning after 1986, the 25% limit remains unchanged. However, the dollar limit has been tied to the dollar limit for defined benefit plans. It is now the greater of $30,000 or one-quarter of the dollar limit (subject to cost-of-living adjustments) for defined benefit plans.

Defined benefit plans. Defined benefit plans are any qualified employee benefit plans that are not defined contribution plans. In general, this type of plan must identify the final benefit that will be paid. Also, the employer's contributions to the plan must not be based on the employer's profits. Defined benefit plans include pension plans and annuity plans.

The maximum benefit that may be paid under a defined benefit plan is the lesser of $90,000, or 100% of the average compensation of the person covered by the plan for the highest 3 consecutive years during which he or she was covered by an employer retirement plan.

For years before 1987, the maximum limit was reduced for benefits beginning before age 62 and increased for benefits beginning after age 65.

For years beginning after 1986, however, the maximum limit is reduced for benefits beginning before the social security retirement age (now 65) and increased for benefits received after that age. This reduction or increase in the $90,000 limit (but not the 100%-of-compensation limit) is figured actuarially so that the dollar limit is equal to an annual benefit of $90,000 beginning at the social security retirement age.

The $75,000 floor that applied previously for benefits for early retirement beginning at or after age 55 has been repealed. For years beginning after 1986, this dollar limit will be determined under regulations that are consistent with the reduction for early retirement under social security.

Leased Employees

Qualified employer pension plans must generally meet certain standards concerning minimum participation, nondiscrimination against lower-paid employees, and minimum vesting. For purposes of applying these standards, an employer's pool of employees must also include *leased employees* who provide services to the employer if:

1) The services are provided under an agreement between the recipient of the services and an organization that leases employees (temporary help agency, etc.).
2) The leased employee has performed such services for recipient on a substantially full-time basis for at least a year.
3) The services are a type historically performed in the business field of the recipient by employees.

If these leased employees are included in the recipient's pool of employees for pension plan purposes, contributions or benefits provided by the leasing organization are combined with those provided by the recipient in determining whether the qualification tests for pension plans maintained by the recipient are satisfied.

However, leased employees performing services for a recipient are **not** included in the recipient's pool of employees for pension plan purposes if they are covered under a safe harbor plan maintained by the leasing organization. Previously, a pension plan of a leasing organization would qualify as a safe harbor plan if it was a money purchase pension plan with a nonintegrated employer contribution rate of at least 7% and it provided for immediate participation and for full and immediate vesting.

The requirements have been tightened for a safe harbor plan of a leasing organization for services performed after 1986. As a result, some employers will no longer be able to exclude leased employees covered by leasing organizations' pension plans for their employee pools. Under the new rules, if leased employees make up more than 20% of the recipient's nonhighly compensated work force, the employer may only exclude the leased employees from the employee pool if the leasing organization's pension plan provides a nonintegrated employer contribution rate of at least 10% of compensation for each participant, and provides for immediate participation and full and immediate vesting.

Example: Doctor Jones has incorporated his individual medical practice that maintains an office employing a total of 5 nurses, technicians, and clerical personnel. During 1986, Doctor Jones' corporation entered into an agreement with an employee leasing organization whereby the 5 office personnel became employees of the leasing organization, which undertook to supervise them and to handle all details of payroll bookkeeping and employment taxes. The leasing organization covered the employees under a money purchase pension plan with an employer contribution rate of 7% and immediate participation and vesting.

After entering into the employee leasing arrangement, Doctor Jones' corporation set up a retirement plan covering only the doctor, with the maximum allowable contribution rate. The corporation was able to do this because the former employees were covered under a safe harbor plan of the leasing organization and thus could be excluded from the pool of those required to be covered under the corporate plan.

Beginning in 1987, Doctor Jones' corporation must contribute an additional amount to its former employees' retirement accounts, to make up the difference between the 7% contribution provided by the leasing organization and the contribution rate under the corporate retirement plan, for the corporate plan to maintain the maximum allowable contribution rate and still qualify under the nondiscrimination rules. This is so because the pension plan of the leasing organization no longer qualifies as a safe harbor plan. It no longer qualifies as a safe harbor plan for two reasons: first, the contribution rate is 7% instead of 10%, and second, the doctor's leased employees make up more than 20% of his nonhighly compensated work force. However, contributions by the leasing organization may be added to any contributions by Doctor Jones' corporation in satisfying the nondiscrimination requirements for the corporate plan.

Reversion of Plan Assets to Employer

If an employer who maintains a qualified retirement plan receives any cash or other property from the plan, the employer is liable for a nondeductible excise tax of 10% of the amount of the reversion received. This tax is imposed on property that reverts to the employer after 1985, unless the reversion takes place under a plan termination that occurred before 1986.

The excise tax on reversion of plan assets does **not** apply to:

1) Reversions from a retirement plan maintained by a tax-exempt organization or a governmental organization.

2) Distributions to or for any employee (or the employee's beneficiaries) if the amount distributed could have been distributed before the termination of the plan without disqualifying the plan.

3) Distributions to the employer that are allowed because of certain mistakes of law or fact, the return of a withdrawal liability payment, the failure of the plan to initially qualify, or the failure of contributions to be deductible.

4) Transfers from a qualified plan to an employee stock ownership plan (ESOP), if:

   a) The amount transferred is invested in employer securities within 90 days after the transfer.

   b) These employer securities remain in the ESOP until distribution to participants in the ESOP in accordance with its provisions.

   c) At least half the participants in the retirement plan are also participants in the ESOP.

   d) The amount transferred is either allocated to accounts of the participants in the ESOP or is credited to a suspense account for allocation to the accounts of participants.

The exception in 4) applies only to transfers before 1989, unless the transfers are under retirement plan terminations that take place after March, 1985 and before 1989.

Plan Amendments—Not Required Until 1989

The 1986 Act made numerous changes to the rules covering pension and deferred compensation plans and employee stock ownership plans (ESOPs). Even if amendments are not made, a plan generally will continue to be considered qualified under the new rules for any year beginning after January 1, 1989, provided:

1) The plan operates in compliance with the required changes.

2) The plan makes amendments to comply with the changes no later than the last day of the first plan year beginning after December 31, 1988.

3) The amendments apply retroactively to the effective dates of the changes as provided by the new law.

Collectively bargained plans maintained pursuant to collective bargaining agreements ratified before March 1, 1986, generally have until 1991 to make these amendments.

Employer Must Report Employee's Coverage by Plan

Under new individual retirement arrangement (IRA) rules, an employer must inform employees whether, for IRA purposes, they are considered covered by the employer's retirement plan. For purposes of the new IRA deduction rules, the following types of plans are considered employment retirement plans:

1) A qualified pension, profit-sharing, stock bonus, money purchase, etc., plan.
2) A qualified annuity plan.
3) A plan established for its employees by a federal, state, or local government, or any of their political subdivisions, agencies, or instrumentalities (other than an eligible state deferred compensation plan).
4) A tax-sheltered annuity plan for employees of public schools and certain tax-exempt organizations.
5) A simplified employee pension (SEP).
6) A 501 (c) (18) trust (a certain type of tax-exempt trust created before June 25, 1959), that is funded by employee contributions.

Coverage by Defined Contribution and Defined Benefit Plans

Special rules apply in determining when an employee is considered to be covered by a plan. These rules differ depending on whether the plan is a defined contribution or defined benefit plan.

Defined benefit plan. A person who is not specifically excluded from the eligibility provisions of an employer's plan for the plan year that ends with or within the tax year is considered covered by the plan. This rule applies even if the person declined to be covered by the plan, did not make a required contribution, or did not perform the minimum service required to accrue a benefit.

Example: John, an employee of B, is not excluded from coverage under B's defined benefit plan with a July 1 to June 30 plan year. John leaves B on December 31, 1987. Since John is not excluded from coverage under the plan for its year ending June 30, 1988, he is considered covered by the plan for his 1988 tax year.

Defined contribution plan. An employee is considered covered by a defined contribution plan if employer or employee contributions or forfeitures are allocated to the employee's account for the plan year that ends with or within the tax year.

Example: Company A has a money purchase pension plan, whose plan year ends June 30. The plan provides that contributions must be allocated as of June 30. Bob, an employee, leaves Company A on December 31, 1987. The contribution for the plan year ending on June 30, 1988, is not made until February 15, 1989 (when Company A files its corporate return). In his case, Bob is considered covered by the plan for his 1988 tax year.

Changes in Penalties

FRAUD.

New Law: 75% of the part of any underpayment that is due to fraud.
Old Law: 50% of the underpayment if any part is due to fraud.

NEGLIGENCE.

New Law: Applies to all taxes.
Old Law: Applied only to income taxes, gift taxes, and windfall profits
tax.
Negligence presumed for failure to report interest or dividends shown on
information returns.

FAILURE TO PAY TAX.

New Law: Same, but increases to 1% for each month beginning after the
day levy may be made.
Old Law: 1% of the unpaid tax for each month, or part of a month, the tax
remains unpaid.

FAILURE TO FILE INFORMATION RETURNS. THIS INCLUDES
FAILURE TO FILE ON MAGNETIC MEDIA WHEN REQUIRED, OR TO
FURNISH A STATEMENT TO A PAYEE.

New Law: Same, except for $100,000 maximum.
Old Law: $50 for each failure, $50,000 maximum, no maximum for dividend or interest returns or statements.

FAILURE TO SUPPLY TAXPAYER IDENTIFICATION NUMBER.

New Law: $50 for each failure, $100,000 maximum, no maximum for dividend interest, or royalty returns or statements.
Old Law: $50 for each failure, $50,000 maximum, no maximum for dividend or interest returns or statements.

FAILURE TO INCLUDE ALL REQUIRED INFORMATION OR
CORRECT INFORMATION ON INFORMATION RETURNS OR PAYEE
STATEMENTS.

New Law: $5 for each failure, $20,000 maximum, no maximum for dividend or interest returns or statements.
Old Law: No penalty.

FAILURE TO REGISTER TAX SHELTERS.

New Law: Same, but no maximum.
Old Law: Greater of $500 or 1% of amount invested, $10,000 maximum.

FAILURE TO MAINTAIN LISTS OF INVESTORS IN POTENTIALLY
ABUSIVE TAX SHELTERS.

New Law: Same, except for $100,000 maximum.
Old Law: $50 for each person not listed, $50,000 maximum.

FAILURE TO DEPOSIT TAXES ON TIME.

New Law: 10% of the amount of underpayment.
Old Law: 5% of the amount of underpayment.

SUBSTANTIAL UNDERSTATEMENT OF INCOME TAX.

New Law: 25% of the amount of any underpayment due to the understatement.
Old Law: 10% of the amount of any underpayment due to the understatement.

Accounting Periods and Methods

- Tax year of partnership, S corporation, or personal service corporation may have to be changed to conform to tax year rules.
- Cash method of accounting cannot be used by certain entities.

Before 1987, the tax year of a newly formed partnership or of a partnership changing its tax year generally had to be the same as the tax year of its principal partners (those partners who owned a 5% or more share of the partnership). If the principal partners did not have the same tax year, the partnership's tax year had to be a calendar year. New law changed the requirements for selecting the tax year of a partnership. For tax years beginning after 1986, all partnerships, including existing partnerships, must conform their tax year to their partners' tax years in the following way:

1) If one or more partners own a majority interest (more than a 50% interest in partnership profits and capital), the partnership must adopt the tax year of those partners.

2) If there are no partners who own a majority interest, or if the majority interest partners do not have the same tax year, the partnership is required to change to the tax year of its principal partners.

3) If neither 1) or 2) applies, the partnership must use a calendar year, unless another year is prescribed by regulations.

These requirements do not apply to partnerships that can establish an acceptable business purpose for having a different tax year; for example, a partnership having a natural business year, as described in Rev. Proc. 87-32, 1987—28 I.R.B.14 may be able to use that year.

Any change in a tax year made because of this new provision will be treated as though approved by the IRS, so a partnership should not file a formal application for the change.

A change in the tax year requires a partnership to file two returns for the year of change—a full year return and a short-period return. Any income from the short period may be included in the partners' tax returns ratable over the next 4 years that begin after December 31, 1986. For this 4-year period to apply, the income from the short period must have to be included in a partner's tax return for 1987. However, a partner may elect to include all of the income in the year of change.

S Corporation Tax Year

For tax years beginning after December 31, 1986, **all** S corporations, regardless of when they became S corporations, are required to use as their tax year a year ending December 31, or any other accounting period for which the corporation establishes a business purpose to the satisfaction of IRS. The deferral of income to shareholders is not a business purpose.

Personal Service Corporation Tax Year

Under prior law a personal service corporation generally could adopt any tax year on its federal income tax return that agreed with its annual accounting period. A personal service corporation was required to get permission from IRS if it wanted to change its tax year.

For tax years beginning after 1986, a personal service corporation must use a calendar tax year unless it can establish, to the satisfaction of the IRS, a business purpose for having a different tax year. A deferral of income will no longer be treated as a business purpose.

A personal service corporation is a corporation in which the principal business activity is performing personal services, if the services are substantially performed by employee-owners. Employee-owners of personal service corporations, for the purpose of determining a tax year, are employees who own any outstanding stock on any day during the tax year. The attribution rules of Internal Revenue Code Section 318(a) (2) (C) apply for determining stock ownership. However, the rules are applied without regard to the 50% ownership requirement.

A personal service corporation may not deduct payments made to employee-owners prior to the time that the employee-owner should include the payment in gross income.

Cash Method of Accounting

Under prior law, a taxpayer could generally elect to use any permissible method of accounting provided that method clearly reflected income and was consistently used from year to year in keeping books. However, for tax years beginning after 1986, the cash method of accounting may not be used by the following entities:

1) Corporations (other than S corporations).
2) Partnerships having a corporation (other than an S corporation) as a partner.
3) Tax shelters.

Exceptions.   An exception allows farming businesses (including the raising, harvesting, or growing of trees), qualified personal service corporations, and entities with average annual gross receipts of $5,000,000 or less to continue using the cash method. However, these exceptions do not apply to tax shelters.

A qualified personal service corporation is a corporation that meets both a *function test* and an *ownership test*. The function test is met if substantially all of the activities of the corporation are the performance of service in the fields of health, law, engineering, architecture, accounting, actuarial science, performing arts, or consulting. The ownership test is met if substantially all (at least 95%) of the value of the stock of the corporation is owned, directly or indirectly by:

1) Employees performing services for the corporation in a field qualifying under the function test.
2) Retired employees who performed services in such fields.
3) The estate of an employee described in 1) and 2).
4) Any other person who acquired the stock by reason of the death of an employee referred to in 1) and 2).

Under an additional exception, taxpayers may elect to continue to report income from the following transactions by using the cash method:

1) Loans, leases, and transactions between related parties entered into before September 26, 1985.
2) Contracts for the acquisition and transfer of real property.
3) Contracts for services related to the acquisition or development of real property.

Items 2) and 3) apply only if the contracts were entered into before September 25, 1985, and the only part of the contract not completed as of that date is payment for the property or services.

Allocation of Sales Price of Business Assets

The new law requires both the buyer and seller of a business to use the residual method to allocate the sales price of the business to the various business assets. This method determines the amount of gain or loss from the transfer of each asset and how much of the sales price is considered received for goodwill and going concern value. It also determines the buyer's basis in the assets of the business.

The residual method must be used for any transfer of a group of assets that constitutes a trade or business and for which the buyer's basis is determined only by the amount paid for the assets. This applies to both direct and indirect transfers, such as the sale of a business, or the sale of a partnership interest in which the basis of the buyer's share of the partnership assets is adjusted for the amount paid. A group of assets constitutes a trade or business if goodwill or going concern value could, under any circumstances, attach to the assets.

This rule applies to any qualifying transfer after May 6, 1986, unless the transfer was made under a binding contract in effect on May 6, 1986, and at all times after that date.

Residual method.   The residual method provides for the sales price to be allocated first among the business' various assets in a specified order, and then for the remainder of the sale price to be allocated to goodwill or going concern value.

The allocation must be made among the following assets in proportion to (but not in excess of) their fair market values in the order specified.

1) Cash and demand deposits and similar accounts.
2) Certificates of deposit, U.S. Government securities, readily marketable stock or securities, and foreign currency.
3) All other assets, both tangible and intangible, except goodwill or going concern value.

After making this allocation, the remainder of the sales price of the business is considered goodwill or going concern value.

Example: The total amount paid in the sale of Company SKB is $21,000. No cash or demand deposits were sold. The company's U.S. Government securities had a fair market value of $3,200, and other business assets had a fair market value of $15,000. Of the $21,000 paid for Company SKB, $3,200 is allocated to U.S. Government securities, $15,000 to other business assets, and the remaining $2,800 to goodwill or going concern value.

Reporting requirements. Both the buyer and the seller involved in the sale of business assets must report to the IRS the allocation of the sales price among goodwill and the other business assets. The buyer and seller should each attach Form 8584, *Asset Acquisition Statement* to their federal income tax returns for the year in which the sale occurred.

Transactions Between Related Parties

The new law changed and expanded the definition of related parties as used in determining the treatment of sales and exchanges of depreciable property between related taxpayers. Taxpayers who are considered related parties may not report sale of depreciable property under the installment method.

Under prior law, the term *related parties* for this purpose included:

1) A taxpayer and an 80% owned entity.
2) Two 80% owned entities.
3) A taxpayer and any trust in which the taxpayer or the taxpayer's spouse was a beneficiary, unless the taxpayer's interest was a remote contingent interest. (A remote contingent interest is an interest that, if computed actuarially, is 5% or less of the value of the trust.)

For sales after October 22, 1986, the term *related parties* includes:

1) A taxpayer and a controlled entity.
2) A taxpayer and any trust in which the taxpayer or the taxpayer's spouse is a beneficiary, unless the taxpayer's interest in the trust is a remote contingent interest.
3) Two corporations that are members of the same controlled group.
4) Two S corporations if the same persons own more than 50% in value of the outstanding stock of each corporation.
5) An S corporation and a corporation that is not an S corporation if the same persons own more than 50% in value of the outstanding stock of each corporation.
6) A corporation and a partnership if the same persons own more than 50% in value of the outstanding stock of each corporation.

A controlled entity is a partnership in which the taxpayer owns, directly or indirectly, more than 50% of the interest in its capital or profits, or a corporation in which the taxpayer owns, directly or indirectly, more than 50% of the value of the outstanding stock.

To determine whether an individual indirectly owns any of the outstanding stock of a corporation, the following rules are applied:

1) Stock owned by or for a corporation, partnership, estate, or trust is indirectly owned proportionately by or for its shareholders, partners, or beneficiaries.

2) An individual indirectly owns the stock owned by or for the individual's spouse, brothers and sisters (including half-brothers and half-sisters), lineal descendants, and ancestors.

For purposes of applying rules 1) and 2), a person is considered to actually own stock that he or she indirectly owned by applying rule 1). But if an individual indirectly owns stock by applying rule 2), he or she does not own the stock for the purpose of again applying rule 2) to make another person the indirect owner of the same stock.

Sales after October 22, 1986, made under a binding contract in effect on August 15, 1986, are treated as sales before October 22, 1986.

All payments on an installment sale of depreciable property between related parties are considered received in the year of sale. For sales after October 22, 1986, the payments to be received include the total amount of all payments that are determinable as to amount and the fair market value of any payment the amount of which is not determinable.

For all payments which are not determinable as to amount and for which the fair market value is not reasonably ascertainable, the basis is recovered ratably. The purchaser may not increase the basis of any property acquired in the sale by any amount before the time the seller includes the amount in income.

Employment Taxes—Independent Contractor

Under a relief provision, a taxpayer is not liable for employment taxes on the payments to a worker (even though, under common-law standards, the worker is an employee) if the taxpayer has a reasonable basis for not treating the worker as an employee (for example, past industry practice). To get this relief, the taxpayer must meet certain requirements.

For wages paid and services performed after 1986, this relief provision does not apply to a worker who, under an arrangement between a taxpayer, such as a technical services firm and a client, provides services for the client as a technical service specialist. A technical service specialist is an engineer, designer, drafter, computer programmer, systems analyst, or other similarly skilled worker engaged in a similar line of work. (A taxpayer who directly contracts with a technical service specialist to provide services for himself or herself rather than for another person may still be entitled to the relief provision.)

This new rule does not automatically convert technical service specialists to employees for employment tax purposes. The common-law standards control whether the specialist is treated as an employee or an independent contractor.

Generally, under common-law standards, an individual is an employee if he or she performs services that are subject to the control of an employer, both as to what work must be done and how the work must be done. If the employer has the right to control only the result of the work and not the means of accomplishing the result, the individual, generally, is an independent contractor.

Real Estate Reporting

Information reporting is now required on certain real estate transactions. For closings after 1986, a person treated as a real estate broker is required to file a Form 1099 to report the sale or exchange of "one-to-four-family" real estate transactions.

The following information must be reported on Form 1099:

1) The broker's name, address, and taxpayer identification number (TIN).
2) The name, address, and TIN of the transferor.
3) A description of the real estate.
4) The date of the closing (the settlement date).
5) The gross proceeds of the transaction, which include cash, amount of liabilities taken over by the transferee (buyer) and notes received from the buyer. If the total consideration includes other property or services the broker must indicate this on Form 1099, in accordance with the instructions to the form.

Reportable real estate transactions. Reporting on real estate transactions is required only if the transaction consists of the sale or exchange of one-to-four-family real estate for money, indebtedness, property, or services. One-to-four-family real estate includes:

1) Any structure designed principally to house up to four families, such as a house, townhouse or condominium unit, duplex, or four-unit apartment building.
2) Stock in a cooperative housing corporation.

Real estate broker. The person generally treated as a real estate broker and required to file Form 1099 is the person designated in a qualifying designation agreement, or if there is no designation agreement, the person responsible for closing the transaction is the person listed as settlement agent on a HUD-1 Settlement Statement, or if that statement is not used, the person preparing the closing statement. If no closing statement is used, the person responsible for closing, in the order listed, is:

1) The transferee's attorney who significantly participates in the transaction.
2) The transferor's attorney who significantly participates in the transaction.
3) The title or escrow company that is most significant in disbursing the gross proceeds of the transaction.

If no one is responsible for closing the transaction, the real estate broker is, in the following order:

1) The mortgage lender.
2) The transferor's broker.
3) The transferee's broker.
4) The transferee.

Partnerships and S Corporations: Meals, Travel, and Entertainment Expenses

Many items of income, deductions, and credits must be separately stated on Form 1065, *U.S. Partnership Return of Income,* and on Form 1120S, *U.S. Income Tax Return for an S Corporation.* This is necessary because certain limits or special treatment apply to these items on the partner's or shareholder's return.

The Tax Reform Act of 1986 limits the amount that may be deducted for meals and entertainment expenses, skyboxes, and other luxury box seat rentals, and luxury water transportation expenses that are paid or incurred after 1986. Partnerships and S corporations with fiscal years that include December 31, 1986, must report these expenses paid or incurred after 1986 as a separate item to the partners or shareholders.

Each expense must be listed separately on an attachment to the appropriate schedule with any additional information the partner or shareholder needs to determine the deductibility and the limited amount to claim on his or her individual tax return for 1987. Although a portion of an expense is not deductible, the partner or shareholder is still required to reduce his or her basis by the full amount stated on the schedule.

Capitalizing Sales Tax

For tax years beginning after 1986, taxpayers can no longer deduct state and local sales tax as an itemized deduction. However, if a taxpayer pays or accrues sales tax on the purchase of property, the tax is treated as part of the cost of the property.

Thus, if a taxpayer acquires depreciable property for use in a business, any sales tax paid or accrued on the purchase is added to the basis of the property and treated as part of the property's cost for depreciation purposes.

If a taxpayer buys a nondepreciable item that is deductible as a business expense, the sales tax on the purchase is still deductible as a business expense.

IV

Updates—S Corporations, Partnerships, Depreciation, Interest Expense, Corporate Net Operating Losses, Deducting Business Expenses, RICs, REITs, REMICs, Change in Accounting Methods, Basis of Assets

S CORPORATION ORGANIZATION AND TAX REQUIREMENTS

A corporation is taxed on its income under corporate tax rules. When it distributes dividends to its shareholders, the shareholders include these already taxed amounts in their income. In effect, corporate income is taxed twice, once to the corporation and again to the shareholders.

However, an eligible domestic corporation can avoid double taxation by electing to be treated as an *S corporation* under the rules of Subchapter S of the Internal Revenue Code. In this way, the S corporation passes its items of income, loss, deduction, and credits through to its shareholders to be included on their separate returns. Individual shareholders may benefit from a reduction in their taxable income during the first years of the corporation's existence when it may be operating at a loss.

Only qualifying corporations may elect S corporation status. This section of the *Supplement* discusses:

1) How to become an S corporation.
2) How an S corporation may be taxed.
3) How income is distributed to shareholders.
4) How to terminate an S corporation.

A corporation can become an S corporation if:

1) It meets the requirements of S corporation status.
2) All of its shareholders consent to S corporation status.
3) It uses a permitted tax year, or elects to use a tax year other than a permitted tax year.
4) It files Form 2553, *Election by a Small Business Corporation,* to indicate it chooses S corporation status.

To qualify for S corporation status, a corporation must meet **all** of the following requirements:

1) It must be a domestic corporation. It must be a corporation that is either organized in the United States, or organized under federal or state laws. The term *corporation* includes a joint-stock company, certain insurance companies, or an association that has the characteristics of a corporation.
2) It must have only one class of stock.
3) It must have **no more than 35 shareholders**.
4) It must have as shareholders only individuals, estates (including estates of individuals in bankruptcy) and certain trusts. Partnerships and corporations cannot be shareholders in an S corporation.

5) It must have shareholders who are citizens or residents of the United States. Nonresident aliens cannot be shareholders.

Certain domestic corporations are ineligible to elect S corporation status. They are:

1) A member of an affiliate group of corporations. Generally, an affiliated group means one or more chains of corporations connected through stock ownership with a common parent corporation that is also part of the group. The common parent must directly own stock that possesses at least 80% of the total voting power of the stock of at least one of the corporations, and the stock must have a value equal to at least 80% of the total value of the stock of that corporation. Stock does not include certain preferred stock. A corporation is a member of an affiliated group if it directly owns 80% or more of the total combined voting power of stock entitled to vote and 80% or more of the total value of all other stock, except preferred stock, of another corporation.

2) A **DISC** (*Domestic International Sales Corporation*) or former DISC.

3) A corporation that takes the Puerto Rico and possessions tax credit for doing business in a United States possession.

4) A financial institution that is a bank, including mutual savings banks, cooperative banks, and domestic building and loan associations.

5) An insurance company taxed under Subchapter L of the Internal Revenue Code.

One class of stock generally means that the outstanding shares of the corporation must be identical as to the right of the holders in the profits and in the assets of the corporation. Stock may have differences in voting rights and still be considered one class of stock.

A stock purchase agreement executed between an S corporation and its shareholders that does not affect the shareholders' right in the corporation's profits and assets will not create a second class of stock.

Debt obligations of a corporation that are actually contributions of equity capital may be treated as a second class of stock. However, straight debt will not be considered a second class of stock. The term *straight debt* means any written unconditional promise to pay a fixed amount on demand or on a specific date if:

1) The interest rate and interest payment dates are not contingent on profits, the borrower's discretion, or similar factors.

2) The debt cannot be converted directly or indirectly into stock.

3) The creditor is an individual, estate, or trust eligible to hold stock in an S corporation.

Authorized but unissued stock and treasury stock are not considered in determining if a corporation has more than one class of stock. Nor is special stock issued to the Federal Housing Administration considered when making this determination. The existence of outstanding options, warrants to acquire stock, or convertible debentures will not, by itself, be considered a second class of stock.

When counting shareholders, an S corporation cannot have more than 35 shareholders. The following rules apply when counting shareholders:

1) Count the persons who are considered shareholders if the stock is actually held by a trust. Do not count the trust itself as a shareholder.
2) Count a husband and wife, and their estates, as one shareholder, even if they own stock separately.
3) Otherwise, count everyone who owns any stock, even if the stock is owned jointly with someone else.

The following *trusts,* other than foreign trusts, can be shareholders of an S corporation:

1) A trust all of which is treated as owned by an individual who is a United States citizen or resident. The individual, not the trust, is treated as the shareholder.
2) A trust that qualified under 1) before the owner's death, and continues in existence after the owner's death, may continue to be an S corporation shareholder for stock held by the trust when the owner died, but only for a period no longer than 60 days, beginning on the day of the owner's death. However, if the entire corpus of the trust is included in the owner's gross estate, the 60-day period becomes a 2-year period. The owner's estate is treated as the shareholder.
3) A trust created primarily to exercise the voting power of stock transferred to it. Each beneficiary of the trust is treated as a shareholder.
4) Any trust to which stock is transferred according to the terms of a will, but only for 60 days, beginning with the day the stock was transferred to the trust under the will. The estate of the person leaving the will is treated as the shareholder.

Qualified Subchapter S Trusts. A qualified Subchapter S trust means a trust the terms of which require that:

1) During the life of the current income beneficiary, there shall be only one income beneficiary of the trust.
2) Any corpus distributed during the life of the current beneficiary may be distributed only to such beneficiary.
3) The income interest of the current beneficiary in the trust shall terminate on the earlier of such beneficiary's death or the termination of the trust.

4) Upon the termination of the trust during the life of the current income beneficiary, it shall distribute all of its assets to such beneficiary.

5) All of the income of which is distributed or required to be distributed currently to one individual who is a citizen or resident of the United States.

An S corporation cannot have a subsidiary that would cause it to be a member of an affiliated group of corporations. However, this rule may not apply if the subsidiary is inactive, a former DISC, or a foreign corporation. An *inactive subsidiary* is one that during any period in a tax year:

1) Has not begun business at any time on or before the close of that period.

2) Does not have gross income for that period.

A corporation that holds a foreign corporation or former DISC as a subsidiary is not eligible to be an S corporation unless it qualified under the *grandfather rules* of the Subchapter S Revision Act of 1982.

A corporation's election of S corporation status is valid only if **all** shareholders consent to the election. A shareholder's consent is binding and may be withdrawn only if shareholders who collectively own more than 50% of the outstanding shares in the S corporation stock consent to a revocation. The consenting shareholders must own their stock in the S corporation at the time the revocation is made.

A *permitted tax year* is a calendar year, or any other accounting period for which the corporation establishes a business purpose to the satisfaction of the IRS. In addition, an S corporation may elect to have a tax year other than the permitted tax year. A corporation electing S corporation status does not need IRS approval to choose a calendar year as its tax year. An electing S corporation should use Form 2553 to request a tax year other than a calendar year, or to make a Section 444 election.

When figuring *S Corporation Income and Expenses,* the S corporation's items of income, loss, expense, and credit are divided into two categories:

1) Separately stated items.

2) Items used to figure nonseparately stated income or loss.

Because the shareholders of an S corporation rather than the S corporation itself are taxed on its income, and some income and expense items are subject to special rules, it is necessary to divide the items of income, loss, expense, and the S corporation into two categories. One category consists of items that are separately stated items subject to special rules. The other category consists of combined items resulting in **net** amount.

The items of income, loss, expense, and credit that must be separately stated are those items that, when separately treated on the shareholder's income tax return (not as part of a lump-sum amount) could affect the shareholder's tax liability. The list of items that must be separately stated includes (but is not limited to):

1) Net income or loss from rental real estate activity.
2) Net income or loss from other rental activity.
3) Portfolio income or loss—interest income, dividend income, royalty income, short-term capital gain or loss, long-term capital gain or loss.
4) Section 1231 net gain or loss.
5) Charitable contributions.
6) Health insurance premiums.
7) Expenses related to portfolio income or loss.
8) Credits—low-income housing credit, qualified rehabilitation expenses, other credits.
9) Investment interest expense.
10) Tax preference and adjustment items needed to figure shareholder's alternative minimum tax.

Indirect deductions through an S corporation of amounts that are **not allowable** as deductions if paid or incurred directly as an individual are not allowed. For example, an individual cannot avoid the 2% floor on miscellaneous itemized deductions or the limits on personal interest by allowing an S corporation in which he or she is a shareholder to pay and deduct these amounts.

If an S corporation distributed borrowed funds to a shareholder, the corporation should separately state the *interest expense* on these funds and list as *interest expense allocated to debt-financed distributions* under other deductions on the shareholder's Schedule K-1. The shareholder deducts this interest on his or her tax return depending on how the shareholder uses the funds.

Nonseparately stated income or loss. Nonseparately stated income or loss is the net income or loss (gross income minus allowable deductions) of the corporation stated after excluding all the items that must be separately stated.

If an S corporation, or any predecessor, was a regular corporation for any of the 3 immediately preceding tax years, the S corporation is required to adjust tax preference items. In determining its income or loss from operations for tax purposes, these items, which are also items subject to alternative minimum tax and are considered tax preference items, must be adjusted. If an adjustment is made to a tax preference amount, an approximate adjustment must be made to reduce the tax preference item for purposes of the alternative minimum tax.

An S corporation may elect to *amortize corporate organizational costs* over a period of not less than 60 months. Corporation organizational costs are those that are directly connected with the creation of the corporation. They include the cost of temporary directors, organizational meetings, state incorporation fees, and accounting services related to setting up the organization. They also include the cost of legal services, such as drafting the charter, bylaws, terms of the original stock certificates, and minutes of organizational meetings.

To qualify for amortization, an organizational cost must meet **all** three of the following tests:

1) It must be incidental to the creation of the corporation. The cost must be incurred before the end of the first tax year in which the corporation is in business. A corporation using the cash method may amortize organizational expenses incurred within the first tax year even if it does not pay them in that year.
2) It must be a cost that is chargeable to a capital account.
3) It must be a cost that could be amortized over the life of the corporation, if the corporation has a fixed life. Once an amortization period is elected, it cannot be changed.

In deciding on the *ownership* of any of the outstanding stock of a corporation, the following rules apply:

1) Stock owned, directly or indirectly, by or for a corporation, partnership, estate, or trust is treated as being owned proportionately by or for its shareholders, partners, or beneficiaries.
2) An individual is treated as owning the stock owned, directly or indirectly, by or for his or her family.
3) Any individual owning (other than applying paragraph 2) any stock in a corporation is treated as owning the stock owned, directly or indirectly, by or for his or her partner.
4) The family of an individual includes only his or her brothers and sisters, half-brothers or half-sisters, spouse, ancestors, and lineal descendants.
5) Stock constructively owned by a person under paragraph 1, for applying paragraphs 1, 2, or 3, is treated as actually owned by that person. But stock constructively owned by an individual under paragraphs 2 or 3 is not treated as owned by him or her, for again applying either paragraph 2 or 3, to make another person the constructive owner of that stock.

If an S corporation is a shareholder in another corporation, the S corporation is treated as an individual. For example, if an S corporation receives a distribution of property based on the stock it holds, the tax consequences of the distribution are figured as if the S corporation is an individual and not a corporation.

The S corporation, like any other business, pays its own excise and employment taxes. However, it is subject to income taxes only in certain instances. An S corporation may be subject to the following taxes:

1) The tax on *excess net passive investment income.* Passive investment income includes gross receipts from royalties, rents, dividends, interest, annuities, and sales or exchanges of stock or securities. If the corporation's earnings and profits at the end of a tax year and its passive investment income are more than 25% of its gross receipts, the S corporation may be subject to a tax on excess net passive income.

If passive investment income is more than 25% of gross receipts for 3 consecutive tax years and the corporation has pre-S corporation earnings and profits at the end of each of those tax years, the corporation's S corporation status will be terminated. (*Gross receipts* means the total amount an S corporation receives or accrues under the method of accounting it uses to figure its taxable income).

An S corporation will not be subject to the tax on excess net passive income if it has been an S corporation for each of its tax years.

2) The tax on certain *capital gains.* An S corporation that elected S corporation status **before** 1987 may be liable for a capital gains tax if:

a) Its net long-term capital gain exceeds its net short-term capital loss by more than $25,000.

b) The excess is more than 50% of the corporation's taxable income.

c) The taxable income is more than $25,000.

3) The tax on built-in gains. If an S corporation has a net recognized *built-in gain* for any tax year beginning in the recognition period, a tax is imposed on the income of the S corporation for that tax year. The *recognition period* is the 10-year period beginning with the first day of the first tax year the corporation was an S corporation.

The net recognized built-in gain for any tax year in the recognition period is the **lesser** of:

a) The amount that would be taxable income of an S corporation for the tax year if only recognized built-in gains and recognized built-in losses were taken into account.

b) The amount that would be taxable income of the corporation if it were not an S corporation. Taxable income is the gross income of the corporation minus most deductions, including the amortization deduction for corporate organization costs allowed a corporation. But it does not include the net operating loss deduction or other special deductions for corporations, such as the dividend-received deductions.

4) The tax from recomputing a *prior-year investment credit* may apply if the corporation claimed investment credit on a prior year's corporate income tax return before it became an S corporation. If the S corporation makes an early disposition of the property the S corporation, not its shareholders, will be liable for payment of the tax.

5) The S corporation must make **Estimated Tax Payments** if the S corporation's tax liability for net unrecognized built-in gain, net passive income, and recapture of investment credit total $500, or more. The S corporation must then pay quarterly estimated tax payments which must equal 25% of the required annual estimated tax.

The annual estimated tax is the lesser of:

a) 90% of the tax shown on the return for the tax year, or if no return is filed, 90% of these taxes for the year.

b) The sum of 90% of the investment credit recapture and the tax on net recognized built-in gain, or the tax on certain capital gains shown on the tax return for the tax year or, if no return is filed, 90% of these taxes for the year.

c) 100% of any tax on excess net passive income shown on the corporation's return for the preceding year.

6) An S corporation may be liable for the *LIFO Recapture Tax* if the corporation made an election to be an S corporation after December 17, 1987, and used the LIFO inventory pricing method for its last tax year before its S election became effective. A LIFO recapture amount must be included in gross income; the recapture amount is the amount, if any, by which the amount of inventory using the FIFO method exceeds the inventory amount of such assets under the LIFO method.

When figuring *shareholder taxable income,* each shareholder reports a pro rata share of each item of income, loss, deduction, or credit that is separately stated and a pro rata share of nonseparately stated income or loss on his or her income tax return.

When it is reported on the shareholder's income tax return, the character of any item included in a shareholder's pro rata share is determined as if the item were realized directly from the source from which the S corporation realized it, or incurred in the same manner in which the corporation incurred it.

A shareholder's gross income is considered to include the shareholder's pro rata share of the gross income of the corporation. To calculate pro rata share:

1) Divide the item by the number of days in the S corporation's tax year. The resulting figure is the daily amount of the item.

2) Multiply the daily amount of the items by the percentage of stock owned by the shareholder on that day to figure the shareholder's daily part of the daily amount of the items.

3) Total the shareholder's daily parts of the daily amount of the item to figure the shareholder's pro rata share of the item for the tax year.

If there is no change in shareholders or in the percentage of stock each shareholder owns during the tax year, each shareholder's pro rata share of an item is the amount of the item times the percentage of stock owned by the shareholder during the year

Distribution to shareholders. How S corporation distributions to a shareholder are taxed first depends on whether the corporation has earnings and profits. An S corporation is not considered to have earnings and profits for tax years beginning after 1982 for which it was an S corporation. However, the corporation may have accumulated earnings and profits from years before 1983 or from tax years before an S corporation election was made.

Distributions from an S corporation that does not have any earnings and profits generally will be a nontaxable return of the shareholder's basis in the corporate stock. However, if the distributions are more than the shareholder's adjusted basis in the stock, the excess is taxable as a sale or exchange of property. If an S corporation has earnings and profits, the distributions may be taxable dividends, or they may be nontaxable or taxable as a sale or exchange of property. A shareholder who receives a distribution from an S corporation must wait until the close of the corporation's tax year to be able to figure the tax treatment of the distribution.

The S corporation's distributions may be in the form of cash or property. If the corporation distributes cash, the shareholder uses the amount received to figure the tax effect and the adjusted basis of his or her stock. If property other than cash is distributed, the amount the shareholder uses as a distribution is the fair market value of the property.

If an S corporation distributes appreciated property, the S corporation will be treated as if it has sold the property to the shareholders at fair market value. Appreciated property is S corporation property that has a fair market value that is more than its adjusted basis to the S corporation.

The amount the shareholder uses as a value to figure the tax treatment of the property distribution is the same fair market value that the S corporation used when it treated the property as if it had been sold to the shareholder for fair market value.

S corporation with no earnings and profits. If an S corporation has no earnings and profits, any distribution a shareholder receives is a return of basis in the shareholder's stock in the S corporation; as such, it reduces the adjusted basis of his or her stock in the S corporation. At the close of S corporation's tax year, the shareholder must adjust his or her basis in the S corporation's stock for all increases or decreases. This does not include the decrease to adjusted basis for any distributions during the S corporation's tax year. The shareholder then uses the adjusted basis to figure the tax treatment of any distributions received during the S corporation's tax year.

If the distributions are **less than or equal to** the adjusted bases, they are a return of capital and the adjusted basis of the shareholder's stock after being reduced for the distributions is next year's beginning adjusted basis. If the distributions are **more than** the adjusted basis of the shareholder's stock, the excess is a gain from the sale or exchange of property. As such, the gain is generally long- or short-term capital gain. The next year's beginning basis for shareholder's stock is zero.

For example, ABC, an S corporation, has no earnings and profits. ABC distributes $80,000 to its only shareholder, John Smith. His *adjusted basis* in the stock is $50,000. The amount of the distribution that exceeds his adjusted basis in the stock, $30,000 ($80,000 − $50,000), is taxable as a gain from the sale or exchange of property.

S corporation with earnings and profits.   The existence of earnings and profits is important to an S corporation if it has passive investment income or makes distributions. The presence of earnings and profits can mean that a distribution is a taxable dividend or the corporation is liable for a tax on its excess net passive income. An S corporation is not considered to have earnings and profits for tax years beginning after 1982 in which it was an S corporation. However, an S corporation can have earnings and profits from:

1) Liquidations, redemptions, and reorganizations governed by the rules of Subchapter C of the Internal Revenue Code.
2) Tax years in which the corporation was not an S corporation.
3) Any of the S corporation's tax years that begin before 1983.
4) A corporate acquisition that results in a carryover of earnings and profits under Section 381 of the Internal Revenue Code.

Earnings and profits can be reduced by an S corporation for payment of the tax from recomputing a prior-year's investment credit. This reduction of earnings and profits may affect the tax treatment of distributions by an S corporation to its shareholders. If an S corporation has earnings and profits, it may also have previously taxable income. In that case, a shareholder's treatment of a distribution is more complex than the treatment for S corporations with no earnings and profits. There is a general treatment for distributions of S corporations with earnings and profits and previous taxable income, and another treatment for S corporations that elect, with the consent of their shareholders, to first distribute earnings and profits.

Retained earnings accounts contain accumulated earnings and profits of the corporation. If the corporation has accumulated earnings and profits, it must maintain separate accounts for previously taxed income and the *accumulated adjustments account (AAA)*. The S corporation should maintain an AAA which is adjusted each year for income, losses, and expenses. The AAA is adjusted in a similar way as the shareholder's basis in the stock of the S corporation, except that no adjustments are made for tax-exempt income or related expenses. However, the amounts of any tax-exempt interest or related expenses are adjustments to the adjusted basis of the stock.

If the accumulated earnings and profits were accumulated before the corporation became an S corporation, the corporation may be liable for the tax imposed on excess net passive income. If a corporation has accumulated earnings and profits, the retained earnings and accumulated earnings and profits usually will not be the same because of the special rules for computation of retained earnings. If the earnings and profits were accumulated after the corporation became an S corporation, the rules in effect before 1983 would apply in figuring accumulated earnings and profits.

An S corporation's status can be **terminated** in any of the following ways:

1) By revoking the election.
2) By ceasing to qualify as an S corporation.
3) By violating the passive investment income restrictions on S corporations with pre-S corporation's earnings and profits.

Terminations are generally effective on the date of the terminating event.

If a corporation's status as an S corporation has been terminated, it generally must wait 5 years before it can again become an S corporation unless it gets special permission of the IRS.

An S corporation's election may be **revoked** by the corporation for any tax year. It can be revoked only if shareholders who collectively own more than 50% of the outstanding shares in the S corporation's stock consent to the revocation. The consenting shareholders must own their stock in the S corporation at the time the revocation is made.

The revocation must be made by the corporation in the form of a statement. The statement must provide:

1) That the corporation is revoking its election to be treated as an S corporation under section 1362(a) of the Internal Revenue Code.
2) The number of shares of stock, including nonvoting stock, outstanding at the time the revocation is made.
3) The date the revocation is to be effective for revocations that specify a prospective revocation.

The statement should be signed by someone authorized to sign the S corporation return. It should be sent to the service center where the corporation filed its election to be an S corporation. Attached to the revocation should be a statement of consent, signed by each consenting shareholder. It should also provide the number of shares of outstanding stock, including nonvoting stock, held by each shareholder at the time the revocation is made.

The revocation is effective:

1) On the first day of the tax year if the revocation is made by the 15th day of the 3rd month of the same tax year.
2) On the first day of the following tax year if the revocation is made after the 15th day of the 3rd month of a tax year.
3) On the date specified if the revocation specifies a date on or after the day the revocation is made.

A corporation that specifies a prospective date for revocation that is other than the first day of the tax year will **create** an S termination year.

Any termination that is effective during the tax year on a date other than the first day of that tax year will create an S termination year. The part of the S termination year ending on the date before the effective date of the termination is an 1120S (S corporation) short tax year. The part of the S termination year beginning on the first day on which the termination is effective is an 1120C (C corporation) short tax year.

After the S termination year is divided into an 1120S short year and an 1120C short year, the separately stated items of income, credit, and deductions, and the amount of the nonseparately stated income or loss must be divided between the periods. There are two methods that can be used to make the division.

1) A *pro rata* allocation.
2) An allocation based on *normal tax accounting rules.*

After the separately stated items and the nonseparately stated income or loss are divided, one set of amounts is used for the 1120S short year and the other set of amounts is used for the 1120C short year.

The corporation will have to file two returns to cover the S termination year. One covers the 1120S short year and one covers the 1120C short year. The S termination year will count only as one tax year for figuring carrybacks and carryforwards even though two returns are filed for the year.

The following pro rata method of allocation must be used unless the shareholders and S corporation specifically indicate they choose to use the other allocation method. The pro rata allocation is made in the following way:

1) Determine for the entire S termination year the amount of each separately stated item of income, loss, deduction, or credit and the amount of the nonseparately stated income or loss.
2) Divide each amount by the number of days in the S termination year.
3) Multiply the amounts from step 2) by the number of days in the Form 1120S short year. These amounts are used for the Form 1120S filed for the 1120S short year.
4) Multiply the amounts from step 2) by the number of days in the 1120C short year. These amounts are used for the Form 1120C filed for the 1120C short year.

The pro rata allocation cannot be made if 50% or more of the corporation's stock is sold or exchanged during the S termination year.

The alternate method of allocation is an allocation based on *normal accounting rules.* It can be used if the corporation chooses to use it and all persons who are or were shareholders at any time during the 1120S short year and on the first day of the 1120C short year consent to the choice.

The corporation makes the choice by filing a statement with the return for the 1120C short year, which should include the following:

1) That it chooses to have the pro rata allocation rules not apply.
2) The cause and date of the termination.
3) The signature of the person authorized to sign Form 1120S.
4) A separate statement of consent signed by each person who is, or was, a shareholder at any time during the 1120S short year and on the first day of the 1120C short year.

Under the alternate method of allocation, the corporation will report all items of income, loss, deduction, or credit based on the corporation's books and records, **including worksheets**. Therefore, the items will be split between the 1120S short year and the 1120C short year according to the time they were realized or incurred based on the corporation's books and records.

The alternate method of allocation must be used by the corporation if there is a sale or exchange of 50% or more of the stock of the corporation during the S termination year.

Form 1120S for the 1120S short year is due at the same time as Form 1120C is due for the 1120C short year, including extensions. To figure the tax on the Form 1120C for the Form 1120C short year, the taxable income for the 1120C tax year must be annualized, computed in the following way:

1) Multiply the taxable income of the 1120C short year by the number of days in the S termination year.
2) Divide the amount from step 1) by the number of days in the 1120C short year.
3) Figure the tax on the amount from step 2).
4) Multiply the tax from step 3) by the number of days in the 1120C short year.
5) Divide the amount from step 4) by the number of days in the S termination year.

To figure the corporate alternative minimum tax for the short year, the following adjustments must be made:

1) The alternative minimum taxable income for the short period is placed on an annual basis by multiplying that amount by 12 and dividing the result by the number of months in the short period.
2) The *tentative minimum tax* for the tax year will have the same relation to the tax figure on the annual basis as the number of months in the short period has to 12.

If the corporation is terminated because it **inadvertently** ceased to qualify as an S corporation or because it inadvertently violated the restriction on passive investment income, the IRS may waive the termination. The termination may be waived if the IRS determines that the termination was inadvertent, the corporation takes steps to correct the event within a reasonable period of time, and the corporation and its shareholders agree to be treated as if the event had not happened.

The S corporation may request a determination in the form of a ruling request whether the termination was inadvertent by setting forth all relevant facts pertaining to the termination event, including the date of the corporation's election to be an S corporation, a detailed explanation of the event causing termination, when and how the event was discovered, and the steps taken to return the corporation to small business corporation status.

PARTNERSHIPS

This section explains how the tax law applies to partnerships and to partners. A partnership does not pay tax on its income but passes through any profits or losses to its partners. Partners are required to include partnership items on their tax returns. The rules cited apply to both general and limited partnerships.

Definition.   A *partnership* is the relationship between two or more persons who join together to carry on a trade or business. Each person contributes money, property, labor, or skill, and each expects to share in the profits and losses. "Person" when used to describe a partner means an individual, a corporation, a trust, an estate, or another partnership.

For income tax purposes, the term "partnership" includes a syndicate, group, pool, joint venture, or similar organization that is carrying on a trade or business, and that is not classified as a trust, estate, or corporation. A *joint undertaking* to share expenses is not a partnership. Mere co-ownership of property that is maintained and leased or rented is not a partnership. However, if the co-owners provide services to the tenants, a partnership exists. If spouses carry on a business together and share in the profits and losses, they might be partners whether or not they have a formal partnership agreement.

Partnership agreement.   The partnership agreement includes the original agreement and any modifications of it. The modifications must be agreed to by all the partners or adopted in any other manner provided by the partnership agreement. The agreement or modifications can be oral or written.

Partners can modify the partnership agreement for a particular tax year after the close of the year but not later than the date for filing the partnership return for that year. The filing date does not include any extensions of time. A partner's share of income, gains, losses, deductions, or credits is usually controlled by the partnership agreement. However, the partnership agreement or any modification of it will be disregarded if the allocation of income, gains, losses, deductions, or credits to a partner under the agreement does not have substantial economic effect.

If the partnership agreement, or any modification of it, is silent on any matter, the provisions of local law are treated as a part of the agreement.

Some partnerships may be completely or partially *excluded* from being treated as partnerships for federal income tax purposes if all the partners agree. The exclusion applies only to certain investing or operating agreement partnerships where there is no active conduct of a business. It applies to the joint production, extraction, or use of property, but not to the sales of services or sales of property produced or extracted. The members of such an organization must be able to figure their income without having to figure partnership taxable income.

The partners of excluded partnerships are not exempt from partnership provisions that limit a partner's distributive share of a partnership loss, or the requirement of a business purpose for the adoption of a tax year for the partnership which is different from its required tax year. In certain circumstances, even though a choice for exclusion was not made, it will be considered to have been made if the members can show that at the time of the organization's formation, they intended to be excluded from partnership treatment. To choose *complete exclusion,* the partnership must file a partnership return for the first year it chooses to be excluded. The return must be filed by the due date for filing the return. The return needs to contain only the name, or other identification, and the address of the organization. The return or a separate statement attached to the return must contain all of the following:

1) The names, addresses, and identification numbers of all members of the organization.
2) A statement that the organization is an investing or operating agreement partnership.
3) A statement that all the members have chosen the exclusion from partnership treatment.
4) A statement indicating where a copy of the operating agreement is available.

Required tax year.   A partnership generally must conform its tax year to its partners' tax years as follows:

1) If one or more partners having the same tax year owns an interest in partnership profits and capital of more than 50% (a majority interest) the partnership must use the tax year of those partners (the *majority tax year*). The partnership determines if there is a majority interest tax year, usually the first day of the partnership's current tax year. If a partnership is required to change to a majority interest tax year, it will not be required to change to another year for 2 years following the year of change.

2) If there is no majority interest tax year, the partnership is required to use the tax year of all its principal partners. A *principal partner* is one who has a 5% or more interest in the profits or capital of the partnership.

3) If there is no majority interest tax year or the principal partners do not have the same tax year, the partnership must generally use a tax year that results in the least aggregate deferral of income to the partners. This will almost always be the same as the tax year of at least one of the partners.

The least aggregate deferral of income is determined by comparing the deferral that all the partners would get if the partnership used the tax year of one of its partners. A computation must be made for each partner whose tax year is different from the other partners as follows:

1) Determine the number of months of deferral using one partner's tax year. The months of deferral are found by counting the months from the end of the partnership's tax year forward to the end of that partner's tax year.

2) Multiply the deferral period found in step 1) by each partner's share of his or her interest in the partnership profits for the year.

3) Add the amounts figured in step 2) to get the aggregate which is the total amount of deferral.

4) Repeat steps 1) through 3) for each partner's tax year that is different from the other partners' years.

The partner's tax year that results in the lowest aggregate total number is the tax year that must be used by the partnership. If more than one year qualifies as the tax year that has the least aggregate deferral of income, the partnership may choose any year that qualifies. However, if one of the tax years that qualifies is already the partnership's existing year, the partnership must retain that year.

Example: X and Y have equal shares in a partnership that uses a fiscal year ending June 30. X uses a calendar year while Y has a fiscal year ending November 30. The partnership must change its tax year to a fiscal year ending November 30 because this results in the least aggregate deferral of income to the partners.

There are exceptions to the required tax year rule. One exception allows a partnership to use its natural business year. Another exception allows the partnership to make a Section 444 election.

Natural business year.   If a partnership establishes an acceptable business purpose for having a tax year that is different from its required tax year, the different tax year can be used. The deferral of income to the partners is not considered a business purpose.

Section 444 election.   Under Section 444 of the Code, certain partnerships may elect to use a tax year that is different from their required tax year.

A partnership is eligible to make a Section 444 election if it meets all of the following conditions.

1) It is not a member of a tiered structure. (A tiered structure, for this purpose, occurs when a partnership directly owns any part of another partnership, S corporation, or personal service corporation, or any part of the partnership itself is owned by one of these entities.) If the tiered structure consists only of partnerships, S corporations, or both, the partnership can make a Section 444 election if all the entities have the same tax year.

2) It has not made a Section 444 election before.

3) It does not choose a tax year where the deferral period is more than 3 months or the deferral period of the tax year being changed if this period is shorter.

A partnership should not make a Section 444 election when it wants to establish a business purpose for having a tax year different from its required year. If a Section 444 election is made, the deferral period is the number of months between the end of the elected tax year and the close of the required tax year.

A partnership is **not** a taxable entity, but the partnership must figure its total income and file Form 1065 which provides information on partnership income or losses for the year. A partnership computes its income and files a return in the same way as an individual does, except that a partnership must state certain items of gain, loss, income, etc., separately.

The partnership, not the partners, makes the choices about how to compute income. These include choices for general accounting methods; depreciation methods; accounting for specific items, such as depletion or installment sales; nonrecognition of gain on the involuntary conversion of property; and amortization of certain organization fees and business start-up costs of the partnership.

A partnership does not make estimated tax payments. However, the partners may have to make payments of estimated tax as a result of partnership distributions. If the partnership uses the accrual method of accounting, its deductions for expenses may depend on economic performance.

Neither the partnership nor any partner can deduct amounts paid or incurred to organize a partnership or to promote the sale of, or to sell, an interest in the partnership. The partnership can choose to amortize certain organization fees over a period of not less than 60 months. The 60-month period starts with the month the partnership begins business. If the partnership is liquidated before the end of the 60-month period, the remaining balance in this account can be deductible as a loss, but only if the 60-month amortization election has been made. Amortization applies to expenses that:

1) Are incident to the creation of the partnership.

2) Are chargeable to a capital account.

3) Would be amortized over the life of the partnership if they were incurred for a partnership having a fixed life.

Amortization does not apply to expenses connected with the issuing and marketing of interests in the partnership, such as commissions, professional fees, and printing costs. These expenses are capitalized. Syndication fees can never be deducted by the partnership even if the syndication is unsuccessful.

If a partnership begins or acquires a business, it can elect to amortize over a period of at least 60 months certain start-up expenses. To make this election, attach a statement to the partnership return for the tax year in which the amortization period begins. The amortization period starts with the month the partnership begins the business or the month it acquires a business. The statement must include a description of the expenses, the amount of the expenses, the date the expenses were paid or incurred, the month in which the partnership began or acquired the business, and the number of months in the amortization period.

Start-up expenses are amounts paid or incurred in connection with creating an active trade or business or for investigating the creation or acquisition of an active trade or business. Start-up expenses must be of a type that could be deducted in the tax year they were paid or incurred, if they were paid or incurred to expand an existing trade or business in the same field. Once the partnership chooses a period of time for amortizing start-up expenses and files the election, it cannot change to a different time period.

The original basis of an interest is **increased** by:

1) Additional contributions to the partnership.
2) The partner's distributive share of both taxable and nontaxable partnership income.
3) The excess of the deductions for depletion over the basis of the depletable property.

The original basis is **decreased**, but never below zero, by:

1) The amount of money and the adjusted basis of property distributed to the partner by the partnership.
2) The partner's distributive share of the partnership losses, including capital losses.
3) Nondeductible partnership expenses that are not capital expenditures.
4) The amount of any deduction for depletion for oil and gas wells.
5) The partner's share of any section 179 expenses, even if the partner cannot deduct the entire amount on his or her individual tax return. (Section 179 allows a deduction of up to $10,000 for the cost of depreciable property placed in service during the year.)

Partnership liabilities. A partner's basis includes a partnership liability only if, and to the extent that, the liability:

1) Creates or increases the partnership's basis in any of its assets.
2) Gives rise to a current deduction to the partnership.
3) Decreases the partner's basis in the partnership because it relates to a nondeductible partnership expense that is not a capital expenditure.

The term *assets* includes capitalized items allocable to future periods, such as organizational expenses. Partnership liabilities do not include accrued but unpaid expenses or accounts payable of a cash basis partnership. If the liabilities of a partnership are increased, resulting in an increase in a partner's share of the liabilities, this increase is treated as a contribution of money by the partner to the partnership.

If the liabilities of a partnership are decreased resulting in a decrease in a partner's share of the liabilities, this decrease is treated as a distribution of money to the partner by the partnership.

Example 1: X and Y are equal partners and their partnership borrows $1,000. The basis of the partnership interest of each is increased by $500 since each is considered to have contributed that amount to the partnership. Partners increase their basis regardless of the partnership's method of accounting.

Example 2: X and Y are equal partners and their partnership repays a $10,000 note. The basis of the partnership interest of each is decreased by $5,000 since each is considered to have received a distribution of that amount from the partnership.

Partner's share.   A partner's share of partnership liabilities depends on whether the liability is a recourse or nonrecourse liability. A liability is a *recourse liability* of the partnership to the extent that any partner has an economic risk of loss for that liability. A partner's share of such liability equals that partner's share of the economic risk of loss. A *limited partner* generally has no obligation to contribute additional capital to the partnership and, therefore, does not have an economic risk of loss in partnership liabilities.

A liability is a *nonrecourse liability* of the partnership if no partner has an economic risk of loss for that liability. A partner's share of such liability generally is determined by the partner's ratio for sharing partnership profits.

A partner has an economic risk of loss if that partner is obligated (whether by agreement or operation of law) to make a net payment to the creditor or a contribution to the partnership with respect to the liability if the partnership is constructively liquidated. A partner that is the creditor for a liability that would otherwise be a nonrecourse liability has an economic risk of loss in that liability.

Generally, in a constructive liquidation, all partnership assets (including cash) are assumed to become worthless and all partnership liabilities are assumed to become due and payable in full. Therefore, the partnership lacks the assets needed to pay off the liability and the partner or partners who have to pay it off have an economic risk of loss.

Example: X and Y form a general partnership with cash contributions of $20,000 each. Under the partnership agreement, they share all partnership profits and losses equally. They borrow $60,000 to purchase business equipment. This indebtedness qualifies as a partnership liability.

If neither partner has an economic risk of loss in the liability, it is a nonrecourse liability. Each partner's basis would include his share of the liability, $30,000 each.

If X, under the agreement, had to pay the creditor if the partnership defaulted, he would have an economic risk of loss in the liability. His basis in the partnership would be $80,000, while Y's basis would be $20,000 (the amount of Y's original contribution to the partnership).

Liquidation of partner's interest.
When payments are made by the partnership to a retiring partner or to a successor in interest of a deceased partner in return for the partner's entire interest in the partnership, the payments may have to be allocated between payments in liquidation and other payments.

For income tax purposes, a retired partner or a successor in interest to a deceased partner is vested as a partner until his or her interest in the partnership has been completely liquidated.

Payments in liquidation of a partner's entire interest, to the extent that they are made in exchange for the interest in partnership property, are treated as distributions to the partner by the partnership. Amounts paid for unrealized receivables, or for goodwill, are not treated as distributions. However, if the partnership agreement provides for payments for goodwill, these payments are treated as distributions.

Generally, the partners' valuation of a partner's interest in partnership property in an arm's length agreement will be treated as correct. If the valuation reflects only the partner's net interest in the property (total assets less liabilities), it must be adjusted so that both the value of and the basis for the partner's interest include the partner's share of partnership liabilities.

The remaining partners' distributive shares are not reduced by payments in exchange for a retired partner's interest in partnership property.

Closing of partnership year.
Generally, the partnership's tax year is not closed because of the sale, exchange, or liquidation of a partner's interest; the death of a partner; or the entry of a new partner. If a partner sells, exchanges, or liquidates his or her entire interest, the partnership's tax year is closed for that partner.

If a partner disposes of his or her entire interest in a partnership, the partner must include his or her distributive share of partnership items in taxable income for the tax year in which membership in the partnership ends. To compute the distributive share of these items, the partnership's tax year is considered ended on the date that the partner disposed of the interest. To avoid an interim closing of the partnership books, the partners can agree that the distributive share can be estimated by taking a prorated part of the amount of the items the partner would have included in income if he or she remained a partner for the entire partnership tax year.

A partner who sells or exchanges only part of an interest in a partnership, or whose interest is changed (whether by entry of a new partner, partial liquidation of a partner's interest, gift, or otherwise), reports his or her distributive share of partnership items by taking into account his or her varying interests during the partnership year.

Example: XYZ is a calendar year partnership with three partners, A, B, and C. Under the partnership agreement, profits and losses are to be shared in proportion to their contributions. As of January 1, this was 90% for A, 5% for B, and 5% for C. On December 1, B and C each contributed additional amounts so that the new profit and loss sharing ratios were 30% for A, 35% for B, and 35% for C. For its tax year ended December 31, the partnership had a loss of $1,200. This loss occurred equally over the partnership's tax year. The loss is divided among the partners as follows:

Partner	Profit or Loss Percent		Part of Year Held		Total Loss		Share of Loss
A	90	×	11/12	×	$1,200	=	$990
	30	×	1/12	×	1,200	=	30
B	5	×	11/12	×	1,200	=	55
	35	×	1/12	×	1,200	=	35
C	5	×	11/12	×	1,200	=	55
	35	×	1/12	×	1,200	=	35

If any partner's interest in a partnership changes during the tax year, each partner's share of certain cash basis items of the partnership must be determined by prorating the items on a daily basis. Then that daily portion is allocated to the partners in proportion to their interests in the partnership at the close of each day. This rule applies to the following items for which the partnership uses the cash method of accounting.

1) Interest.
2) Taxes.
3) Payments for services or for the use of property.
4) Any other item for which it is appropriate to use this rule in order to avoid significant misstatements of the partners' income.

Deceased partner.   If a partner dies, the partner's estate or other successor in interest reports in its return the decedent's distributive share of the partnership items for the partnership year ending after the death occurred. If the partnership year terminates with the death of the partner, the deceased partner's share of income for that year will be included in the deceased partner's final return.

Every partnership must file a return showing its income, deductions, and other information required. This is an information return and must be signed by one partner. The return must be filed for every tax year of the partnership even though it has no income for the year. However, the first return is not required to be filed before the first tax year in which the partnership has income or deductions.

Form 1065 must be filed on or before April 15 following the close of the partnership's tax year if the accounting period is the calendar year. A fiscal year partnership generally must file its return by the 15th day of the 4th month following the close of its fiscal year.

Partner's Income

1) Gains and losses from sales or exchanges of capital assets.

2) Gains and losses from sales or exchanges of certain property used in a trade or business and from involuntary conversions (for example, casualties, thefts, or condemnations).

3) Charitable contributions.

4) Dividends for which corporate partners can claim a deduction.

5) Certain taxes paid or accrued to foreign countries and to possessions of the United States.

6) Depletion allowances for partnership oil and gas properties.

7) Intangible drilling and development costs.

8) Recoveries of tax benefit items.

9) Gains and losses from wagering.

10) Soil and water conservation expenses.

11) IRA, Keogh, or SEP payments; alimony payments; medical insurance for a partner, a partner's spouse, and dependents; and any penalty on early withdrawal of savings.

12) Interest and taxes paid to cooperating housing corporations.

13) Any item of income, gain, loss, deduction, or credit that is allocated under the partnership agreement in a way that differs from the partnership's usual allocation of taxable income or loss.

14) Interest expense allocated to debt-financed distributions.

15) Amounts paid by the partnership that would be an itemized deduction on a partner's income tax return if paid by the partner, such as medical and dental expenses; dependent care expenses; and meal, travel, and entertainment expenses.

16) Any amount that would result in a different income tax liability for a partner if it were taken into account separately rather than as part of the total income or loss.

17) Taxable income or loss of the partnership, determined without the items requiring separate computations.

To determine the allowable amount of any deduction or exclusion that is limited, a partner must combine the amounts of any separate deductions or exclusions on their income tax return with the distributive share of partnership deductions or exclusions before applying the limit.

Basis of partner's interest.   The adjusted basis of a partner's partnership interest is ordinarily computed at the end of a partnership's tax year. However, if there has been a sale or exchange of all or a part of the partner's interest or a liquidation of his or her entire interest in a partnership, the adjusted basis is computed on the date of the sale, exchange, or liquidation.

The adjusted basis of a partner's interest is determined without considering any amount shown in the partnership books as a capital, equity, or similar account.

Example: X contributes property to a partnership that has an adjusted basis of $400 and a fair market value of $1,000. His partner contributes $1,000 cash. While under the partnership agreement each has a capital account in the partnership of $1,000, which will be reflected in the partnership books, the adjusted basis of X's interest is only $400 and his partner's basis is $1,000.

Original basis.   The original of a partnership interest is the money a partner contributed plus the adjusted basis of any property he or she contributed. If the property contribution results in taxable income to the partner, the income generally will be included in the basis of the partner's interest. Any increase in a partner's individual liabilities because of an assumption of partnership liabilities is also treated as a contribution of money to the partnership by the partner.

If the property contributed is subject to indebtedness or if a partner's liabilities are assumed by the partnership, the basis of that partner's interest is reduced by the liability that is assumed by the other partners. This partner must reduce his or her basis because the assumption of the liability is treated as though they had made a contribution of money to the partnership.

Example 1: John acquired a 20% interest in a partnership by contributing property that had an adjusted basis to him of $8,000 and was subject to a $4,000 mortgage. Payment of the mortgage was assumed by the partnership. The adjusted basis of John's interest is:

Adjusted basis of the property contributed.................... $8,000
Minus: Part of mortgage assumed by his partners that
    must be treated as a distribution of money to
    him, 80% of $4,000 3,200
Basis of John's partnership interest......................... $4,800

Example 2: If, in the above example, the property John contributed had a $12,000 mortgage, the adjusted basis of his partnership interest would be zero. The difference between the amount of the mortgage assumed by the other partners, $9,600 (80% × $12,000), and his basis of $8,000 would be treated as a gain to him from the sale or exchange of a capital asset. However, this gain would not increase the basis of John's partnership interest.

The original basis of an interest is **increased** by:

1) Additional contributions to the partnership.
2) The partner's distributive share of both taxable and nontaxable partnership income.
3) The excess of the deductions for depletion over the basis of the depletable property.

The original basis is **decreased**, but never below zero, by:

1) The amount of money and the adjusted basis of property distributed to the partner by the partnership.
2) The partner's distributive share of the partnership losses, including capital losses.
3) Nondeductible partnership expenses that are not capital expenditures.
4) The amount of any deduction for depletion for oil and gas wells.
5) The partner's share of any Section 179 expenses, even if the partner cannot deduct the entire amount on his or her individual tax return. (Section 179 allows a deduction of up to $10,000 for the cost of depreciable property placed in service during the year.)

DEPRECIATION

What can be depreciated?   Depreciable property is property for which a depreciation deduction is allowed. Many different kinds of property can be depreciated, for example, machinery, buildings, vehicles, patents, copyrights, furniture, and equipment. Property is depreciable if it meets the following requirements:

1) It must be used in business or held for the production of income.
2) It must have a determinable life, and that life must be longer than one year.
3) It must be something that wears out, decays, gets used up, becomes obsolete, or loses value from natural causes.

If property does not meet all three of these conditions, it is not depreciable.

Depreciable property can be tangible or intangible. Tangible property is any property that can be seen or touched. Intangible property is property, such as a copyright or franchise, that is not tangible. Depreciable property can be *real* or *personal*. Personal property is property, such as machinery or equipment, that is not real estate. Real property is land and generally anything that is erected on, growing on, or attached to land. However, land itself is never depreciable.

Depreciation can be deducted on tangible property only if it can wear out, decay, or lose value from natural causes; be used up; or become obsolete. Intangible property can be depreciated if its useful life can be determined. The straight-line method must be used. Patents and copyrights are two kinds of intangible property that can be depreciated. The useful life is granted by the government for a patent or copyright. If a patent or copyright becomes valueless in any year before it expires, the undepreciated cost or other basis can be deducted in that tax year.

It should be noted that *goodwill* is not depreciable because its useful life cannot be determined.

When to claim depreciation.   A business can begin to claim depreciation on property when it is placed in service in a trade or business or for the production of income. Depreciation of property is continued until the basis in the property is recovered, disposed of, or use of the property for business or investment purposes has stopped.

Depreciation not deducted.   If, in an earlier year, depreciation was not claimed for property for which deduction could be taken, the basis of the property must be reduced by the amount of the depreciation that was not deducted. The unclaimed depreciation cannot be deducted in the current year, or in any later tax year. However, the depreciation for an earlier year can be claimed on an amended return. The amended return must be filed within 3 years from the date the original return was filed, or within 2 years from the time the tax was paid, whichever is later.

Section 179 deduction.   All or part of the cost of certain qualifying property can be treated as an expense rather than as a capital expenditure. The taxpayer decides for each item of qualifying property whether to deduct, subject to the yearly limit, or capitalize and depreciate a property's cost. If an election is made for a deduction, a limited amount of the cost of qualifying property purchased for use in a trade or business is deductible in the first year the property is placed in service. For the 179 deduction, property is considered placed in service in the tax year in which the property is first placed in a condition or state of readiness and availability for a specifically assigned function, whether in a trade or business, in the production of income, in a tax-exempt or personal activity.

The determination of whether property is qualifying property is made in the first year the property is placed in service. Therefore, if property is placed in service in a tax year and the property does not qualify for the Section 179 deduction, no 179 deduction is ever allowed for the property even though the property becomes qualifying property in a later tax year.

Example: In 1989 a new car is purchased and used entirely for personal purposes. In 1990 the car is used in a trade or business. No Section 179 deduction is allowed for the car. The car was placed in service in 1989 when it was used for personal purposes.

Qualifying property.   A Section 179 deduction can be claimed on depreciable property that is Section 38 property and that is purchased for use in the active conduct of a trade or business. Property held merely for the production of income cannot be deducted. The following property does not qualify for a Section 179 deduction:

1) Property acquired by one member of a controlled group from another component member of the same group.

2) Property acquired from another person and the basis in that property is determined in whole or in part by reference to the adjusted basis of the property in the hands of the person from whom the property was acquired, or under the stepped-up basis rules for property acquired from a decedent.

3) Property acquired from a related person if the relationship to the related person would result in the disallowance of losses.

Section 38 property.   Section 38 property is property with a useful life of at least 3 years. It includes:

1) Tangible personal property (except heating or air-conditioning units).

2) Other tangible property, except most buildings and their structural components.

3) Elevators and escalators built or acquired new.

4) Single purpose livestock or horticultural structures.

5) Storage facilities (excluding buildings and their structural components) that are used in connection with distribution of petroleum or any primary product of petroleum.

Tangible personal property.   Tangible personal property is tangible property **other than** real property. Machinery and equipment are examples of tangible personal property.

Land and land improvements, such as buildings and other permanent structures and their components, are real property and, therefore, do not qualify as tangible personal property. For the same reason, swimming pools, paved parking areas, wharfs, docks, bridges, fences, and similar property also do not qualify as tangible personal property.

All business property, other than structural components, contained in or attached to a building is tangible personal property. Some property that is tangible personal property under local law may not qualify as tangible personal property for Section 179 purposes, and some property that may be real property under local law, such as fixtures, may be considered tangible personal property for Section 179 purposes. Transportation and office equipment, printing presses, testing equipment, and signs are tangible personal property. A car or truck used in a business also qualifies.

Section 38 property **does not** include:

1) Buildings and structural components.

2) Property used for lodging.

3) Certain property used predominantly outside the United States.

4) Property used by a tax-exempt organization other than a farmer's cooperative unless it is used predominantly to produce unrelated business taxable income which is subject to tax.

5) Certain property completed outside the United States or property for which less than 50% of the basis is attributable to value added within the United States.

6) Property used primarily for lodging. This includes most property used in the operation of an apartment house and most other facilities where sleeping accommodations are provided and rented (property used by a hotel, motel, inn, or similar establishment that primarily serves *transient* guests, i.e., the rental period is normally less than 30 days, or property used in nonlodging commercial facilities, such as a restaurant).

Amount to deduct. The total cost that can be elected to deduct for a tax year cannot exceed $10,000. While the maximum amount that can be deducted is $10,000, there are certain provisions that can reduce the maximum. For each dollar of cost of Section 179 property placed in service in excess of $200,000 in a tax year, the $10,000 maximum is reduced (but not below zero) by one dollar.

Example: In 1990 X Company placed in service machinery with a cost of $207,000. Since the cost of the machinery exceeds $200,000 by $7,000, Company X must reduce the maximum deduction allowed ($10,000) by $7,000. A Section 179 deduction for 1990 of $3,000 is allowed.

The total cost that can be deducted in each tax year is limited to the taxable income which is from the active conduct of any trade or business of the taxpayer during the tax year. Taxable income is figured as usual, but without taking a deduction for the cost of any Section 179 property. The amount of any cost that is not deductible in one tax year under Section 179 because of this limit can be carried to the next tax year and added to the cost of qualifying property placed in service in that tax year.

Example: Company X places in service in 1990 a machine that cost $8,000. X's taxable income from the business for 1990 is $6,000. X's Section 179 deduction is limited to $6,000. The $2,000 cost that is not allowed because of the taxable income limit can be carried to 1991.

Carryover of unallowable deduction. If the cost of Section 179 property placed in service during the tax year is $210,000 or more, a Section 179 deduction cannot be taken and cannot be carried over.

If the cost of Section 179 property placed in service during the tax year is less than $210,000, the maximum dollar limit of $10,000 is reduced by the amount, if any, by which the cost of Section 179 property placed in service during the tax year exceeds $200,000.

If the cost of Section 179 property placed in service during the tax year is $10,000 or less, the maximum dollar limit is the cost of Section 179 property placed in service during the tax year.

After determining the maximum dollar amount that applies, but never more than $10,000, the taxable income limit must be calculated. The taxable income limit is determined by figuring the taxable income from the active conduct of the business without taking any deduction for the cost of Section 179 property. If this taxable income amount is more than the maximum dollar amount allowed, the Section 179 deduction is the maximum dollar amount that can be taken, and there is no carryover to the next tax year.

If the taxable income amount is less than the maximum dollar amount, the Section 179 deduction is the taxable income amount. The carryover is the excess of the maximum dollar amount over the Section 179 deduction; the amount of the carryover will be taken into account in determining the section 179 deduction next year.

Example: John Smith, a sole proprietor of an active business, places in service in 1990 Section 179 property with a cost of $201,000. He files his return based on the calendar year. He figures that his taxable income for the limit is $6,000.

John computes his maximum dollar limit. His Section 179 property for 1990 exceeds $200,000 by $1,000. Therefore, his maximum dollar limit is $9,000 ($10,000 less $1,000). Because his taxable income of $6,000 is less than his maximum dollar limit of $9,000, his 1990 Section 179 deduction is $6,000. His carryover to 1991 is $3,000 which is the excess of his maximum dollar limit, $9,000, over his 1990 Section 179 deduction of $6,000.

MACRS—Assets Placed in Service After 1986

The *modified accelerated cost recovery system* (MACRS), also referred to as the *General Depreciation System* or (GDS), applies to all tangible property placed in service after 1986. A business could have made a property-by-property election to use MACRS for tangible property placed in service after July 31, 1986, and before January 1, 1987.

Transition property. Transition property must have a class life of at least 7 years or be residential rental or nonresidential real property that is placed in service **before:**

- 1989 if it has a class life of at least 7 but less than 20 years.
- 1991 if it has a class life of 20 years or more, or is residential rental or nonresidential real property.

To qualify it must be:

1) Property constructed, reconstructed, or acquired under a written contract that was binding on March 1, 1986.

2) Property constructed or reconstructed by the taxpayer if:

   a) The lesser of $1,000,000, or 5% of the cost of the property had been incurred or committed by March 1, 1986; **and**

   b) The construction or reconstruction of the property began by March 1, 1986;

3) An equipped building or plant facility if construction was started by March 1, 1986, under a written specific plan and more than one-half of the cost had been incurred or committed by March 1, 1986.

A *plant facility* is a facility that does not include any building, or for which buildings are an insignificant portion, and that is:

1) A self-contained single operating unit or processing operation.

2) Located on a single site.

3) Identified as a single unitary project as of March 1, 1986.

Property classes under MACRS. Each item of property depreciated under MACRS is assigned to a property class. The property classes establish the recovery periods over which the basis of items in a class are recovered. The classes of property are:

- 3-year property.
- 6-year property.
- 7-year property.
- 10-year property.
- 15-year property.
- 20-year property.
- Nonresidential real property.
- Residential rental property.

The class to which property is assigned is determined by its class life. The class life of an item of property determines its recovery period and the method of depreciation that is used. Class lives for most assets are listed in a table labeled *Table of Class Lives and Recovery Periods*. The table has a description of assets included in each asset class. At the end of each asset class description are listed the class life, the MACRS recovery period, and the alternate MACRS recovery period for the property described.

The asset class is first determined for an item of property by reading the description for the assets included in the asset class. Once the asset class into which the property fits has been determined, the MACRS recovery period assigned to that asset class is used. If the property does not fit into any of the asset classes, the property has not been assigned a class life. Property without a class life is assigned to the 7-year property recovery class.

Example: X is a building contractor. In 1990 X purchases and places a tractor in service in the business. Reading the tables, X's accountant comes to asset class 15.0 for construction assets. Since the class life is 6 years, the tractor is in the 5-year property class. The MACRS recovery period for the tractor is 5 years and the alternate MACRS recovery period is 6 years.

Recovery periods. Under MACRS, tangible property that is placed in service after 1986, or after July 31, 1986, if elected, falls into one of the following classes:

3-year property. This class includes property with a class life of 4 years or less. It includes tractor units for use over-the-road.

5-year property. This class includes property with a class life of more than 4 years but less than 10 years. It includes taxis, buses, heavy general purpose trucks, computers and peripheral equipment, and office machinery (typewriters, calculators, copiers, etc.), and any automobile, light general purpose trucks, and any property used in connection with research and experimentation.

7-year property. This class includes property with a class life of 10 years or more but less than 16 years. It includes office furniture and fixtures and any property that does not have a class life and that has not been designated by law as being in any other class.

10-year property. This class includes property with a class life of 16 years or more but less than 20 years. It includes vessels, barges, tugs, and similar water transportation equipment and any single purpose agriculture or horticultural structure and any tree or vine bearing fruits or nuts.

15-year property. This class includes property with a class life of 20 years or more but less than 25 years. It includes roads, shrubbery, wharves (if depreciable), and any municipal wastewater treatment plant.

20-year property. This class includes any property with a class life of 25 years or more. It includes farm buildings and any municipal sewers.

Nonresidential property. This class includes any real property that is not residential rental property and any real property that is section 1250 property with a class life of 27.5 years or more. This property is depreciated over 31.5 years.

Residential rental property. This class includes any real property that is a rental building or structure (including mobile homes) for which 80% or more of the gross rental income for the tax year is rental income from dwelling units. If any part of the building or structure is occupied by the taxpayer, the gross rental income includes the fair rental value of the part the taxpayer occupies. This property is depreciated over 27.5 years.

A *dwelling unit* is a house or an apartment used to provide living accommodations in a building or structure, but does not include a unit in a hotel, motel, inn, or other establishment where more than half of the units are used on a transient basis.

For depreciation purposes, property is considered *placed in service* when it is in a condition or state of readiness and availability for a specifically assigned function whether in a trade or business, in the production of income, in a tax-exempt activity, or in a personal activity. However, depreciation applies only to property placed in service in a trade or business or in production of income. For example, if property is placed in service in a personal use, no depreciation would be allowable. If the use of the property is changed to a business or income producing activity, depreciation would begin at the time of the change in use.

Example 1: On November 22, 1989, Smith purchased a machine for his business. The machine was delivered on December 7, 1989. However, the machine was not installed and in operation until January 3, 1990. Since the machine was not operational until 1990, it is considered placed in service in 1990. If the machine had been ready for use when it was delivered in 1989, it would be considered placed in service in 1989, even if not actually used until 1990.

Example 2: On April 6, 1989, Jones purchased a house to use as residential rental property. Jones made extensive repairs to the house and had the house ready for rent on July 5, 1989, at which time Jones began to advertise the house for rent. Jones began to rent the house on September 1, 1989. The house is considered placed in service in July when it was ready and available for rent. Jones can begin to depreciate the house in July.

Basis. To deduct the proper amount of depreciation each year, the basis in the property must first be determined. The basis used for figuring MACRS depreciation is the original basis for the property reduced by any Section 179 deduction claimed on the property. The original basis is usually the purchase price. However, if the property is acquired in some other way, such as inheriting it, or getting it as a gift, the original basis may have to be calculated another way.

Additions or improvements to property, including leased property, are treated as separate property items for depreciation purposes. The recovery period begins on the later of either the date the addition or improvement is placed in service, or the date the property to which the addition or improvement is made is placed in service. The recovery class of the addition or improvement is the recovery class that would apply to the underlying property if the underlying property were placed in service at the same time as the addition or improvement.

Example: Smith owns a residential rental house that he is depreciating under MACRS. If he puts an addition on the house which he places in service on January 31, 1989, he uses MACRS for the addition. Under MACRS, the addition is depreciated as residential rental property because the house to which the addition is made would be residential rental property if it had been placed in service on January 31, 1989.

Computing MACRS deductions.   The MACRS deduction can be computed in one of two ways. It can actually be computed using the applicable depreciation method and convention over the recovery period. In the alternative, the MACRS percentage table can be used. One deduction is the same under both methods.

Depreciation methods.   For property in the 3-, 5-, 7-, or 10-year class, use the double (200%) declining balance method over 3, 5, 7, or 10 years and a half-year convention. For property in the 15- or 20-year class, use the 150% declining balance method over 15 or 20 years and a half-year convention. For these classes of property, change to the straight-line method for the first tax year for which that method when applied to the adjusted basis at the beginning of the year will yield a larger deduction. Always use the straight-line method and a midmonth convention for nonresidential real property and residential rental property.

Instead of using the declining balance method, the *straight-line method* can be elected with a half-year or midquarter convention over the recovery period. The election to use the straight-line method for a class of property applies to all property in that class that is placed in service during the tax year of the election. Once made, the election to use the straight-line method over the recovery cannot be changed.

Half-year convention.   Under MACRS, the half-year convention treats all property placed in service, or disposed of, during a tax year as placed in service, or disposed of, on the midpoint that tax year.

A half-year of depreciation is allowable for the first year property is placed in service, regardless of when the property is placed in service during the tax year. For each of the remaining years of the recovery period, a full year of depreciation can be taken. If the property is held for the entire recovery period, a half-year of depreciation is allowable for the year following the end of the recovery period. If the property is disposed of before the end of the recovery period, a half-year of depreciation is allowable for the year of disposition.

Midquarter convention.   If during any tax year the total bases of depreciable property placed in service during the last 3 months of that year exceed 40% of the total bases of all depreciable property placed in service during that tax year (whether or not all of the property is subject to MACRS) a midquarter convention is used instead of a half-year convention. In determining the total bases of the property, do not include basis of either:

- Residential rental property.
- Nonresidential real property.
- Property placed in service and disposed of in the same tax year.

Under a midquarter convention, all property placed in service, or disposed of, during any quarter of a tax year is treated as placed in service, or disposed of, on the midpoint of the quarter. To figure a MACRS deduction for property subject to the midquarter convention, first calculate the depreciation for the full tax year and then multiply by the following percentages for the quarter of the tax year the property is placed in service.

Quarter of the Tax Year	Percentage
First	87.5%
Second	62.5%
Third	37.5%
Fourth	12.5%

For nonresidential real and residential rental property, a midmonth convention is used in **all** situations. Under a midmonth convention all property placed in service, or disposed of, during any month is treated as placed in service, or disposed of, on the midpoint of that month.

ACRS—Assets Placed in Service After 1980 and Before 1987

ACRS (accelerated cost recovery system) was mandatory for most tangible depreciable assets placed in service after 1980 and before 1987. MACRS must be used for assets placed in service after 1986, except for transition property and certain excluded property.

ACRS allows a recovery of the unadjusted basis of recovery property over a recovery period. The property's recovery period is determined by the class life of the property. The class life of the property places it in a 3-, 5-, 10-, 15-, 18-, or 19-year class. A recovery percentage for each year of the recovery period is prescribed for figuring the ACRS deduction. The deduction is figured by multiplying the unadjusted basis of the property by the applicable recovery percentage.

ACRS cannot be used for property placed in service before 1981 or after 1986. ACRS also cannot be used for intangible depreciable property. For depreciation purposes, property is considered placed in service when it is in a condition or state of readiness and availability for a specifically assigned function whether in a trade or business, in the production of income, in a tax-exempt activity, or in a personal activity.

Depreciation-dispositions. A *disposition* is the permanent withdrawal of property from use in a trade or business or in the production of income. A withdrawal may be made by sale, exchange, retirement, abandonment, or destruction. A gain or loss is usually recognized on the disposition of an asset by sale. If property is physically abandoned, a loss can be deducted on the adjusted basis of the asset at the time of its abandonment. There must be an *intent* to discard the asset so that it will not be used again, retrieved for sale, exchange, or other disposition.

If an asset is disposed of before the end of its specified recovery period, it is referred to as an *early disposition*. When an early disposition occurs, the depreciation deduction in the year of disposition depends on the method of depreciation used for the property and the class of property involved. If depreciated under MACRS, a depreciation deduction for the year of disposition is allowed. The depreciation deduction for the year of disposition is determined by using a half-year, midquarter, or midmonth convention.

For residential rental and nonresidential real property, a mid-month convention is always used. For all other depreciated property under MACRS, either a half-year or midquarter convention is used depending on the convention that was used when the property was placed in service.

For property for which a half-year convention was used, the deduction for the year of disposition is half of the depreciation determined for the full year.

For property for which the midquarter convention was used, first determine the depreciation for the full year and then multiply by the following percentages for the quarter of the tax year in which the property was disposed of.

Quarter of the Tax Year	Percentage
First	12.5%
Second	37.5%
Third	62.5%
Fourth	87.5%

Depreciated recapture.   All gain on the disposition of property, other than residential rental and nonresidential real property, depreciated under MACRS is recaptured as ordinary income to the extent of previously allowed depreciation deductions. For purposes of this rule, any Section 179 deduction claimed on the property is treated as depreciation. For residential rental and nonresidential real property, there is no recapture of previously allowed depreciation.

Property under ACRS.   A gain or loss will generally be recognized for property disposed of that is section 1245 recovery property and depreciated under ACRS. Gain on the disposition is ordinary income to the extent of prior depreciation deductions taken. This recapture rule applies to all personal property in the 3-, 5-, and 10-year classes.

If section 1250 real property is disposed of at a gain, the property is treated as section 1245 recovery property; gain will be recognized as ordinary income to the extent of prior depreciation deductions taken. This rule applies to all section 1250 real property **except:**

1) 15-, 18-, 19-year real property that is residential rental property.

2) 15-, 18-, 19-year real property for which depreciation was elected using the ACRS method.

3) 15-, 18-, 19-year real property that is subsidized low-income housing.

For purposes of these recapture rules, the Section 179 deduction and 50% of the investment credit which reduced the basis are treated as depreciation.

Before the ACRS method was enacted, other depreciation methods were used. If property placed in service before 1981 does not qualify for ACRS or MACRS, the methods in place must continue to be used; however, those methods cannot be used for property that qualifies for ACRS or MACRS.

There are many different methods of figuring depreciation that are acceptable. Any method is acceptable that is reasonable and applied consistently. The two most common methods used are the straight line method and the declining balance method. If ACRS or MACRS does not apply, either of these methods can be used. For both of these methods, three factors must first be determined:

1) The property's basis.

2) The property's useful life.

3) The property's estimated salvage value at the end of its useful life.

The amount of the depreciation deduction in any year will depend on which method of depreciation is applied. If the method of depreciation is changed, the change is usually the result of a change in accounting method. IRS approval of a change must be obtained, except a change from the declining balance method to the straight-line method at any time during the useful life of the property can be made without permission from the IRS. Once the change to the straight-line method is made, a change back to the declining balance method, or to any other method of depreciation, cannot be made for a period of 10 years without written permission from the IRS.

INTEREST EXPENSE

Definitions. The following terms defined are frequently used in the personal tax laws covering the deductibility of nonbusiness and noninvestment kinds of interest expense.

Acquisition Debt—Any loan secured by a main or second home and used to buy, build, or improve a home.

Allocation of Interest—The method of tracing the use of loan proceeds to determine how much interest can be deducted for federal income tax purposes.

Amortization of Interest—A deductible expense allowed by spreading the cost of an asset over a period of time.

Below-Market Interest Rate Loan—A loan on which no interest is charged or on which interest is charged at a rate below the federal rate.

Capitalized Interest—Interest added to the cost of personal property, rather than deducting it on the taxpayer's return.

Debt—An obligation to pay a sum of money by certain and express agreement.

Demand Loan—A loan payable in full at any time upon the lender's demand.

Eligible Debt—Includes all debt **except** any debt with:

1) Permanently nondeductible interest, such as tax-exempt interest.
2) Personal interest.
3) Qualified home mortgage interest.
4) Interest incurred by a tax-exempt organization.
5) Interest attributable to a debt between a taxpayer and certain related parties, or between the parties themselves, if the rate of interest is less than the applicable federal interest rate.

Foregone Interest—The amount of interest that would be payable on a loan if the interest were figured at the applicable federal rate over the amount of interest actually paid on the loan.

Gift Loan—A loan where the foregoing of interest is treated as a gift.

Graduated Payment Mortgage (GPM)—Monthly mortgage payments that increase each year for a certain number of years, then remain at the same level.

Home Acquisition Debt—Any loan secured by a person's main or second home and used to buy, build, or improve the home.

Home Equity Debt—Any loan secured by a person's main or second home that is not acquisition debt. The interest on home equity debt is fully deductible on indebtedness of $100,000 or less ($50,000 or less if married filing a separate return). The debt may not exceed the fair market value of the main or second home reduced by any acquisition debt on that home.

Installment Plan Purchase—The purchase of an item on credit that allows the taxpayer to pay a portion of the amount owed every month, or other specified period. The amount owed is the cost of the item plus interest on the credit purchase.

Interest—The amount paid for the use of borrowed money.

Investment Interest Expense—The interest paid or accrued on a loan the funds from which were allocable to investment property.

Main Home—A taxpayer has only one main home, which is the property lived in most of the time. It may be a house, condominium, cooperative, mobile home, boat or similar property. It must provide basic living accommodations including sleeping space, toilet, and cooking facilities.

Mortgage Prepayment Penalty—An amount charged to a borrower who pays off a mortgage early.

Passive Activity Interest—Interest on a loan used to invest in a passive activity. (A passive activity, generally, is any activity involving the conduct of any trade or business in which the taxpayer does not **materially** participate).

Personal Interest—Any interest paid on a loan the proceeds of which are used for personal reasons; for example, to pay for a car, boat, furniture, or a vacation.

Points (paid by the borrower)—A general term used to describe the charges paid by a borrower when getting a home mortgage. Points are also known as loan origination fees, maximum loan charges, or premium charges.

Points (paid by the seller)—Also known as loan placement fees. The seller sometimes must pay this fee to the lender to arrange financing for the buyer.

Portfolio Expenditure Interest—Interest on a loan, the proceeds of which are generally used to purchase stocks or bonds.

Production Period—For real property, the production period begins when physical activity is first performed on the property.

Reverse Mortgage Loan—A loan in which the lender pays the borrower the loan proceeds in installments over a period of time. If the borrower is a cash method taxpayer, only the interest actually paid on this type of loan can be deducted.

Second Home—Property which has been selected to be a second home. It may be a house, condominium, cooperative, mobile home, boat or similar property. It must provide basic living accommodations, including sleeping space, toilet and cooking facilities.

Shared Appreciation Mortgage (SAM)—This type of loan involves the borrower paying a fixed rate of interest as well as a contingent interest. The contingent interest is based on the appreciation in the value of the home.

Term Loan—A loan the maturity of which is usually longer than 5 years.

Traced Debt—Debt allocated to a particular cost by tracing payments made from the debt's proceeds to that cost.

Unstated Interest (imputed interest)—Interest that is treated as paid on certain loans that do not provide adequate stated interest payments.

Allocation of Interest

The rules for deducting interest vary, depending on whether it is used for business, personal home, mortgage, investment or passive activities. If the proceeds of a loan are used for more than one expense, an allocation must be made to determine the amount of interest for each use of the loan's proceeds.

The most advantageous way to allocate interest is to keep the proceeds of a particular loan separate from any other funds. If the proceeds are deposited in an account containing other funds, or received in cash, the loans should generally be used for a specific purpose within 15 days if they are not intended to allocate interest.

In general, the interest on a loan is allocated in the same way as the loan itself is allocated. This is true even if the funds are paid directly to a third party. Loans are allocated by tracing disbursements to specific uses. If the interest expense must be allocated, use the following categories:

1) A loan is allocated according to the use of its proceeds. The interest on a loan is allocated in the same way as the loan is allocated for the same time period. Loan proceeds and the related interest are allocated only by reference to the use of the proceeds. The allocation is not affected by the use of property that secures the loan.

   For example, when property is used in a trade or business as security for a loan and the proceeds used to buy an auto for personal use, the interest expense on the loan must be allocated to the personal expenditure for the auto even though the loan is secured by business property.

2) A loan is allocated to a particular use from the date the proceeds are used to the earlier, the date the loan is repaid or the date the loan is reallocated to another use.

3) If at the time any part of a loan is repaid, and the loan is allocated to more than one use, the loan is treated as repaid in the following order:

   a) Amounts allocated to personal use.

   b) Amounts allocated to investments and passive activities (other than those included in c) below).

   c) Amounts allocated to passive activities in connection with a rental real estate activity in which the taxpayer actively participates.

   d) Amounts allocated to former passive activities.

   e) Amounts allocated to a trade or business use and to expenses for certain low-income housing projects.

Special rules apply to the allocation of interest expense in connection with debt-financed acquisition of, and distributions from, *Partnerships and S corporations*. These rules will not apply if the partnership or S corporation is formed or used for the principal purpose of avoiding the interest allocation rules.

Debt-financed Acquisitions is the use of loan proceeds to purchase an interest in an entity or to make a contribution to the capital of the entity. If an interest in an entity is purchased, the loan proceeds and the interest expense are allocated among all the assets of the entity. The allocation can be based on the fair market value, book value, or adjusted basis of the assets, reduced by any debts allocated to the assets.

If the taxpayer contributes to the capital of an entity, the allocation is based on the assets or by tracing the loan proceeds to the entity's expenditures. A purchase of an interest in an entity is treated as a contribution to capital to the extent the entity receives any proceeds of the purchases.

For example, an interest in a partnership is purchased for $20,000 using $75,000 of borrowed funds. The partnership's only assets include machinery used in its business valued at $60,000, and stocks valued at $15,000. The loan proceeds are allocated based on the value of the assets. Therefore, $16,000 of the loan proceeds ($60,000/$75,000 × $20,000) and the interest expense on that part are allocated to trade or business use. $4,000 ($15,000/$75,000 × $20,000) and the interest on that part are allocated to investment use.

If *debt-financed distributions* are allocated to partners or shareholders, the distributed loan proceeds and related interest expense must be reported to the partners and shareholders separately. This is because the loan proceeds and the interest expense must be allocated depending on how the partner or shareholder uses the proceeds. For example, if a shareholder uses distributed loan proceeds to invest in a passive activity, that shareholder's portion of the entity's interest expense on the loan proceeds is allocated to a passive activity use.

If the lender pays a *third party* for the borrower, the borrower allocates the loan based on the reason the third party received the funds. If the loan proceeds are not given directly to the borrower, the loan is allocated based on the use of the funds. This would apply if the borrower pays for property, services, or anything else by incurring a loan, or if the borrower takes property subject to debt.

For example, John Smith, a calendar year taxpayer, borrows $100,000 on January 4 and immediately uses the proceeds to open a checking account that pays no interest. No other amounts are deposited in the account during the year, and no part of the loan principal is repaid during the year. On April 1, John uses $20,000 of the loan proceeds held in the account for a passive activity expenditure. On September 1, John uses an additional $40,000 of the loan proceeds held in the account for a personal expenditure.

Under the interest allocation rules, the entire $100,000 loan is allocated to an investment expenditure for the period January 4 through March 31. From April 1 through August 31, John must allocate $20,000 of the loan to the passive activity expenditure, and $80,000 of the loan to the investment expenditure. From September 1 through December 31, he must allocate $40,000 of the loan to the personal expenditure, $20,000 to the passive activity expenditure, and $40,000 to the investment expenditure.

The *order of funds spent from an account* that are loan proceeds deposited in an account generally are treated as used (spent) **before** any unborrowed amounts in the same account and before any amounts deposited after the loan proceeds.

If the proceeds of a loan are received in *cash,* any expenditure up to the amount of the loan is treated as being paid from the loan's proceeds, if the expenditure is made within **30 days** before or after the proceeds of the loan are received. The expenditure can be made from any account or from cash. Also the expenditure can be treated as made on the date the cash is received. Otherwise, loan proceeds received in cash are treated as personal loans.

If the borrower has a line of credit or similar arrangement for *continuous borrowings,* all borrowings on which interest accrues at the same fixed or variable rate are treated as a single loan, and borrowings or parts of borrowings on which interest accrues at different fixed or variable rates are treated as different loans. These loans are treated as repaid in the order in which they are treated as repaid under the loan agreement.

Interest capitalization. Under the uniform capitalization rules, interest on debt must generally be capitalized if used to finance the production of real or tangible personal property. The property must be used in a trade or business or held for sale to customers. Interest on a debt on property that was acquired and held for resale does not have to be capitalized. Interest paid or incurred during the product period must be capitalized if the property produced is *qualified property.* Qualified property is:

1) Real property.
2) Personal property with a class life of 20 years or more.
3) Personal property with an estimated production period of more than 2 years.
4) Personal property with an estimated production period of more than one year, if the estimated cost of production is more than $1,000,000.

Property is considered to be *produced property* if constructed, built, installed, manufactured, developed, improved, created, raised, or the property is grown.

Capitalized interest is treated as a cost of the property produced. This interest is recovered when the property is sold, used, or otherwise disposed of under the rules that apply to such transactions. Capitalized interest is recovered through cost of goods sold, an adjustment to basis, depreciation, or other method.

Interest capitalization applies to interest paid or incurred on any debt allocable to the costs of producing qualified property that must be capitalized. For example, these costs would include planning and design activities which are generally incurred before the production period begins, as well as the costs of raw land and materials acquired before the production period begins. Also included are any costs incurred under a contract for property produced by a third party.

Interest on a debt incurred to finance any asset used in the production of property (for example, manufacturing equipment and facilities) must also be capitalized to the extent the interest is paid or incurred during the production of the property. If an asset is used in the production of property and for other purposes, capitalize only the portion of the interest associated to the production activity.

Partnership and S corporations. The interest capitalization rules are applied first at the level of the partnership or S corporation, and then at the level of the partners or shareholders. These rules are applied to the extent that the partnership or S corporation has insufficient debt to support production or construction costs.

A shareholder in an S corporation may have to capitalize interest incurred during the tax year for the production costs of the S corporation. A partner in a partnership may have to capitalize interest incurred during the tax year with respect to the production costs of the partnership. Similarly, interest may have to be capitalized if incurred by the partnership with respect to the partners' own production costs.

CORPORATION NET OPERATING LOSSES

Figuring a net operating loss (NOL). A corporation's NOL is figured the same way as its taxable income. Start with the corporation's gross income and subtract its deductions. If the deductions are more than the gross income, the result is an NOL. However, there are rules for computing the NOL that either limit what can be deducted, or permit deductions that are not ordinarily allowed. These rules are:

1) Dividends received can be deducted without limiting to a percentage of the corporation's taxable income.

2) Dividends paid on certain preferred stock of public utilities can be deducted without limiting to the taxable income for the year.

Dividends-received deduction. A corporation can take a deduction for 80% of dividends received or accrued if it owns 20% or more of the stock of the paying domestic corporation. If a corporation owns less than 20% of the paying domestic corporation, it can take a deduction for only 70% of dividends received or accrued.

Generally, the amount of the dividends-received deduction is limited to 70% or 80% of the taxable income of the corporation receiving the dividend. However, if a corporation sustains an NOL for a tax year, the limitation of 70% or 80% of the taxable income does not apply. In determining if a corporation has an NOL, the dividends-received deduction is figured without regard to the 70% or 80% of taxable income limitation.

Example: A corporation had $500,000 gross income from business operations and $625,000 of allowable business expenses. It also received $150,000 in dividends from a domestic corporation in which it was a 20% owner. The NOL is figured as follows:

Income from business........................	$500,000
Dividends....................................	150,000
Gross income...............................	$650,000
Deductions (expenses)........................	625,000
Taxable income before special deductions........	$ 25,000
Minus: Deduction for dividends received (not limited to 80% of taxable income), 80% of $150,000...........................	$120,000
Net operating Loss.........................	($ 95,000)

Using an NOL. A corporation figures how much of its NOL to deduct in the year it is carried to by **subtracting** from the NOL the modified taxable income of any earlier carryback or carryover years. If the NOL available for a carryback or carryover year is greater than the taxable income for that year, the corporation must modify its taxable income to figure how much of the NOL is used up in that year and how much may be carried to the next tax year.

Unless a corporation elects to forego the carryback period, it must first carry the entire NOL to the earliest carryback year, then carry any excess NOL after subtracting modified tax income, to the net carryback year, and so on.

Modified taxable income. Modified taxable income is figured in the same way as taxable income, but the corporation must figure the corporation's deduction for charitable contributions without considering any NOL carrybacks. Modified taxable income is used only to figure how much of an NOL is used up in the carryback or carryover year, and how much to carry to the next year. It is not used to fill out the corporation's tax return or figure its tax.

Ownership change. A corporation that has an ownership change is limited in the amount of taxable income that can be offset by NOL carryovers arising before the date of the ownership change. This limit applies to any year ending after the change.

NOL worksheets. Two NOL worksheets are available to help the tax-payer figure an NOL deduction and how much of an NOL is used up in a carry-back or carryover year. There are two worksheets because the computations required for years ending before 1987 are different from those required for years ending after 1986. For example, if a business loss was sustained in 1989 which required an NOL to be carried back to 1986, 1987, and 1988, a separate NOL worksheet for each of those tax years would be used. One NOL worksheet would be marked "for carryback or carryover years ending before 1987," for 1986. For 1987 and 1988, two separate worksheets would be used marked "For carryback or carryover years ending after 1986."

Do not use a worksheet if an NOL to be carried to a year is equal to or less than taxable income (taxable income minus the zero bracket amount for 1986) for that year. If the NOL is equal to or less than the taxable income for the year, the whole amount is deductible for the year to which the loss is carried.

If an NOL to be carried to a year is more than taxable income (taxable income minus the zero bracket amount for 1986) for that year, the NOL worksheets that follow can be used to figure the amount of the loss used in that year and the unused part of the loss to be carried to the next tax year.

The following steps can be used as a guide to figuring and using an NOL.

1) If it is determined that the business has an NOL, decide whether to carry it back and claim a refund of taxes paid in a prior year, or whether to forego the carryback period and only carry the loss forward.

2) If the taxpayer does not choose to forego the carryback period, carry the 1989 NOL back 3 years to 1986. If the taxpayer elects to forego the carryback period, the NOL will first be used in 1990.

3) Figure how much of the NOL is used up in the year it is first carried to, and how much to carry on to another year.

4) Deduct the NOL. If the NOL was carried back, refigure the tax for the carryback year and file either the corporate Form 1139 or Form 1120X.

DEDUCTING BUSINESS EXPENSES

Business expenses are the normal and current costs of carrying on a trade, business, or profession, and are usually deductible, provided that the business is operated to make a profit.

This review covers the kinds of expenses that can be deducted, the year in which the expenses can be deducted, and the limits on how much can be deducted. It is important to distinguish costs that are capital expenses from costs that are deductible expenses. Otherwise, the entire amount spent may be required to be capitalized, even if part of the cost can be deductible as an expense.

To be deductible, a business expense must be both ordinary and necessary. An **ordinary** expense is one that is common and accepted in the particular field of business, trade, or profession claiming the expense deduction. A **necessary** expense is one that is helpful and appropriate for the specific trade, business, or profession. An expense does not have to be indispensable to be considered necessary.

It is important to separate business expenses from 1) the expenses used to figure the cost of goods sold, and 2) capital expenses. In addition, business expenses must be kept separable from personal expenses. If an expense is partly for business and partly personal, the expense must separate the personal part from the business part.

Cost of goods sold.   If the business manufactures products or purchases them for resale, some of the expenses are for the products that are sold.

These expenses are used to figure the cost of the goods sold during the taxable year. Cost of goods sold is subtracted from the total amount the business takes in to figure its gross profit for the year. If an expense is used to figure cost of goods sold, it cannot be deducted again as a business expense. Among the expenses that go into figuring cost of goods sold are:

1) The cost of products or raw materials in inventory, including the cost of having them shipped to the business.
2) The cost of storing the products that are sold.
3) Direct labor costs (including contributions to pension or annuity plans) for workers who produce the products.
4) Depreciation on machinery used to produce the products.
5) Factory overhead expenses.

Under the uniform capitalization rules, all indirect costs incurred because of production and resale activities are required to be included in cost of goods sold. Indirect costs include rent, interest, taxes, storage, purchasing, processing, repackaging, handling, and general and administrative costs. This rule on indirect costs does not apply to personal property acquired for resale if the average annual gross receipts for the business for the preceding 3 tax years are not more than $10 million.

Capital expenses.   Some costs must be capitalized rather than deducted. These costs are considered a part of the investment in the business and are called *capital expenses*. There are, in general, three types of costs that must be capitalized:

1) Going into business.
2) Business assets.
3) Improvements.

The costs of *getting started in business* and before actual business operations are begun are all capital expenses. These expenses are treated as capital expenses and are a part of the investor(s) basis in the business. Capital expenses become a part of the **basis** in the business and its assets. Basis is a way of measuring an investment in an asset for tax purposes. The basis is used to figure depreciation deductions, casualty losses, and gain or loss on an eventual sale of an asset.

What is spent for any asset for use in the business for more than one year is a *capital expenditure*. There are many different kinds of business assets, i.e., land, buildings, machinery, furniture, trucks, patents and franchise rights. The full cost of an asset, including freight and installation charges, must be capitalized. Under the uniform capitalization rules, direct and indirect costs incurred in producing real or tangible personal property for use in the trade or business must be capitalized.

The cost of making **improvements** to a business asset are capital expenses, if the improvements add to the value of the asset, appreciably lengthen the time the asset can be used, or adapt the asset to a different use. Ordinarily, the cost of the improvement is added to the basis of the improved property. Improvements include such items as new electric wiring, a new roof, a new floor, new plumbing, strengthening for a wall, and lighting improvements.

How much can be deducted?   A business cannot deduct more for an expense than the amount actually spent. There is no other limit on how much can be deducted provided that the amount is reasonable. If deductions are large enough to produce a net business loss for the year, the amount of tax loss may be limited. If the deductions for an investment or business activity are more than the income it brings in, a net loss results. There may be limits on how much, if any, of the loss can be used to offset income from other sources. If a business activity is carried on with the intention of not making a profit, the loss from the activity cannot be used to offset other income. In general, a deductible loss from a business or investment activity is limited to the amount of investment that is *at-risk* in the activity. Any money invested in the business is considered to be at-risk. Amounts borrowed for use in the business are considered to be at-risk. Deductions from passive activities can be used only to offset the income from the passive activities. Any excess deductions cannot be deducted against other income. A passive activity can be defined as any activity that involves the conduct of any trade or business, and in which the investor(s) does not materially participate. (Any rental activity is a passive activity even if the owner(s) materially participates in the activity.)

When can an expense be deducted?   Under the cash method of accounting, business expenses are deducted in the tax year they are actually paid—even if they were incurred in an earlier year. Under the accrual method of accounting, business expenses are deductible when the business becomes liable for them—whether or not they are paid in the same year that they are incurred. All events that set the amount of the liability must have happened, and the expense must be figured with reasonable accuracy.

Economic performance rule.   Under the accrual method, business expenses are usually not deductible until economic performance occurs. If the expense is for property or services provided, or for the use of property by the business, economic performance occurs as the property or service is provided, or as the property is used. If the expense is for property or service that the business provides to others, economic performance occurs when the property or service is provided.

Expenses paid in advance cannot be deducted in advance, under either the cash or the accrual method. For example, assume a business signs a 10-year lease and immediately pays rent for the first 3 years. Even though the rent is paid in advance, only the rent for the current tax year can be deducted. The rent for the remaining two years must be deducted the following year and the year after. This same rule applies to prepaid interest, prepaid insurance premiums, and any other expense that is paid far enough in advance to, in effect, create an asset extending substantially beyond the end of the current tax year.

Not-for-profit activities.   If a business activity, or an activity which an individual has invested in, is not carried on to make a profit, the deductions for it are limited and no loss will be allowed to offset other income. Activities done as a hobby, or mainly for sport or recreation, come under this limit. So would an investment activity that is intended only to produce tax losses for the investors.

The limit on not-for-profit losses applies to individuals, partnerships, estates, trusts, and S corporations. It does not apply to corporations other than S corporations.

In determining whether an activity is carried on for profits, all the facts in regard to the activity are taken into account. No one factor alone is decisive. Among the factors to be considered are:

1) Whether you carry on the activity in a businesslike manner.

2) Whether the time and effort the taxpayer puts into the activity indicate that the intent is to make the activity profitable.

3) Whether the income from the activity is used for the livelihood of the owner of the business.

4) Whether the losses from the activity are due to circumstances beyond the owner's control, or are normal in the start-up phase of the business.

5) Whether the methods of operation are changed in an attempt to improve the profitability of the activity.

6) Whether the organizers of the activity have the knowledge needed to carry on the activity as a successful business.

7) Whether the organizers of the activity have been successful in making a profit in similar activities in the past.

8) Whether the activity makes a profit in some years, and how much profit it makes.

9) Whether future profit can be expected from the appreciation of the assets used in the activity.

Limits on deductions and losses.   If the activity is not carried on for profit, deductions are allowed only in the following order, only to the extent stated in the three categories, and only if the deductions are itemized on Schedule A of Form 1040.

Category 1. Deductions that can be taken for personal as well as for business activities are allowed in full. All nonbusiness deductions, such as those for interest, taxes, and casualty losses, belong in this category and are deducted on the appropriate lines of Schedule A, Form 1040.

Category 2. Deductions that do not result in an adjustment to the basis of property are allowed next, but only to the extent that the taxpayer's gross income from the activity is more than the deductions he/she has taken, or could take for it, under Category 1. Most business deductions belong in this category.

Category 3. Business deductions that decrease the basis of property are allowed last, but only to the extent that the gross income from the activity is more than deductions taken, or could be taken, under the first two categories. The deductions for depreciation, amortization, and the portion of a casualty loss not deductible in Category 1 belong in this category. Where more than one asset is involved, depreciation and these other deductions must be divided proportionally among those assets.

Example:

Gross Income		$3,200
Less Expenses:		
Real estate taxes	$700	
Interest on mortgage	$900	
Insurance	$400	
Utilities	$700	
Maintenance	$200	
Depreciation on auto	$600	
Depreciation on machine	$200	
Total Expenses		$3,700
Loss		$ 500

The interest on the mortgage is deductible in full. The deductions are limited to $3,200, the amount of gross income earned from the activity. The limit is reached in category 3), as follows:

Limit on Deduction		$3,200
Category 1. Taxes and Interest	$1,600	
Category 2. Insurance, utilities,		
maintenance	1,300	2,900
Available for Category 3		$ 300

The $300 for depreciation is divided between the automobile and the machine as follows:

$600/$800 × $300 = $225 automobile depreciation.
$200/$800 × $300 = $ 75 machine depreciation.

The basis of each asset is reduced accordingly.

Employees' pay.   Salaries, wages, and other forms of pay given to employees are deductible business expenses. However, a deduction for salaries and wages must be reduced by any jobs credit determined for the tax year.

Employees' wages and salaries paid to produce real or tangible personal property or to acquire property for resale generally must be capitalized or included in inventory. Personal property acquired for resale is not subject to this rule if gross receipts are $10,000,000 or less. Salaries and other expenses incurred for constructing capital assets cannot be deducted. They should be included in the basis of the constructed asset and covered through depreciation allowances.

Mining and manufacturing businesses include most of their salaries, wages, or other compensation expenses as part of cost of goods sold. They cannot deduct such items as current business expenses. To be deductible, employees' pay must meet four tests, i.e., ordinary and necessary, reasonable, for services performed, paid or incurred. Employers can be asked to prove that salaries, wages, and other payments for employees' services are ordinary and necessary expenses directly connected with the trade or business. What is reasonable to pay is determined by the facts. Usually, it is the amount that ordinarily would be paid for these services by similar enterprises under similar circumstances.

The employer must prove that the payments were made for services actually performed. The payments must actually have been made or incurred during the tax year. If the cash method of accounting is used, the expense for salaries and wages can be deducted only during the tax year.

Vacation pay.   Vacation pay is any amount paid or to be paid to an employee while the employee is on vacation. Vacation pay also includes amounts paid an employee when the employee chooses not to take a vacation. Vacation pay does not include amounts for sick pay or holiday pay. If the cash basis of accounting is used, vacation pay can be deducted when the employee is paid. If an accrual basis of accounting is used, vacation pay earned by employees can be deducted in the year earned only if the amount is paid at the close of the tax year, or if the amount is vested within 2 months after the close of the year. If it is paid later than this, it is deducted in the year actually paid.

Meals and entertainment.   A business generally can deduct 80% of business-related meal and entertainment expenses. This limit applies to employers even if they reimburse their employees for 100% of the expenses.

The 80% limit applies to meal expenses incurred while traveling away from home on business, in entertaining business customers at the place of business or a restaurant, or in attending a business convention or reception, business meeting, or business luncheon at a club. The limit may apply to meals furnished on the premises to employees. Taxes and tips relating to a meal or entertainment activity are included in the amount subject to the 80% limit. However, the cost of transportation to and from a business meal or entertainment activity that is otherwise allowable is not subject to the 80% limit.

The 80% limit on meal and entertainment expenses applies if the expense is otherwise deductible. The limit applies to trade or business expenses, to expenses incurred for the production of income including rental or royalty income, and to deductible education expenses.

It must be shown that meal and entertainment expenses are directly for, or associated with, the conduct of the trade or business, or are covered by one of the exceptions. (Some of the exceptions to the 80% limit must still meet other restrictions.) To be deductible, the expense must be an ordinary and necessary expense of carrying on the trade or business, and the taxpayer must be able to prove the expense.

Costs chosen to deduct or to capitalize.   There are certain costs that a business can choose **either** to deduct or to capitalize. The choice usually depends upon when it is best for the business to recover the costs. If a cost is deducted as an expense, it is recovered in full, i.e., recovered from income. If a cost is capitalized it can be recovered through a Section 179 deduction or periodic deductions for depreciation, amortization, or depletion. The costs that can be deducted or capitalized include:

1) Certain carrying charges on property.
2) Research and experimental costs.
3) *Intangible* drilling and development costs for oil, gas, and geothermal wells.
4) Exploration costs for new mineral deposits.
5) Mine development costs for a new mineral deposit.
6) Costs of increasing the circulation of a newspaper or other periodical.
7) Costs of making public transportation vehicles, buildings, and other facilities more accessible.

The decision to capitalize or to deduct belongs to the business entity—the sole proprietor, partnership, corporation, estate, or trust. Individual partners, shareholders, and beneficiaries do not make the choice themselves (except for exploration costs for a new mineral deposit).

Amortization.   A **part** of certain capital expenses can be deducted each year as amortization. Amortization allows these certain expenses to be recovered in a way that is similar to straight-line depreciation. Only certain specified expenses can be amortized for federal income tax purposes.

Since amortization sometimes allows a write-off of costs that are not ordinarily deductible, a taxpayer may want to recover eligible costs by electing to take amortization deductions. Business start-up costs, pollution control facilities, and research and experimental costs are costs that are commonly amortized. (They must be amortized over a period of *not less than 60 months.*)

If a taxpayer owns mineral property, an oil, gas, or geothermal well, or standing timber, a deduction can be taken for *depletion.* The taxpayer must have an economic interest in the mineral deposits or standing timber.

RICs, REITs, REMICs

- RIC—*regulated investment company*
- REIT—*real estate investment trust*
- REMIC—*real estate mortgage investment conduit*

A *regulated investment company* is any domestic corporation

1) Which at all times during the taxable year is registered as an investment company under the Investment Company Act of 1940 as a management company or unit investment trust, **or** has in effect an election under such Act to be treated as a business development company; **or**
2) Which is a common trust fund or similar fund excluded by the Act from the definition of "investment company" and is not included in the definition of a *common trust fund* by Section 584(a).

A regulated investment company's (RIC) income from a partnership or trust will be treated as derived from RIC business only when it can be shown to qualify as income. Here, the 30% test can be applied to specified sales or dispositions not specifically involved with the company's principal business. Any profits occurring after the adoption of a plan of complete liquidation are not taken into account under this test when the RIC liquidation comes about in the year when the plan was adopted. In some instances, a fund belonging to a series would not be disqualified under the 30% test on sales resulting from, and occurring within, five days of abnormal redemptions.

REIT.   The term *real estate investment trust* means a corporation, trust, or association which meets the qualifying conditions. In order for a REIT to qualify, it must be an organization:

1) Which is managed by one or more trustees or directors.
2) The beneficial ownership of which is evidenced by transferable shares or by transferable certificates of beneficial interest.
3) Which would be taxable as a domestic corporation but for the provisions of Section 856, Chapter 1, Subchapter M, Part 11 of the Code.
4) Which in the case of a taxable year beginning before October 5, 1976, does not hold any property, other than foreclosure property, primarily for sale to customers in the ordinary course of its trade or business.
5) Which is neither a financial institution to which Section 585, 586, or 593 apply, nor an insurance company to which Subchapter L applies.
6) Beneficial ownership of which is held by 100 or more persons.
7) Which would not be a personal holding company as defined in section 542, if all of its gross income constituted personal holding company income as defined in section 543.
8) Which is not closely held as determined under Section 856(h).

The IRS may waive a real estate investment trust (REIT) dividend distribution quota for a year if the REIT is not in a position to meet the quota because distribution was made to get around Code Sec. 4981 excise tax on undistributed income. Additionally, when specific conditions are satisfied, sums received or accrued from a tenant could be treated as rents from real property. A similar rule relates to interest.

A REIT may reduce its capital gain net income by the amount of REIT net ordinary losses. Computation of REIT taxable income includes the net income resulting from the sale of foreclosed property.

REMIC. The term *real estate mortgage investment conduit* means any entity:

1) To which an election to be treated as a *REMIC* applies for the taxable year and all prior taxable years.
2) In which all of the interests are regular interests or residual interests.
3) Which has one (and only one) class of residual interests and all distributions, if any, with respect to such interests are *pro rata.*
4) Of which substantially all of the assets consist of qualified and permitted investments as of the close of the third month beginning after the startup day and at all times thereafter.
5) Which has a taxable year that is a calendar year.
6) And with respect to which there are reasonable arrangements designed to ensure that:
   a) Residual interests in such entity are not held by disqualified organizations as defined in Section 860E(e)(5);
   b) Information necessary for the application of Section 860E(e) will be made available by the entity.

When applied to real estate mortgage investment conduits (REMIC), the asset test for a business electing REMIC status is continuous after the end of the third month after its startup, but not applicable during the qualified liquidation period.

CHANGE IN ACCOUNTING METHODS

Either the IRS or the taxpayer may require a change in the accounting method utilized. If the IRS requires the change, the altered approach must conform to the method required by law. The taxpayer, with a few exceptions, must obtain IRS approval whether the changes conform to GAAP (APB Opinion 20) or to the tax law.

Following are examples of changes requiring IRS approval:

1) Gross income and expenses, switched from cash to accrual method.
2) Altered basis for inventory valuation.

3) A change in depreciation method.

4) Changes in the reporting entity. Realignment of subsidiary-parent organizations may result in the creation of different entities for accounting purposes.

5) Changes in method for a material item. Any items that involve the proper time for inclusion of said items in income or the taking of a deduction are considered material items.

Following are items **not** considered to be changes in method.

1) Correction of mathematical errors.

2) Improper posting corrections.

3) Depreciation schedule adjustments.

4) Alterations in circumstances and facts governing the current method.

A special rule applies to dealers in personal property. A dealer may adopt the installment method of accounting at the time of a transaction, or make a change to the installment method without IRS consent. However, a dealer may **not** change from the installment method to any other method without IRS consent.

Under present procedure, Form 3115 application for permission to change an accounting method or practice is filed within the first 180 days of the year to which the change is to apply. Resulting adjustments are generally apportioned over a 10-year period as prescribed by the Commissioner. When the taxpayer agrees to the 10-year spread, or whatever time frame is suggested by IRS, the application is usually approved.

When a taxpayer desires to discontinue the LIFO method of inventory valuation, the 10-year readjustment period is normally allowed; however, the taxpayer may **not** revert to LIFO during the previously approved readjustment without IRS consent.

BASIS OF ASSETS

Basis of assets is the amount of investment (equity) in property for tax purposes. Use the basis of property to figure the deductions for depreciation, depletion, and casualty losses. Also use it to figure gain or loss on the sale or other disposition of property.

The following are the meanings of the terms used in the tax regulations to report the basis of assets.

Agreement not to compete—An agreement (intangible property) made by the seller of a business not to be in competition with the buyer.

Amortization—A ratable deduction for the cost of certain intangible property over the period specified by law. Research and mining costs are examples of costs that can be amortized.

Business Assets—Property used in the conduct of a trade or business, such as business machinery and office furniture.

Capital Assets—Generally, everything owned for personal purposes or investment is a capital asset. This includes a home, personal car, or stocks and bonds. It does not include inventory or depreciable property.

Capital Expenses—Costs that must be added to (increase the basis of) business investments or capital assets.

Capitalization—Adding costs, such as improvements, to the basis of assets.

Depletion—Yearly deduction allowed to recover investments in minerals, in-place or standing timber. To take the deduction, the business must have the right to income from the extraction and sale of the minerals or from the cutting of timber.

Goodwill—Intangible property that represents the advantage or benefit acquired in a business beyond the value of its other assets. It is not confined to a name but can be attached to a particular area where business is transacted, to a list of customers, or to other elements of value in a business as a going concern.

Intangible Property—Property such as goodwill, patents, copyrights, etc.

Like-kind Property—Items of property with the same nature or character. The grade or quality of the properties does not matter. An example of like-kind properties are two vacant plots of land.

Nonbusiness Assets—Property used for personal purposes, such as a home or family car.

Personal Property—Property, such as machinery, equipment, or furniture, that is not real property.

Real Property—Land and generally anything erected on, growing on, or attached to land; i.e., a building.

Recapture—Amount of depreciation that must be reported as ordinary income when property is sold at a gain.

Section 179 Deduction—A special deduction allowed against the cost of certain property purchased for use in the active conduct of a trade or business.

Tangible Property—Property that can be seen or touched, such as furniture and buildings.

Unstated Interest—The part of the sales price treated as interest when an installment contract provides for little or no interest.

The *basis of property* is usually its *cost*. The basis in some assets cannot be determined by cost, such as property received by a gift or inheritance. It also applies to property received in an involuntary exchange, and in certain other circumstances. If the asset is used in a trade or business or an activity conducted for profit, many direct and indirect costs must be capitalized (added to the basis) as part of the cost basis.

The original basis in property, whether cost or other, is increased or decreased by certain events. If improvements to the property are made, the basis is increased. The basis is reduced if deductions for depreciation or casualty losses are taken.

The basis of property is usually its cost, as stated above; the *cost* is the amount paid in cash or in other property or services. Cost also includes amounts paid for sales tax charged on the purchase, freight charges to obtain the property, and installation and testing charges. In addition, the cost basis of real property and business assets will include other items.

Loans with low or no interest. If business or investment property is bought on any time-payment plan that charges little or no interest, the basis of the property is the stated purchase price, less the amount considered to be unstated interest. Unstated interest is an interest rate less than the applicable federal rate.

The cost basis of *stocks and bonds* is the purchase price plus the costs of purchase, such as commissions and recording or transfer fees. There are other ways to determine the basis of stocks or bonds depending on how they are acquired. Some ways in which stock can be acquired are by automatic investment programs, dividend reinvestments, and stock rights. An average basis of shares in a regulated investment company can be used if the shares are acquired at different times and prices, and the shares are kept by a custodian or agent.

When *real property* is bought and the buyer agrees to pay certain taxes the seller owed on it, the taxes are treated as part of the cost of the property. These payments cannot be deducted as taxes. If the seller is reimbursed for taxes paid for the buyer, the buyer can deduct that amount. That amount cannot be included in the cost of the property.

Settlement fees and other costs, such as legal and recording fees, are some of the settlement fees or closing costs included in the basis of property. Some others are abstract fees, charges for installing utility services, surveys, transfer taxes, title insurance, and any amounts the seller owes that are paid by the buyer, such as back taxes or interest, recording or mortgage fees, charges for improvements or repairs, and sales commissions.

These fees and costs must be allocated between land and improvements, such as buildings, to figure the basis for depreciation of the improvements. Allocate the fees according to the market values of the land and improvements at the time of purchase. Settlement fees do not include amounts placed in escrow for the future payment of items such as taxes and insurance.

Fair market value (FMV) is the price at which the property would change hands between a buyer and a seller, neither being required to buy or sell, and both having reasonable knowledge of all necessary facts. Sales of similar property, on or about the same date, may be helpful in figuring the FMV.

If the buyer of property becomes liable for an existing mortgage on the property, the basis is the amount paid for the property plus the amount to be paid on the assumed mortgage. If a building, for example, is bought for $40,000 and the mortgage on it to be paid is $60,000, the cost basis is $100,000.

Business assets.   If property is purchased to use in a business, the basis is usually the actual cost. If property is constructed, built, or otherwise produced, the business may be subject to the uniform capitalization rules to determine the basis of the property. The *uniform capitalization rules* specify the costs to be added to basis in certain circumstances. A business is subject to the uniform capitalization rules if it:

1) Produces real property or tangible personal property for use in a trade or business.
2) Produces real property or tangible personal property for sale to customers.
3) Acquires property for resale.

Property is produced if it is constructed, built, installed, manufactured, developed, improved, created, or anything raised or grown on the property. Property produced under a contract is treated as produced to the extent that payments are made or otherwise are incurred for the property. Tangible personal property includes films, sound recordings, videotapes, books, and other similar property.

Under the uniform capitalization rules, direct costs and an allocable part of most indirect costs that benefit or are incurred because of production or resale activities must be capitalized. This means that certain expenses incurred during the year will be included in the basis of property produced or in inventory costs, rather than claimed as a current deduction. These costs are recovered through depreciation, amortization, or cost of goods sold when the property is used, sold, or otherwise disposed of.

Any cost which is not used in figuring taxable income for any tax year is not subject to the uniform capitalization rules. The uniform capitalization rules also do not apply to:

1) Property produced that is not used in the trade or business or an activity conducted for profit.
2) Costs paid or incurred by an individual other than as an employee, or a qualified employee-owner of a corporation in the business of being a writer, photographer, or artist.
3) Certain developments and other intangible costs of oil and gas, or geothermal wells, or other mineral property allowable as a deduction.
4) Property produced under a long-term contract.

5) Research and developmental expenses allowable as a deduction.

6) Cost incurred for the production of property for use in a trade or business if substantial construction of the property occurred before March 1, 1986.

7) Costs for personal property acquired for resale if the average annual gross receipts do not exceed $10 million.

8) Costs of raising, growing, or harvesting trees, (including costs associated with the land under the trees) other than ornamental trees or trees bearing fruit, nuts, or other crops. Ornamental trees do not include evergreens over 6 years old when severed from the roots.

9) Costs, other than circulation expenses, subject to 10-year amortization under the alternative minimum tax.

Direct costs.   Direct material costs and direct labor costs incurred for production or resale activities must be capitalized. Direct material costs include the cost of materials that become an integral part of the asset plus the cost of materials used in the ordinary course of the activity.

Direct labor costs include the cost of labor that can be identified or associated with a particular activity. This includes all types of compensation: basic; overtime; sick; vacation; etc.; as well as payroll taxes and payments to a supplemental unemployment plan.

Indirect costs.   Indirect costs include all costs other than direct material and labor costs. Certain types of costs may directly benefit, or be incurred because of a particular activity even though the same costs also benefit other activities. These costs require allocation to determine the part for each of the activities.

Indirect costs that must be capitalized for production or resale activities include but are not limited to amounts incurred for:

1) Repair and maintenance of equipment or facilities.

2) Utilities related to equipment or facilities.

3) Rent of equipment, facilities, or land.

4) Indirect labor and contract supervisory wages including payroll taxes and payments to supplemental unemployment benefit plans.

5) Indirect materials and supplies.

6) Tools and equipment not otherwise capitalized.

7) Quality control and inspection.

8) Taxes otherwise allowable as a deduction (other than state, local, and foreign income taxes) that relate to labor, materials, supplies, equipment, land, or facilities. Taxes as part of the cost of property are not included.

9) Depreciation, amortization, and cost recovery allowance on equipment and facilities to the extent allowable as a deduction.

10) Depletion, whether or not in excess of cost.

11) Administrative costs, whether or not performed on a job site, but not including any cost of selling, or any return on capital.

12) Insurance on plant, machinery, or equipment; or insurance on a particular activity.

If materials, labor, or services are provided by a *related person* for a price less than the arm's length charge for the items, special rules apply.

Interest.   Interest must be capitalized for all items produced but not for property acquired for resale. Interest paid or incurred during the production period must be capitalized if the property produced is:

1) Real property.

2) Personal property with a class life of 20 years or more for determining depreciation.

3) Personal property with an estimated production period of more than 2 years.

4) Personal property with an estimated production period of more than 1 year if the estimated cost of production is more than $1 million.

The production period begins on the date the production of the property begins, and ends on the date the property is ready to be placed in service or is ready to be held for sale.

Costs not capitalized.   Costs which are not required to be capitalized for production or resale activities include amounts incurred for:

1) Marketing, selling, advertising, and distribution expenses.

2) Bidding expenses incurred in the solicitation of contracts not awarded to the bidding company.

3) General and administrative expenses, and compensation paid to officers for the performance of services not directly benefiting, or not incurred, because of a particular production activity.

4) Research and experimental expenses.

5) Casualties, thefts, and other losses allowed by Section 165 of the Internal Revenue Code.

6) Depreciation, amortization, and cost recovery allowances on equipment and facilities that have been placed in service but are temporarily idle.

7) Income taxes.

8) Costs attributable to strikes.

9) Repair expenses that do not relate to the manufacture or production of property.

Intangible assets. Intangible assets include goodwill, copyrights, trademarks, grade names, and franchises. The basis of an intangible asset is usually its cost. If a number of assets are acquired for a lump-sum price, for example a going business, the basis of the individual assets is determined by allocating the total purchase price among the individual assets.

Goodwill. The basis of goodwill usually is its cost if it is bought. However, if a going business is bought with the intent to continue the business, goodwill can be included in the price.

Patents. If the individual gets a patent for an invention, the basis is the cost of development, such as research and experimental expenditures, drawings, working models, and attorneys and government fees. If the research and experimental expenditures are deducted as current business expenses, they cannot be included in the cost of the patent. The value of the inventor's time spent on an invention is not a part of the basis.

Copyrights. When a copyright is bought, the basis is the amount paid for it. However, if the person is an author, the basis usually will be the cost of getting the copyright plus copyright fees, attorneys' fees, clerical assistance, and the cost of plates that remain in the author's possession. The basis does not include the value of the author's time.

Franchises, trademarks, and trade names. The basis is the cost of the franchise, trademark, or trade name.

Trade or business acquired. If a group of assets are acquired that are a trade or business to which goodwill or going concern value is attached, the following method to allocate the purchase price to the various assets must be used. Allocate the purchase price to:

1) Cash, demand deposits, and similar accounts.
2) Allocate the remaining purchase price to the following assets by allocating to each asset an amount proportionate to, but not in excess of, its fair market value in the following order:
   a) Certificates of deposit, U.S. Government securities, readily marketable stock or securities, and foreign currency.
   b) All other assets except goodwill and going concern value.

Any remainder of the purchase price, after making these allocations, is the basis for goodwill and going concern value.

If the buyer and seller agree *in writing* to the allocation of any consideration, or on the fair market value of any asset, the agreement is binding on both the buyer and seller unless the IRS determines the allocation, or fair market value, is not appropriate.

Land and buildings.   If buildings and the land on which they stand are bought for a business and a lump-sum price is paid for them, allocate the basis of the whole property among the land and buildings in order to figure the depreciation allowable on the buildings. When the cost between land and buildings is allocated, the part of the cost that is used as the basis of each asset is the ratio of the FMV of that asset to the FMV of the whole property at the time of purchase. If uncertain about the FMV of the land and buildings, allocate the cost among them based on their assessed values for real estate tax purposes.

Demolition of building.   The costs of demolition and other losses incurred for the demolition of any building are added to the basis of the land on which the demolished building was located, rather than claimed as a current deduction.

Subdivided lots.   If a tract of land is bought and subdivided into individual lots, allocate the basis to the individual lots based on the FMV of each lot to the total price paid for the tract. This allocation is necessary because the gain or loss on the sale of each individual lot must be figured. If a mistake is made in figuring the cost of subdivided lots that were sold in previous years, the mistake cannot be refigured for years for which the statute of limitations has expired. Figure the cost basis of any remaining lots by allocating the correct original cost basis of the entire tract among the original lots.

Example: A tract of land is bought for $15,000 and is subdivided into 15 building lots of equal size. The cost basis of each lot is divided equally to $1,000. The sale of each lot was treated as a separate transaction and figured gain or loss separately on each sale.

Several years later it was determined that the original cost basis in the tract was $22,500 instead of $15,000. Eight of the lots had been sold using $8,000 of basis in years for which the statute of limitations had expired. Only a basis of $1,500 can be taken into account for figuring gain or loss on the sale of each of the remaining 7 lots ($22,000 basis divided among all 15 total lots). The basis of the 8 lots sold in tax years barred by the statute of limitations cannot be refigured.

Before figuring a gain or loss on a sale, exchange, or other disposition of property, or to figure depreciation, depletion, or amortization, certain adjustments must usually be made that increase or decrease the basis of the property. The result of these adjustments to the basis is the *adjusted basis*.

Increases to basis.   Increase the basis of any property by all items added to a capital account. This includes the cost of any improvements having a useful life of more than 1 year and amounts spent after a casualty to restore the damaged property. Rehabilitation expenses also increase the basis, but any rehabilitation credit allowed for these expenses must be subtracted before adding them to the basis. If any of the credit has to be recaptured, the basis is increased by the amount of the recapture.

If additions or improvements are made to business property, separate accounts must be kept for these and depreciate the basis of each according to the depreciation rules in effect when the addition or improvement is placed in service. Some items that are added to the basis of property are:

1) The cost of extending utility service lines to the property.
2) Legal fees such as the cost of defending and protecting title.
3) Legal fees for obtaining a decrease in an assessment levied against property to pay for local improvements.
4) Zoning costs.
5) The capitalized value of a redeemable ground rent.

Assessments for local improvements.   Assessments for items such as streets and sidewalks, which tend to increase the value of the property assessed are added to the basis of the property and not deducted as taxes. Assessments for maintenance, repair, or meeting interest charges on the improvements are deductible.

Example: If the city changes the street in front of an owner's store into an enclosed pedestrian mall, and assesses the owner for the cost of the conversion, add the assessment to the basis of the property. The amount of the assessment is a depreciable asset.

Deducting vs. capitalizing costs.   Costs that are deductible as current expense cannot be added to the basis of property. There are certain costs that can either be deducted or capitalized. If capitalized, these costs are included in the basis. If deducted, they cannot be included in the basis. Costs which may be chosen to deduct or to capitalize are:

1) Carrying charges, such as interest and taxes, that are paid to own property.
2) Research and expenditure costs.
3) Intangible drilling and development costs for oil, gas, and geothermal wells.
4) Exploration costs for new mineral deposits.
5) Mine development costs for a new mineral deposit.
6) The cost of increasing the circulation of a newspaper or other periodical.
7) The cost of removing architectural and transportation barriers to the handicapped and elderly.

Decreases to basis.

1) Election to expense certain depreciable business assets.
2) Nontaxable dividends.

3) Deductions previously allowed, or allowable, for amortization, depreciation, and depletion.

Casualty and theft losses decrease the basis of property by the amount of any insurance or other reimbursement. Increase the basis for amounts spent after a casualty to restore the damaged property.

The amount received for granting an easement is usually considered to be from the sale of an interest in real property. It reduces the basis of the affected part of the property. If the amount received is more than the basis of the part of the property affected by the easement, the basis is reduced to zero and the excess is recognized as a gain.

Decrease the basis of property by the *depreciation* that could have been deducted on the tax returns under the method of depreciation selected. If less depreciation is taken than could have been taken under the method selected, decrease the basis by the amount that could have been taken under that method. If a depreciation deduction is not taken, the adjustments to basis for depreciation that could have been taken are made using the accelerated cost recovery system (ACRS) or the modified accelerated cost recovery system (MACRS). Use the straight-line method for property not depreciable using ACRS or MACRS.

If more deductions are taken than permissible, decrease the basis by the amount that should have been deducted, plus the part of the excess deducted that actually resulted in a decrease in the tax liability for any year.

In decreasing a basis for depreciation, be careful to take into account not only the amount deducted on the tax return as depreciation, but also any depreciation required to be capitalized under the uniform capitalization rules.

Nontaxable exchanges. A nontaxable exchange is an exchange in which any gain is not taxed and any loss cannot be deducted. If property is received in a nontaxable exchange, its basis is usually the same as the basis of the property exchanged.

An exchange must meet the following conditions to be nontaxable:

1) The property must be business or investment property. The property exchanged and the property received must be held for business or investment purposes. Neither a home nor family car can be exchanged for personal purposes.

2) The property must be *like-kind property*. For exchanges after April 10, 1991, depreciable tangible property can be either "like-kind" or "like-class." The exchange of real estate for real estate or personal property or similar property is a trade of like property. The exchange of an apartment house for a store building, or a panel truck for a pickup truck, is a like-kind exchange. The exchange of a piece of machinery for store building is not a like-kind trade. The exchange of real property located in the United States for real property located outside the United States is not a like-kind exchange. The exchange of a personal computer for a printer is a *like-class exchange.*

3) The property may be either tangible or intangible. The exchange rules do not apply to exchanges of stocks, bonds, notes, certain other intangible property, or interests in a partnership.

4) The property must not be property held for sale. The property exchanged and the property received must not be property for sale to customers, such as merchandise. It must be property held for use in a business or for investment.

5) The property received must meet identification requirements. The property to be received in the exchange must be identified on or before the day that is 45 days after the date of transfer of the property that is exchanged.

6) The trade must meet the completed transaction requirement. The property to be received in the exchange must be received the earlier of the 181st day after the date of transfer of the property exchanged, or the due date, including extensions, for the tax return for the tax year the property exchanged is transferred.

If property is traded in a nontaxable exchange and an additional amount is paid, the basis of the property received is the basis of the property exchanged, increased by the additional amount paid.

Related persons are ancestors, lineal descendants, brothers and sisters of whole and half blood, a spouse, two or more corporations, an individual and a corporation, and a grantor and fiduciary. Generally, when related persons exchange like-kind property the nontaxable exchange rules apply. For exchanges made directly or indirectly between related persons after July 10, 1989, the exchange is disqualified from nontaxable exchange rules if either party disposes of the like-kind property within 2 years after the exchange. Each related person must report any gain or loss not recognized on the original exchange on a tax return filed for the year in which the later disposition occurred. The basis in the property received in the original exchange will be its fair market value. These rules generally do not apply to dispositions due to the death of either related party, involuntary conversions, or exchanges whose main purpose is not the avoidance of federal income tax.

Exchange of businesses. The exchange of assets of one business for the assets of another business is an exchange of multiple assets and cannot be treated as a disposition of a single property. The various assets that comprise each business must be checked to determine which are like-kind exchanges. The assets treated as transferred in exchange for like-kind property are excluded from the allocation rules. Property that is not like-kind property is subject to the allocation rules.

To figure the basis of property *received as a gift,* the adjusted basis to the donor must be known just before it was given to the recipient of the gift. Its FMV at the time it was given and the amount of the gift tax paid on it must also be known. If the FMV of the property was less than the donor's adjusted basis, the basis for depreciation, depletion, and amortization, and for gain on its sale or other disposition, is the same as the donor's adjusted basis. The basis for loss on its sale or other disposition is its FMV at the time the gift is received. If the donor's adjusted basis is used for figuring a gain and results in a loss, and then the FMV basis is used for figuring a loss that results in gain, there is neither gain nor loss on its sale or disposition.

Example: An acre of land is received as a gift. At the time of the gift, the acre had a FMV of $8,000. The donor's adjusted basis was $10,000. If the recipient later sells the property for $12,000, the gain is $2,000 because the donor's adjusted basis at the time of the gift was $10,000, which is used as the basis for reporting the gain. If the property is sold for $7,000, the recipient has a loss of $1,000 because the FMV of $8,000 at the time of the gift is used to report a loss.

If the sale price is between $8,000 and $10,000, the taxpayer has neither a gain or a loss. For instance, if the sale price was $9,000 and a gain was computed using the donor's adjusted basis of $10,000, there would be a loss of $1,000. If a loss was computed using the FMV of $8,000, there would be a gain of $1,000.

Index